FRONT COVER

"IN THE BEGINNING"

PAINTING BY RASSOULI

www.Rassouli.com

THE SHEKHINAH IS COMING

THE SHEKHINAH IS COMING
SECRETS OF THE DIVINE

Valjean Tchakirides
2010

Trafford Publishing
Bloomington, IN

Order this book online at www.trafford.com
or email orders@trafford.com

Most Trafford titles are also available at major online book retailers.

Printed in the United States of America.

ISBN: 978-1-4269-5074-2 (sc)
ISBN: 978-1-4269-5075-9 (hc)

Library of Congress Control Number: 2010919275

Trafford rev. 01/14/2011

www.trafford.com

North America & international
toll-free: 1 888 232 4444 (USA & Canada)
phone: 250 383 6864 • fax: 812 355 4082

DEDICATION

My deepest gratitude to "Spirit" in providing the "light" to guide my Earthly journey

And

My granddaughter—Ryan Skye

For there is nothing hid which shall not be manifested; neither was anything kept secret, but that it should come abroad
Mark 4:22

TABLE OF CONTENTS

LIST OF APPENDIXES

WHAT IF WE STEPPED OUTSIDE THE BOX?

Over the millennia, every culture has put forth myths or legends related to the Divine. There have been various titles, various names, and certainly different forms of worship. But, *what if* there are threads of truth that flow through these various stories? And *what if* that information could be presented as "truth"?

The ancients considered their myths to be the vehicle for passing on the accumulated knowledge and traditions that were accepted as literal truths. It was their way of remembering how the world was created, how to explain nature, and the appropriate moral codes to live by. Their heroes embodied the ideal form and attributes of their society. Myths were their way to understand divinity and the sacred which resonated within their hearts and souls.

In *Metaphysics*, Aristotle states, "Our forefathers in the most remote ages have handed down to their posterity a tradition, in the form of a myth, that these bodies are gods, and that the Divine encloses the whole of nature…they have been preserved until the present like relics of the ancient treasure" (*Metaphysics*, Book XII, Part 8).

But, what really is truth? Most people would say that it has to be scientific and proven through various tests that are observable and repeatable. Yet, people of faith accept many things as truth without this scientific evidence.

In ancient times, there was no division between science and religion. They were both a form of language that was attempting to tell the same story. This is a story that began with creation and ends with either Armageddon or life eternal, depending on your own personal beliefs.

Regardless of the language, many of these stories were told using symbolism, which in itself is a language used to express spiritual truths. The ancient civilizations followed an oral tradition where information was passed by word of mouth from master to the student. There was very little placed in a written form until much later as the ancients concealed their sacred truths in rituals, symbols and allegories. That is why the legends and myths must be looked at carefully with their symbolism to find those threads that can be woven together to present a story of *what if? What if* this information is truth?

In *Memories, Dreams, and Reflections*, Carl Gustav Jung (1875–1961) stated, "Meaning makes a great many things endurable—perhaps everything. No science will ever replace myth, and a myth cannot be made out of any science. For it is not that 'God' is a myth, but that myth is the revelation of a Divine life in man. It is not we who invent myth; rather it speaks to us as a word of God. Myths go back to the primitive storyteller and his dreams, to men moved by the stirring of their fantasies. These people were not very different from those whom later generations called poets or philosophers" (Jung 1961, 77).

Let us first consider inventions. An inventor is one who has a thought about something new or different that can improve current processes or the environment. The word invent comes from the Latin word "invenire", which means "to come upon" or "discover". At first, this process takes place in the mind, in the imagination of the person long before pen is put to paper or devices are created and tested.

The word imagination comes from the root word "image", which in Latin "imago" means "a copy or likenesses". It is like looking in the mirror and seeing your own reflection, an image of you.

I have said all of this to allow us to imagine. To allow ourselves to step out of our boxes of structured thought, whether academic, scientific, religious, or socially driven. To allow our imagination to be in the forefront as we read and reflect on what is presented in this book and to give ourselves the opportunity to reflect on *"What If?"*

The great Albert Einstein once said, *"God does not play dice with the Universe."* I think this is why we see such balance and symmetry in nature. And isn't symbolism the language of Nature? It is the Divine's handwriting and it is why man has discovered (invented) so many universal laws. Laws that have guided our lives over the millennia and advanced civilization in many ways, but these laws have also allowed the discovery of destructive devices. One only has to think of the past wars and know what some of these devices are and the devastation that they have produced.

The words "God" or "Allah" are the most accepted references to the majority of believers of the Creator or the Divine Mind. But, when referring to the "Ineffable" that created all that we see as well as all that we don't see, I like to use what Plato defined when referring to the "Absolute".

Plato said, "'ONE' is the term most suitable for defining the 'Absolute', since the whole precedes the parts and diversity is dependent on unity, but unity not dependent on diversity. The 'One' moreover, is before being, for to be is an attribute or condition on the 'ONE'" (Hall 1928, 21)

In other words, the Absolute, Creator, Divine Mind, or whatever label you choose to use, existed prior to anything. Out of that limitless being, "The One", came all that we are aware of in the mineral, plant and animal kingdoms. As Kathryn Breese-Whiting notes, "The ancients have stated that God sleeps in the mineral, awakens in the vegetable, walks in the animal, and thinks in man" (Weber 2009, 120).

Just imagine what other attributes or conditions exist that we are not yet aware of. Just think if we could see beyond our limited boundaries set by cultures or religions to view humanity as a whole rather than its parts.

The Buddha, known as the "Enlightened One" said, "Each of us is a God. Each of us knows all. We need only open our minds to hear our own wisdom."

Siddhartha Gautama (ca. 563 B.C.–483 B.C)
"Supreme Buddha" or "Awakened One"
First Teaching in Deer Park
Sarnath, India

According to Joseph Campbell, enlightenment to the Hindu's was a state in which "the ears have opened to the song of the universe" (Moyers 1988, 25).

Secrets of the Divine

What If our imagination is merely us remembering that we are "spirit" here to experience the mundane-material world? To remember we are a "spark of light" from the infinite "One". Many believe that the evolution of man will be a new species that is a spiritual being of higher consciousness. Will this happen in 2012?

Let our minds be open to what is presented in this work and maybe a change in beliefs will shift our reality. So, *what if* we stepped outside the box? Like a baby learning to walk, change takes place one step at a time.

PREFACE

Seek ye first the kingdom of God, and His righteousness; and all these things shall be added unto you
Matthew 6:33

Straight is the gate, and narrow is the way, which leadeth unto life, and few there be that find it
Matthew 7:14

Approximately, two thousand years ago, Earth was blessed with the presence of one of the greatest enlightened beings. He was known to many cultures by various names, but I prefer to call him Yesuha, the Aramaic Jesus. He is often referred to as the "Way Shower" because he demonstrated and illuminated a way of life through his actions.

By studying the ancient wisdom of Jesus, we begin to open doors that lead us into the order and harmony of the Universe that came out of the primordial substance called "chaos". This is the same order and harmony that keeps the Sun, stars, and planets correctly on their celestial paths.

However, you cannot discuss order and harmony without talking about mathematics and the preciseness of all these celestial objects. But, don't be concerned as this discussion of mathematics or more correctly sacred geometry will not be the boring stuff you learned in school. You will stand in amazement at the awesomeness of what we view every day, yet what hides in plain sight.

Because our lives are so hectic and we are bombarded with radio and television, let alone the internet, we give little thought to the universe and trust that it continues to operate in order and harmony.

We would not only have to return to school to learn this information, but it would take a library of ancient books to sort it all out.

Part of my job as a teacher is to do the research and present it so that it builds the foundation upon which will support the main body of this work. I have included a great deal of detail on various topics that may appear too historical, scientific, or seemingly not related, but I feel this detail is extremely important to give a complete picture and timeline for the information presented. I have also included numerous pictures to not only enhance what is presented, but to allow the unconscious to remember what the symbolism reveals and how ancient wisdom was kept alive through art.

As we are all individuals on different levels of understanding, some of the information presented might be new and some might be redundant, but it is comprehensive. Providing a broad brush picture, the topics presented will allow you, the individual, to delve deeper into those areas that resonate with you. The information and discussion will reveal all the intricacies that surround us and designed to deeply enhance the main material presented as well as to provide a reference work for further research.

Beyond that, the main purpose of this book is to get you to LOOK UP.

Lift up your eyes on high, and behold who hath created these things, that bringeth out their host by number: He calleth them all by names
Isaiah 40:26

Every night, we are awarded the beauty of the night skies with its sparkling stars. Who hasn't been amazed at our own Moon, especially when it is a full Moon? How many love stories, children stories, or songs have been written about the Sun, Moon, and stars? I think that there is a connection. It is a connection deep within our heart and soul that defines how we on Earth fit into the grand scheme of things. I believe that above us is the greatest story ever told. It is *The Stars: His Life in Lights.*

And God made two great lights; the greater light to rule the day, and the lesser light to rule the night; He made the stars also. And God set them in the firmament of the heaven to give light upon the Earth
Genesis 1:16–17

It was on the fourth day that these celestial bodies were placed with precision in the heavenly skies. These celestial bodies were often referred to by the ancients as "lights", "light-bearers", or "luminaries". In Deuteronomy, we are directed to worship and serve these celestial bodies.

And lest thou lift up thine eyes unto heaven, and when thou seest the Sun, and the Moon, and the stars, even all the host of heaven, shouldest be driven to worship them, and serve them, which the Lord thy God hath divided unto all nations under the whole heaven
Deuteronomy 4:19

It is God who has created the night, the day, the Sun, and Moon and has made them swim in a certain orbit
Qur'an 21:33

God Creating the Sun, the Moon, and the Stars
Jan Brueghel the Younger–17th Century

Many of us believe that we are in the "End of Times". If that is true, then we need to return to the origin of life on Earth and remember what was told to us. The lights in the heavens were to be for "signs". The Hebrew word for "sign" is "*oth*" which means "to come".

Biblically, the word "sign" was a pledge or promise of transpiring events. It was God's mark or signature denoting or certifying his genuineness. It is something that is anticipated to happen and sometimes carries the connotation of "wonder" which was translated from four Hebrew words: *mopheth, pala, pele, and temah.*

These "signs" in the heavens are grouped and represented as pictures of men, women, animals, and monsters which have been kept alive by the legends and myths of the ancients. Today, we simply call them constellations.

Blessed is He who has established constellations in the sky and made therein a lamp and a shining Moon
Qur'an 25:61

We will use this information along with the codes of the Bible to decipher what is the story we are being told. As you will see, the story in the constellations is the story of the life of Yesuha (Jesus).

Weather you believe that Yesuha is the son of God or just a great prophet has no bearing on the "signs" in the heavens. All faiths can resonate to a higher truth and open their hearts to this higher reality. While it is my goal not to offend any religion, I will be making references to the whole Bible along with other text. Any references to the King James Bible should be viewed as a reference work only and not as the basis of any religion or religious dogma.

I will also use the terms One, God, God Creator, or Divine Mind when referring to the "Absolute" or the "Ineffable" that created all that we see as well as all that we don't see. It is hard to label an essence that is infinite and truly unknowable. In fact, we can really only study the attributes of the "One" to even understand an infinitesimal part of the creator. It is interesting to note that all ancient traditions used references dealing with "unity" or "oneness" when referring to the creator.

No vision can grasp Him, but His grasp is over all vision; He is above all comprehension, yet is acquainted with all things
Qur'an 6:103

The Shekhinah is Coming

As a seeker of truth, I have studied the Bible, the Torah, the Tanakh, the Talmud, the Qur'an (Koran), the Vedas, the Upanishads, the Dead Sea Scrolls, the Gnostic works of the Nag Hammadi Library, and other ancient material from Egypt. You will find all of these referenced in this book as I honor all religions.

In my view, one of the major differences between the Bible and the Qur'an is that the Bible had many authors in the form of prophets where as the Qur'an, which in Arabic means "the recitation", is a single book with one author named Muhammad ibn Abdallah (c. A.D. 570–632). Islam believes that the Qur'an was given to Muhammad by the Archangel Jibril (Gabriel), meaning "able-bodied one", over a period of twenty-two years from A.D. 610 to 632. The Qur'an consists of one hundred fourteen suras or chapters and within each sura are various ayats or verses.

Mohammed Receiving His First Revelation
From Angel Gabriel
Jami al-Tawarikh (Compendium of Chronicles)
Rashid al-Din–1307
Edinburgh University Library, Scotland

As the holy book of the Islamic faith, the Qur'an exists in its original Arabic language. At the request of Muhammad, the Qur'an was memorized and written down to preserve the Divine utterances as they were revealed. For over fourteen centuries, the Qur'an has remained unchanged which is much different from the Bible that has been modified and translated over the years as we will learn in Chapter 1.

The Shekhinah is Coming

The Qur'an recognizes many of the same prophets in both the Old Testament and New Testament and believes that they were chosen by Allah to teach mankind as these messengers were sent to every nation to model the correct behavior in which to live by. According to the Qur'an the prophets revered the most are Noah (Nuh), Abraham (Ibrahim), Moses (Musa), Jesus (Isa), and Muhammad. These five prophets are known as the *Ulul Azmi* or *Imams* which means "leaders".

We believe in God and what He has revealed to us and to Abraham, Ishmael, Isaac, and their descendants, and what was revealed to Moses, Jesus, and the Prophets from their Lord. We make no distinction among them and to God we have submitted ourselves
Qur'an 2:136

After all my research and study, I most resonate with the Egyptian work for two reasons. One, it is close to the origination of ancient knowledge and two, the hieroglyphs and the ancient drawings found throughout the temples and tombs. These hieroglyphs which in Greek (ἱερογλύφος) means "sacred carving" allows the unconscious to view the symbols displayed. I feel this gets one out of the confines of the mind and opens one up to greater understanding leading to enlightenment which happens at a cellular level, because symbols (signs) were the languages long before the written word.

Happy is the man who finds wisdom, and the man who gets understanding
Proverbs 3:13

Secrets of the Divine

Unfortunately, our existing vocabulary is lacking in the words to describe or explain the intelligence and perfection of the One, Divine Mind that created what we witness each day. Since we only use approximately 10 percent of our brains, we can't even fathom or comprehend what exists in the Universe except the majesty of who created it.

Does not it make sense that if there is a mind far greater than mine, that I should pay attention to it? And if I don't speak the same language, shouldn't I pay attention to what I am shown as "signs" to understand what is being expressed or conveyed?

One of the oldest sciences that studies celestial objects is Astronomy. Observational artifacts and documentation have been found in all cultures and nations. Many of the ancient scholars devoted significant time to studying astronomy and expected the same from their students. By the third century B.C., the Greeks had measured the size of the Earth, Moon, and Sun as well as the distance between these celestial objects.

So, our search for wisdom will begin with looking at the ancient knowledge that has been enshrouded in the mysteries and left for us to uncover as well as the "signs" in the stars. In Chapter 8, we will build on the work which began in 1862 by Frances Rolleston and her book entitled *Mazzaroth* (constellations), a term that was mentioned in the book of Job.

Canst thou bring forth Mazzaroth in his season?
Job 38:32

My work does not promote any religion. I am merely attempting to put forth facts in a concise and structured way to illuminate different topics. The goal of the bridge that I am building is aimed at demonstrating how there is more likeness than differences between beliefs, but how people just don't know and maybe afraid to investigate on their own. Another goal is to break down the barriers between science and religion to show how the disciplines actually walk the same path and enhance each other.

How many people know that the sacred geometry in nature began with creation? How many people know that the three major religions in the world all believe in a second coming? Yes, that does include Christianity, Judaism, and Muslim religions.

THE CHANGING BIBLE

The Bible is the most printed and sold book in the entire world. The etymology of the word "bible" can be traced to the Greek word, "*biblion*" originally meaning "paper" or "scroll", which to the ancients translated as "book". The Latin word for "bible" was "*biblia*" stemming from the Greek translation. The original scriptures had been transmitted orally and it wasn't until A.D. 70 that this information was committed to writing as Christianity was growing very rapidly and it became increasingly difficult to inform the masses.

There were three early Church Fathers called "Apostolic Fathers" as they are believed to have had personal contact with the Twelve Apostles of Jesus. These Apostolic Fathers include Pope Saint Clement of Rome (ca. 1st century–ca. 99), Saint Ignatius of Antioch (ca. 35–ca. 108), and Saint Polycarp of Smyrna (ca. 69–ca. 155).

According to Tertullian (ca. 160–220) who was known as the Latin Father of Christianity due to his prolific writings, Pope Clement (*fl.* 96) was appointed the successor of Saint Peter and is credited with two epistle writings called: 1 Clement and 2 Clement. Saint Ignatius was Bishop of Antioch after Saint Peter and is credited with writing seven letters related to the role of bishops and the sacraments. Saint Ignatius was also known as *Theophorus*, a Greek word meaning "God-bearer", because tradition states that he was one of the children Jesus took into His arms and blessed. The sole surviving work attributed to Saint Polycarp is his Letter to the Philippians which is a reference to the Greek Scriptures.

It was the writings of Saint Irenaeus (ca. 115–202), Bishop of Lyon, France that began to formulate the development of early Christian theology. Irenaeus claims to have met Polycarp and others claiming to have had direct contact with the Apostles. Irenaeus wrote a number of books with the most important one called *On the Detection and Overthrow of the So-Called Gnosis.* This is a five-volume book normally referred to by its Latin title *Against Heresies.* Its purpose was to refute the teachings of various Gnostic groups as Irenaeus considered the Gnostic teachings to be dangerous to Christian sentiments. Interestingly, it was Irenaeus who was the first to write about the number "666" which will be discussed in Chapter 2.

It was recognized that the Church could not be organized until there existed an official document. Deciding what writings would be included in the Bible was a monumental task and there were many changes along the way. The primary factor that influenced inclusion in the Bible was the antiquity of the writings.

The Roman Emperor Constantine (272–337) requested the first organization of the biblical text as he was attempting to maintain order and stabilize his vast kingdom which included Britain, France, Italy, Spain, Germany, Asia Minor, Egypt, and Palestine to name a few. Constantine wanted to unite the people in his recently acquired lands which practiced many so-called pagan beliefs, especially Mithraism. The word pagan comes from the Latin word "*paganus*" meaning "country dweller" or "rustic". A true pagan believed in the rhythm and forces of nature and that one should be living in harmony with them. This included a belief that since everything derived from God, plants could be used for healing. Their reverence for the natural led to polytheism practices prior to Christianity and monotheism becoming popular.

Constantine believed that he had been divinely directed when he invaded Italy in 312. He had a dream/vision in which he saw the Chi-Rho symbol and the words, "By this sign you will conquer".

The Vision of the Cross
Raffaello Sanzio's assistants
Vatican—16th Century

The Chi-Rho symbol is a monogram of the first two Greek letters (X and P) that spell the word "Christ" *(ΧΡΙΣΤΟΣ, or Χριστός)*. Constantine had this holy monogram painted on the shields of his soldiers and proceeded to win his battles. This symbol was also displayed on the "labarum" *(λάβαρον)* which was like a standard or a flag suspended from the horizontal crossbar of a cross. Believed to be an adaptation of the Egyptian ankh, today, this symbol can be seen on many religious vestments.

Chi Rho Cross

Since Constantine was a newly converted Christian, the future of Christianity rested on the debates of the ancient writings and the conflicting stories of Jesus. It is also recorded that Jesus spoke in his Aramaic native tongue and not Hebrew or Greek. This only added to the debates and the mistranslations of the ancient documents.

Constantine believed in religious tolerance and eliminated the religious persecutions of Diocletian, his predecessor. He also allowed the continued reverence of the "Sol Invictus" which helped in uniting the various groups. Shortly before his death, Constantine was baptized in Rome by Pope Sylvester. He was succeeded by his son, Galerius.

The Baptism of Constantine
Raphael's students
1520–1524

The Sun god, Sol Invictus, whose symbol was the "cross of light" was very important to the Romans and became the official emblem of Christianity. It was further incorporated to represent Sunday, the Christian Sabbath.

In recent years, the "cross of light" has been seen by many people. The documentation for this interesting phenomenon can be found at: http://www.shareinternational.org/background/miracles/MI_crosses.htm.

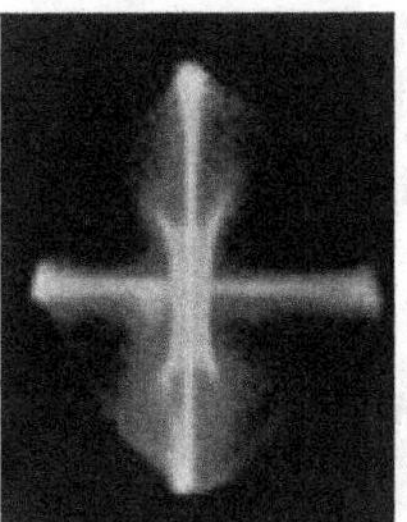

Cross of Light

Sol means "Sun" and "Invictus" is an epithet meaning "unconquered". The Sun God was often depicted as a man with rays of Sun bursting from his head and appeared on ancient coinage. These sunbursts were borrowed from the ancient Egyptian practice of Sun worship.

Akhenaton Worshipping the Sun
Rays of Sun end in Hands
Encyclopaedia Biblica
1903

Shamash
Akkadian—Sun God
"God of Justice"

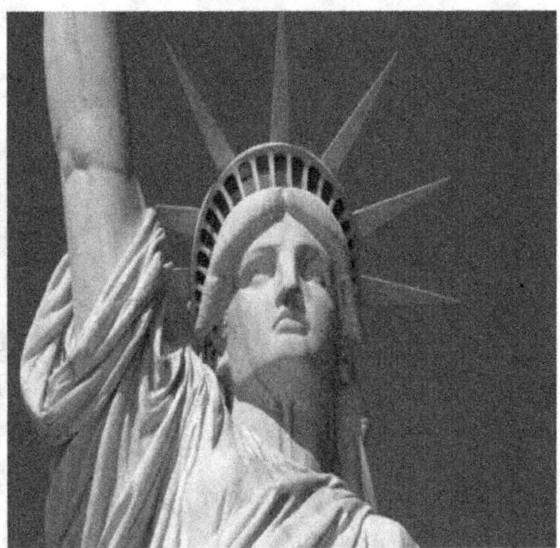

Statue of Liberty
New York, USA

In some pictures, the image looks much like the Statue of Liberty in New York with her seven rays emanating from her head. As Christianity formed, these sun burst became the halos or nimbus that were the glowing disk seen behind the heads of saints or as a radiant light to signify divinity, glory, or majesty.

Coinage of Constantine with Sol Invictus
A.D. 313

Along with the Sun worship, the pagans celebrated the winter and summer solstices with great festivals. So, it was important to design a system that could be embraced by all which became the foundation of the new movement. This included using certain pagan rituals and dates, but cloaking them with a Christian influence. It was all an attempt to bring order to the founding of Christianity.

It is important to remember that history belongs to the conquerors. They have the power to destroy the culture conquered, suppress the knowledge of the culture, and enforce their own beliefs. They can then write their "truth" about history as we have seen happen with many culture's rise and fall throughout time. The word "history" actually comes from the Greek work "*historia*" meaning "inquiry, knowledge acquired by investigation". Regarding history, the great English critic and novelist Aldous Huxley once said, "Facts do not cease to exist because they are ignored" (Huxley 1929, 15).

It is no secret that the ancient churches were built upon the foundations of the ancient pagan teaching temples that were either closed or razed to the ground. Many of these sites were related to nature or natural phenomenon like hot springs or huge holes in the Earth. These churches are usually aligned towards the rising Sun on the morning of the Saint's birth date for which the church is dedicated. Some even believe that the Vatican's chair of Saint Peter, used by the Pope, once belonged to the pagans and used during pagan rituals.

There were different ideas and versions as to who Jesus was, what he said, and his works. Only the gospels of Mathew, Mark, Luke, and John were allowed in the Bible with all other gospel versions banned. The word "gospel" comes from a German root meaning "good" and the Old English "god-spell" meaning "good tidings". The Greeks used the word *"euangelion" (εύαγγέλιον)* meaning "eu—good" and "angelion—message".

The Shekhinah is Coming

This was another influence by Saint Irenaeus as he was insistent that there be only four gospels as he writes in *Against Heresies*:

> "The Gospels could not possibly be either more or less in number than they are. Since there are four zones of the world in which we live, and four principal winds, while the Church is spread over all the Earth, and the pillar and foundation of the Church is the gospel, and the Spirit of life, it fittingly has four pillars, everywhere breathing out incorruption and revivifying men. From this it is clear that the Word, the artificer of all things, being manifested to men gave us the gospel, fourfold in form but held together by one Spirit" (3.11.8).

Irenaeus based this on the analogy of the four corners of the Earth and the four winds. This was taken from Ezekiel 1:10 and Revelation 4:6–10 related to the description of God's throne and the four creatures with four faces. The four living creatures are cherubims or angelic beings with each one having the face of a man and the face of a lion on the right side and on the left side, the face of an ox and the face of an eagle. They were also winged and appeared as a flash of lightening.

The Church Fathers identified the four creatures with the four gospel writers Matthew, Mark, Luke, and John, but not all of them agreed on the same identification as shown in this table:

SAINT	MATTHEW	MARK	LUKE	JOHN
Irenaeus	Human	Eagle	Ox	Lion
Augustine	Lion	Human	Ox	Eagle
Jerome	Human	Lion	Ox	Eagle

Vision of Ezekiel
Raphael
Palazzo Pitti
Florence, Italy

Collectively, these four creatures are referred to as Tetramorphs and universally represent the four elements. The eagle represents the element air, the lion the element fire, the bull the element Earth, and man representing the element water. In Babylonian times, the four cardinal points and their respective zodiac signs were represented by these four creatures. The eagle represents the zodiac sign Scorpio, the lion the zodiac sign Leo, the bull the zodiac sign Taurus, and the man representing the zodiac sign Aquarius. The four creatures have also been found in prehistoric cave paintings around the world. We will discuss these four creatures again in Chapter 5, but you can begin to see how the various beliefs were combined to establish order.

According to Flavius Philostratus (ca. 170–245), a Greek writer, Pythagorean philosopher, and teacher, writes in his book *Life of Apollonius of Tyana* "…in certain traditions the cosmos is composed of four elements: fire, air, water, and earth. To these, some have added a fifth—ether of which the gods are made; for, they say, just as mortal creatures inhale air, so do deities inhale the ether. The elements came into being simultaneously, and not one by one, just as living creatures are born complete and not bit by bit" (Philostratus 200, 3.34.34).

Unfortunately, through this process to define one book, the Bible, many ancient texts were left out or destroyed. It was a select group who decided what writings were inspired by God and which ones were not.

There were many types of councils that took place throughout the ages with the most significant one being the Council of Nicea in A.D. 325, at present day Izeka, Turkey. Constantine ordered the theologians to gather and through this Council, the canons of the Old and New Testaments were established.

The Council of Nicea Fresco
Sistine Salon
Vatican City, Italy
1590

There is a story that relates to Emperor Constantine putting the early Christian father's in a room in which a large table contained all the ancient teachings. These men were not allowed to leave the room until they were ready to present to the Constantine their agreed upon text.

MEMBERS OF THE COUNCIL OF NICE PRESENTING THEIR DECISION TO THE EMPEROR CONSTANTINE: FOURTH CENTURY.
FROM AN EARLY GREEK MANUSCRIPT.

Members from the Council of Nicea
Presenting Emperor Constantine
With their "Bible"
Image from a Greek Manuscript
Fourth Century

Upon Constantine's acceptance of the Bible, he seeks approval from Jesus. This is another image from the same Greek Manuscript.

THE EMPEROR CONSTANTINE PRESENTING THE LABORS OF THE COUNCIL OF NICE TO CHRIST FOR HIS BLESSING.

FROM AN EARLY GREEK MANUSCRIPT.

Out of this council came the Nicene Creed which was modified in A.D. 381. The Creed was a profession of the faith and basically the standard of the "correct belief". The Creed explicitly affirmed the divinity of Jesus, referring to him as God. The Nicene Creed established the "trinity" of the Father, Son, and Holy Spirit and the Creed became the "symbol of faith". For the first time, the terminology of the "divinity of Jesus" and the "trinity" were used. Appendix A contains a table comparing the original and the modified Nicene Creeds.

Constantine and the Christian Fathers Holding the Nicene Creed

The concept of the "trinity" is a major difference between the Bible and the Qur'an, because the Muslims believe in only One God. To Muslims, the idea of the "trinity" is a form of polytheism not monotheism.

Those who say that God is the third of the Three, have, in fact, turned to disbelief. There is no Lord but God, the only One Lord.
Qur'an 2:87

However, the Qur'an is very clear in honoring the great prophets of Christianity as this verse continues:

We gave the Book to Moses and made the Messengers follow in his path. To Jesus, the son of Mary, We gave the miracles and supported him by the Holy Spirit. Why do you arrogantly belie some Messengers and murder others whenever they have brought you messages that you dislike?
Qur'an 2:87

It is clear that the Qur'an honors Jesus as a great prophet glorified by God, but states:

When God asked Jesus, son of Mary "Did you tell men to consider you and your mother as their gods besides God?" Jesus replied, "Glory be to you! How could I say what I have no right to say?
Qur'an 5:116

I believe that the establishment of the "trinity" stems from a more ancient source and the information left by Enoch. As we will discuss in Chapter 4, Enoch introduced the sacred symbol called the "Delta of Enoch", an equilateral triangle where all three sides of the triangle are equal. While the Church fathers did not include the book of Enoch in the Bible, it was important to include this sacred symbol which became the "trinity" of the Godhead.

The Shekhinah is Coming

The success of Emperor Constantine in establishing one core religion created the city of Constantinople, Greece as the capital and center of the Christian movement in A.D. 330. The city was built on the ancient site of Byzantium, known as "The City", that was settled by the Greeks around 671–662 B.C.

Constantine had succeeded in restoring the unity of the Roman Empire and the consolidation of the Christian Church. At one time, the Church of the Holy Apostles in Constantinople held the Temple treasures of Jerusalem originally looted by the Romans in A.D. 70. In 1453, the Turkish Ottomans demolished the Church of the Holy Apostles and replaced it with the Fatih Mosque. In 1930, Constantinople, meaning the "City of Constantine", was renamed to Istanbul, Turkey and is the largest city in Turkey today. It is a thriving city where East meets West and the only city on Earth that borders both Asia and Europe.

The Greek version of the Hebrew Bible was called the Septuagint or simply "LXX". It was translated between the third and first centuries B.C. in Alexandria, Egypt. From the Greek Septuagint, the Bible was translated into Latin by Saint Jerome around A.D. 400 and called the Vulgate. During this translation, Saint Jerome found that many books contained in the Septuagint were not included in the Hebrew Bible. These so called extra texts were named the Apocrypha by Saint Jerome meaning the "hidden" or "secret books" and believed to be the sacred knowledge of the mysteries and disclosed only to the initiated student. Appendix B lists the titles to the thirteen books of the Apocrypha.

Another source of debate during the translation of the Bible from Hebrew to Greek was the Divine name of God. Throughout the Old Testament, the name of God is said to be:

El—Mighty One
Elohim—Gods
El Elyon—God Most High
Adonai—Lord (Master)
El Shaddai—God Almighty
El Olam—God Everlasting
El Gibbor—God of Strength
Kadosh—Holy One
The Eternal One
YHVH—"ha Shem"—The Name

The ancients concealed the name by using terms of reverence or references to Divine attributes or Divine roles as they knew that the creator could not be limited. It is much like the different roles that people engage today. For example, I am a woman, a daughter, a sister, a mother, a boss, and a teacher. I am the same person performing different duties.

Only a chosen few in the priesthood were allowed to pronounce the name of God and never outside the temple as the ancients believed that the sound alone, if pronounced correctly, contained great powers and could be used destructively. Today, the Jews believe that the name of God is so sacred, infinite, and endless that they write it as G–D and skip over the name when they read. Oftentimes, they substitute the word Adonai.

It was the YHVH— יְהֹוָה—(yod, heh, vah, heh), known as the Tetragrammaton, that prevailed in the translations. The Tetragrammaton (from the Greek *τετϱαγϱάμματον)* is known as the four-letter name of God from the root "tetra" meaning "four" and "gramma" meaning "letter". To the Hebrews, the YHVH was the same as Adonai (Lord) which became "Yahweh" and then the English "Jehovah".

The Shekhinah is Coming

Today, the Hebrew claims seventy-two Divine names of God known as the *"Shemhamphorasch"*. This comes from Exodus 14:19–21 as each of these three verses contains seventy-two letters that combine to form seventy-two, three-letter names of God. The number seventy-two is also obtained when the Tetragrammaton is written with the ancient Pythagorean Tetractys symbol as shown in Appendix C. We will discuss the Tetractys more in Chapter 5. According to the *Sefer Yetzirah*, the world was created by the manipulation of the sacred letters that form the names of God. According to the Qur'an, there are ninety-nine most beautiful names of Allah (Qur'an 13:28). The most famous name is *Al-rahman*, "the Merciful".

Related to Jesus, the Greeks translated *Yĕhōšhuă* to *Ἰησοῦς* (*Iēsoûs*). In the Septuagint, the word *Iēsoûs* was used to translate both Hebrew names *Yehoshua* (Joshua) and *Yeshua* (Jesus). From this the Latin derived *Iesus* which became Jesus. Christ was a title from the Greek word *Χριστός* (*Christós*), meaning the "Anointed One" derived from the Hebrew word מָשִׁיחַ meaning "Messiah". To the Hebrews, a Messiah was a king anointed by God or with God's approval.

The Bible as we know it today was somewhat finalized around 1611 when the King James Version was published. The translation was done by forty-seven scholars that were members of the Church of England with the expressed instruction to limit the Puritan influence. The translation of the Old Testament came from the Masoretic Hebrew text and the New Testament was translated from the Textus Receptus. Textus Receptus is Latin meaning "received text". It was the name given to the succession of printed Greek New Testaments by Erasmus. Many scholars believe that King James gave the translated manuscripts to Sir Francis Bacon to edit and that the *Frontispiece* reflects Bacon's symbolism and influence.

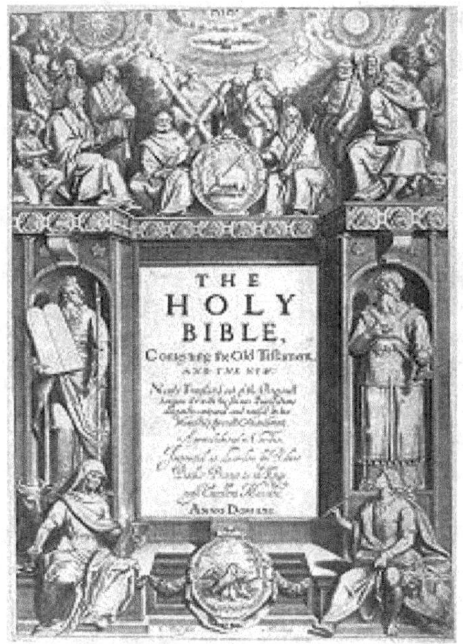

Frontispiece–"The Holy Bible"
King James Bible—1611
Cornelius Boel

Apostles Peter and Paul are seated centrally above the central text which is flanked by Moses and Aaron. In the four corners sit Matthew, Mark, Luke, and John with their symbolic animals. The remaining Apostles stand around Peter and Paul. The Tetragrammaton (יהוה) is at the very top

Prior to the King James Bible, several other versions of the Bible existed. Namely, the Great Bible commissioned during the reign of King Henry VIII (1491–1547), the Matthew Bible of 1537, the Geneva Bible in 1560, and the Bishop's Bible of 1568. The German

Bible was called the "Luther Bible" published in 1534 and included both testaments. Prior to that, the first publication of the German New Testament was in 1522.

Title page–Bishop's Bible
1569

Title page–Luther Bible
1541

British Museum

The Catholic Church was vehemently opposed to the Bible being translated into English, because they did not want their authority challenged by those reading the Bible. They felt that scripture gave the Pope total authority to the understanding and transmittal of the scared message and used this as a way to control the people emotionally, spiritually, and monetarily.

Secrets of the Divine

Just as the ancient priesthood held the secrets to the knowledge and mysteries, the Catholics wanted the same "blind" submission that they alone possessed the key to the sacred knowledge. They believed to be the sole interpreters as they claimed dominion over the truth and the faith of mankind. The Catholic Church's claim to supreme authority comes from the following verse.

And I say also unto thee, that thou art Peter and upon this rock I will build My church; and the gates of hell shall not prevail against it
Matthew 16:18

Throughout the years, non-Catholics have challenged the Catholic Church as the supreme authority over the people which many have written about, especially the Protestants.

It was the invention of the printing press that broke the Catholic Church's monopoly over the sacred knowledge as the information no longer had to be copied by hand. Tradition credits Johannes Gutenberg, a German printer, with the introduction of the modern book printing and the use of moveable type printing around 1439. He published the Gutenberg Bible, which can be seen at the Library of Congress in Washington, D.C.

In 1844, the *Codex Sinaiticus* was discovered by Constantine Tischendorf at St. Catherine's, a Greek Orthodox Monastery at the foot of Mt. Sinai in Egypt. *Codex Sinaiticus* literally means "the Sinai Book" and is known to date to the fourth century A.D. Written on animal skins, it is the earliest known, hand-written complete copy of the Greek Bible to include the New Testament. Today, most of the manuscript resides at the British Museum.

I think one can begin to grasp that all these translations had an impact on the original source of the material. Each successive translation reflected the intentions of those in charge of the masses not necessarily the sacredness of the word. Could the various languages and misunderstandings involved in the translations created the different religions that exist today and the religious conflicts? And wasn't it part of the politics to destroy the history of lands conquered to gain control? A review of ancient world maps will show how often territory changed hands throughout the millennia which always brought new laws to the land.

Acceptance to the contents of the biblical text existed until 1945 when second century documents were discovered in jars buried in Nag Hammadi, Egypt by two brothers, Muhammad and Khalifah 'Ali of the al-Samman clan. The documents had been buried to protect them from those that had burned the greatest and most famous library in antiquity, the Alexandria Library in Egypt.

During the Ptolemaic dynasty, Alexandria flourished as a major center for learning. It is generally accepted that the library was founded in the third century B.C. The library was charged with collecting the entire world's knowledge. They would obtain the original text from various sources, make copies and return the text to the source.

The library was named after Alexander the Great, King of Macedonia, who founded the city in 332 B.C. As a student of Aristotle, Alexander knew the value of ancient documents and collected them from all the areas that he had conquered for what was consider the then known world. As a benevolent ruler, Alexander's desire was to create a culture that incorporated both Greek and Eastern philosophies which was the beginning of Hellenism. Upon his death, Alexander's empire was divided among his three generals: Ptolemy, Antigonus, and Seleucus. It was Ptolemy who ruled Egypt and Israel.

Throughout the ages, it had been the custom to destroy the sacred documents of the lands and cultures conquered as one way to gain control over the people, but Alexander did not do this as Aristotle had taught him the value of wisdom. At the height of its existence, the Alexandria Library contained over five hundred thousand ancient documents from all cultures and was the largest collection in the ancient world. The Library was actually a collection of scrolls, tables of stone, terra cotta, and wood known as *bibliotheke* from the Greek term *βιβλιοθήκη*. Within the great Library, a carved inscription above the documents read, ***"The place of the cure of the soul"***.

The Ancient Library
Alexandria, Egypt
Histoire Generale des Peuples–1880
Hungarian School

The Shekhinah is Coming

There is some controversy over the destruction of the Library with the majority of historians citing Julius Caesar's order in 48 B.C. Other historians cite the decree of Christian Emperor Theophilus I, Bishop of Alexandria, in A.D. 391 when he ordered the destruction of all the "pagan" temples and documents. Others cite the destruction by the Arab army led by Amr ibn al 'Aas in A.D. 642 during the Muslim conquest of Egypt.

I believe that since this was such a great center for learning and the scholars valued the documents, the Library therefore continued regardless of how many times people tried to destroy it. Obviously, the documents were being protected by a higher source for them to come to light in the distance future.

Today, a similar accumulation of ancient documents can be found at the Vatican. The Vatican Secret Archive is a repository of some of the most ancient documents and manuscripts from around the world. It has been publicized that there is an estimated fifty-two miles of shelving containing over thirty-five thousand volumes of text. Access is allowed by permission only for precise documents and you must know in advance that the document exists. A document must be seventy-five years old before it is made available to the public. The Secret Archives are separate, but adjacent to the Vatican Library.

The religious documents found at Nag Hammadi are believed to have been written during the second century A.D. and hidden by monks to avoid being punished for their possession of them. The documents were written on papyrus, a thick paper-like material produced from the pith of the papyrus plant that grew in the Nile Delta of Egypt. The collection consisted of twelve books or codices plus eight pages or leaves to a thirteenth document. Each book was a collection of smaller works which amounted to fifty-two manuscripts or tractates (treatises) in the collection. Unfortunately, one of the books was burned when it was used as fuel for cooking.

The complete collection of the fifty-two tractates is known as the Coptic Gnostic Library and currently resides at the Coptic Museum in Cairo, Egypt. The Coptic language refers to when the Egyptian language is written with the Greek alphabet since the Greek language was widely spoken in the ancient Egyptian city since the time of Alexander the Great.

The Coptic language replaced the use of hieroglyphs which in Greek (ἱερογλύφος) means "sacred carving". It wasn't until Napoleon's troops discovered the Rosetta Stone in 1799 that hieroglyphs could be deciphered and understood. Napoleon had captured the city of Alexandria and held it from 1798 to 1801.

The word "Gnosis" is from the Greek word *"γνῶσις"* meaning "knowledge". The connotation of the word related to more of an "insight" that is divine or a mystical enlightenment of inner illumination. In a sense, it is spiritual wisdom.

The first publication of the Coptic Gnostic Library came in 1959 with the Gospel of Thomas and the complete publication came in 1977. Some scholars feel that the Gospel of Thomas was written in the first century A.D. and one of the oldest gospel texts that exist. Appendix D lists the titles of the fifty-two tractates that comprise the Coptic Gnostic Library.

The world was once again surprised when on 11 April 1948 it was announced that ancient manuscripts had been found by a Bedouin tribe in the caves of Wadi Qumran near Jericho at the northwest end of the Dead Sea in 1946–47. This area had been in the territory of Jordan, but after the Six-day war in 1967 it became the property of Israel.

Caves 4–Dead Sea Scrolls

It might be interesting to note that the Dead Sea is the lowest land on Earth at approximately 1,300 feet below sea level where the concentration of salt is greater than the oceans rendering it lifeless of sea animals. Hence it's name the Dead Sea.

Known as the Dead Sea Scrolls, the original find was of seven scrolls two of which were of the Book of Isaiah, one being entirely intact—all sixty-six chapters and is dated approximately 120 B.C. Most scrolls were written in ancient Hebrew and Aramaic on animal skins or papyrus. There were a few scrolls written in Greek.

The manuscripts include every book of the Hebrew Bible with the exception of the Book of Esther, which has yet to be found. It is felt that the documents found date to the first century of the Common Era. The Psalms Scroll found in Cave 11 clearly displays the Tetragrammaton (YHVH) six times in column nineteen.

Since the original discovery, many additional manuscripts in various caves have been found. Today, the Dead Sea Scrolls are on display in the Shrine of the Book Museum in Jerusalem. According to Gregg Braden, "The entire Isaiah Scroll is unrolled and mounted upon a vertical cylinder displayed at the museum. Considered irreplaceable, the exhibit is designed to retract into a vault covered by steel doors to preserve the scroll for future generations in the event of nuclear attack" (Braden 2000, 2).

It is interesting to note that this museum is built in the form of the clay jars that contained the hidden scrolls found at Qumran. You see the lid of the jar above ground with the rest of the jar below ground. The above ground portion is set within and surrounded by a reflecting pool of water. Appendix E lists the titles of all the Dead Sea Scrolls.

The Shrine of the Book Museum
(Sitting in a square of reflecting water)

The Shekhinah is Coming

I was fortunate to view some of the Dead Sea Scrolls when a select few traveled to San Diego, CA for a viewing at the Balboa Museum. I find the Dead Sea Scrolls truly amazing in their content. Within them are unknown stories about angels, Enoch, Noah, and Abraham. It will be the Book of Enoch that we will discuss in Chapter 4.

THE BIBLE CODES

But thou, O Daniel, shut up the words and seal the book until the time of the End
Daniel 12:4

In Luke 11:52, Jesus is chastising the Pharisees, scribes, and lawyers. He states, ***"Ye have taken away the key of knowledge."*** There is a similar verse in the Gospel of Thomas where Jesus states,

The Pharisees and the scribes have taken the keys of knowledge and have hidden them. They have not entered, nor have they allowed those who want to enter to do so. As for you, be as shrewd as snakes and as innocent as doves
Gospel of Thomas
Saying # 39

Jesus is clearly angry about what the priestly hierarchy has kept from the people. What I believe to be the teachings that lead one to enlightenment. Even in 1Corinthians 13:2, Paul makes reference to understanding all the mysteries and knowledge. Again, Paul references the ***"mysteries that have been hid from ages and generations"*** in Colossians 1:26.

What are these mysteries and knowledge? According to Manly P. Hall, "the mysteries were devoted to instructing man concerning the operation of Divine law in the terrestrial sphere…and there were three kinds of knowledge: knowledge of the name of each thing, of its cause, and of its influence" (Hall 1928, 41).

The Shekhinah is Coming

These ancient teachings were guarded very closely just as state secrets and nuclear information is guarded today. These teachings must be very important and powerful, because the Church has taken drastic means to keep this information from the masses. It is interesting that these secret teachings are known as the "Gnostic" information since it comes from the Greek term *"gnosis"* meaning a "higher knowledge of spiritual things" as was mentioned previously.

Saint Irenaeus was the first to write about the Gnostics, because they claimed to possess an advanced form of scared teachings. Saint Hippolytus (ca. 170–236), one of the most prolific writers of his time, also wrote against the Gnostics in his book, *Refutation of all Heresies.* The writings of Irenaeus and Hippolytus earned them a reputation as "authorities" that greatly influenced the developing Christian movement. With the growing Christian movement, the Gnostic text disappeared and many of their followers went "underground" to avoid being killed.

The battle against Gnostics continued throughout the ages with the worst genocide being the Albigensian Crusades (1209–29) that took place in the south of France, which at that time was known as Gaul. This crusade was against the group called the Cathers also known as "the pure ones". Daily the Cathers read the Bible against the prohibitions of the Church which claimed only the clergy could read the Bible.

It was Pope Innocent III, persuaded by King Philippe II of France who initiated the first genocide of the Cathers to eliminate any of this knowledge being disseminated. The Cathers were a very spiritual group who were tolerant of other religions and a serious rival to the orthodox Christians. The Church was very frightened of them as it was believed that they held a great and sacred treasure related to the ancient knowledge. To maintain control of the masses, the Church could not allow this information to be disseminated or the Cathers to become more powerful. Their goal was to kill every last one of them and destroy all their knowledge. The Church's message was to destroy them all and let God sort out the righteous ones.

In 1997, Michael Drosnin wrote *The Bible Code*. It was the number one best seller in seven different countries and the number two best seller in two additional countries. It is a fascinating read and one that opens the mind to new levels of thought.

The book explains the theory of Equidistant Letter Sequence (ELS). ELS is the selecting of a sequence of equally spaced letters. These selected letters spell out a word or a phase. These are the hidden messages that were encoded in the Bible and known as the Bible Code. While the ancients were aware of the significance of number in scripture, it wasn't until the age of the computers that these algorithms could be run with effectiveness.

ELS was discovered by Dr. Eliyahu Rips, who is an Israeli mathematician and renowned for his work in quantum physics. At the time, Dr. Rips was Associate Professor of Mathematics at the Hebrew University of Jerusalem.

Dr. Rips used the original Hebrew Torah, the first five books of the Bible, to run the ELS. It should be noted that the original Hebrew is a language of consonants and is written without vowels.

1. Genesis—Bereshit (תישארב)
2. Exodus—Shemot (תומש)
3. Leviticus—Vayikra (ארקיו)
4. Numbers—Bamidbar (רבדמב)
5. Deuteronomy—Devarim (םירבד)

The Shekhinah is Coming

In order to use the computer for these computations, the spaces were eliminated in the text yielding one string of letters equaling a length of 304,805 characters. According to the Torah, this was the original format of the Torah that Moses had received from God.

And Moses wrote all the words of the Lord
Exodus 24:4

And the Lord said to Moses: Write these words
Exodus 34:27

And Moses wrote this Torah
Deuteronomy 31:9

Scribes flawlessly and exactly transcribed the Torah from generation to generation. Any errors found by the overseer of the scribes would result in the scribe starting over again as no corrections were allowed on the document. The scribes believed that the Hebrew alphabet was Divine patterns of energy as expressed in the *Sefer Yetzirah 2:3 (Book of Formation)*, "Twenty-two foundation letters: He engraved them with voice, He carved them with breath, He set them in the mouth" (Kaplan 1997, 102).

I actually have the computer software that runs this ELS program. You initially select a "Key Code", a word or phrase that you wish to search. You then determine the range of text in the Bible you want the computer to scan. The computer then uses successive equidistant skip intervals, starting with one and continuing until reaching a maximum number of skips. It continues the scan and produces a resulting Bible text in which the "key code" exists. You can run as many of these "key codes" as you wish. The results will yield the book, the chapter, the verse, the word, and the position in the Bible.

Secrets of the Divine

It is the glory of God to conceal a thing, but the honor of kings is to search out a matter
Proverbs 25:2

Many people do not believe that this so called code exist, but is it really that unbelievable? During WWII, the Nazis used cipher text and encrypted codes to communicate with their troops. These cipher text were an arrangement of letters and numbers and you could not discern the message unless you knew the "key".

The Greek historian, Polybius (ca. 203–120 B.C.), developed a useful tool called the "Polybius square" which allowed letters to be easily signaled using a numerical system. Letters are represented by the numeric coordinates on the square to spell out words. Originally it was used with the Greek alphabet, but can be adapted to other alphabets. A first of its kind recorded in history, it is one of the simplest tools in cryptography and was used as a "knock code" by the American prisoners held during the Vietnam War.

	1	2	3	4	5
1	A	B	C	D	E
2	F	G	H	I	K
3	L	M	N	O	P
4	Q	R	S	T	U
5	V	W	X	Y	Z

Polybius Square

Notice that the "I" and "J" are combined to make it a perfect square. To spell the word "dog", the number code would be "14–34–22".

Documentation on writing in code can be traced back to Caesar who communicated with his armies in what is known as "perfect squares". Today, there are computer algorithms (mathematical formulas) that are used to create encrypted codes by scrambling written text used by some of the most clandestine intelligent agencies in the world. The United States own NSA was created in 1952 by President Truman to monitor these various secret communications.

Today, in the courtyard of the CIA building is a monumental sculpture called Kryptos created in 1990 by Jim Sanborn. Kryptos comes from the Greek word meaning "hidden". The sculpture contains an 865 character cipher code that contains a riddle within a riddle. The answer to the riddle was held in secret by William H. Webster, the former Director of the CIA. As of today, the entire code remains a mystery to some of the greatest minds of our time.

Kryptos
CIA Headquarters
Langley, Virginia

Returning to the Bible Code, one needs to understand a little about the Hebrew alphabet. Originally, the Hebrews did not have any numeral symbols so they used their alphabet to express numbers or arithmetical calculations. Hence, the symbols of the Hebrew alphabet represent letters, numbers, and phrases. The alphabet is viewed as a cipher in understanding the universe. By using the alphabet as numbers, it actually promoted in people the memory or recall of mathematical formulas.

The Hebrew alphabet is represented by twenty-two letters starting with Aleph and ending in Tav (Tau) and is divided into three groupings. These groupings include the three (3) Mothers, the seven (7) Doubles, and the twelve (12) Singles. Each letter is represented by a number and if certain letters fall at the end of the word, the value of the letter is different. These are the letters identified as Doubles. With that in mind, the letters are numerically 1–9, 10–90, and the last four letters represent 100, 200, 300, and 400.

This means that any letter or word in Hebrew can be converted to a numeric value. This value can then be compared to equal numeric values to determine equal or related words or phrases in the Bible. This is an ancient science called Gematria, a Hebrew noun which is probably derived from the Greek word *"geometria"* meaning "geometry". The Greeks called this science Isopsephia and among the Muslims it was called Hisab al-jumal.

It is from this knowledge that gave rise to the hidden meanings being found by comparing numerical values of different words and phrases. The beauty of using Gematria was that numbers could be reversed or scrambled and the results still adds or multiplies to the same value for comparison.

The ancients believed that numbers and their values were important and the foundation principle of the creation process. By using the sacred number code of Gematria, insight into Divine creation can be seen as numbers represent the universal language that eliminates confusion. In a way, the process lends more to an objective approach as opposed to the subjective interpretation, because numbers have one meaning where words can have different connotations.

Secrets of the Divine

The New Testament was written in Greek, an alphabet whose characters also represent letters and numbers. The Greek alphabet differs from Hebrew in that it contains vowels.

The Greek and Hebrew phrases can be compared by numbers expanding the relationship of various words and phrases. These two alphabets were known as a "dual character system" which meant that the characters represented both sound and quantity.

To accurately achieve results with Gematria, use the most ancient language and spelling of words and phrases. Therefore, the Old Testament would be in Hebrew and the New Testament would be in Greek. A table of both the Hebrew and Greek alphabets with their corresponding numbers can be found in Appendix F.

The use of Gematria was documented by Sargon II the ruler of Assyrian in 727–707 B.C. The documentation states that the king built the palace wall "Khorsabad", located in northern Iraq, 16,283 cubits long to correspond to the numerical value of his name.

Entrance of the Palace of Sargon II
Khorsabad, Iraq

According to the rules of Gematria, one unit (value = 1) called a "colel", can be added or subtracted from a word or phrase without changing its meaning. So, a word or phrase that equaled "344 and 345" or "343 and 344" would be comparable.

For example:

Let's review the story of Moses in Numbers 20:8–12. Moses is directed to speak unto the rock before the eyes of the congregation and the rock shall give forth water to them. Instead, Moses takes his rod and strikes the rock twice to produce a flow of water for the congregation to drink. Unfortunately, it was this act that kept Moses from seeing the Promised Land. The name Moses means "out of the water" because the Egyptian princess found the baby Moses in the water and brought him out to safety.

Using the science of Gematria, the numeric values will show the relationship between these two:

The Hebrew word for "Moses", MShH = 345
The Hebrew words for "Water out of the Rock" = 345

By having the same numeric value, we know that these words are related and go together. While this is an easy one to see, its importance is reference by David in Psalms 106:41 and Isaiah 48:21. As we move forward, you will be amazed at what words or phrases can be related to one another.

Moses Brings Water Out of the Rock
Gerard Hoet
Bizzell Bible Collection
University of Oklahoma Libraries

In Psalms 119, you will find the complete Hebrew alphabet in sequential order at the beginning of each verse as well as each line beginning with that same letter. Psalms 119 is not only the longest Psalms, but also the longest chapter in the Bible. The Hebrews revered this Psalms because the number twenty-two is very significant to them.

They cite the number twenty-two as:

- The number of generations from Adam to Jacob

- The number of works of creation
- The number of books in the Jewish canon
- The number of times the name of God is used

(Sources: Josephus; the *Book of Jubilees* 2.23)

It should be noted that when writing or reading Hebrew, you proceed from right to left which differs from English. The Hebrew believes that they write towards their heart. We learned in Chapter 1 that the Hebrew refers to God as YHVH. In Gematria, YHVH has a value of 26 (10 + 5 + 6 + 5 = 26). Interestingly, if you used numerology on the English word God, it would also yield the number 26 (7 + 15 + 4 = 26).

Originally there were twenty-seven letters in the Greek alphabet and the number equivalents were sequential from 1 thru 9, 10 thru 90, and 100 thru 900. Two of these numbers have become extinct. Namely, the number six (6) called Stigma and the number ninety (90) called Qoppa. The letter Qoppa (90) was not used in the New Testament and the letter Stigma (6) was only used once in Revelation giving the number of man and the beast. The original Greek manuscript used the three letters representing 600, 60, and 6.

Here is wisdom. Let him that hath understanding count the number of the beast; for it is the number of a man; and his number is Six hundred threescore and six
Revelation 13:18

Many people have great difficulty with the number 666, but the number 6 is the first perfect number. A perfect number is one that is the sum and product of its factors. This means that 6 = 1 + 2 + 3 and 6 = 1 x 2 x 3. Not many numbers can claim this unique characteristic.

The Shekhinah is Coming

The next perfect number after 6 is 28 followed by the perfect numbers 496 and 8,128. There are only 23 perfect numbers currently known.

An ancient and well known symbol for six is the "Flower of Life". In its basic form, it begins with a central circle surrounded by six other circles all of equal size. As it continues to expand the pattern, many other forms develop and become the process of germination. If you would place a dot at the center of each circle and then connect the dots of the circumference circles along with every other one to the center circle, you would see a "cube" form which we will discuss in Chapter 3?

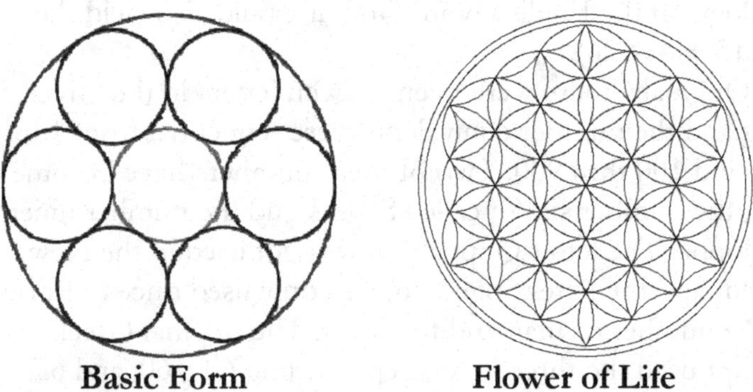

Basic Form **Flower of Life**

This ancient Flower of Life symbol has been found on the Osirion temple walls in Abydos, Egypt.

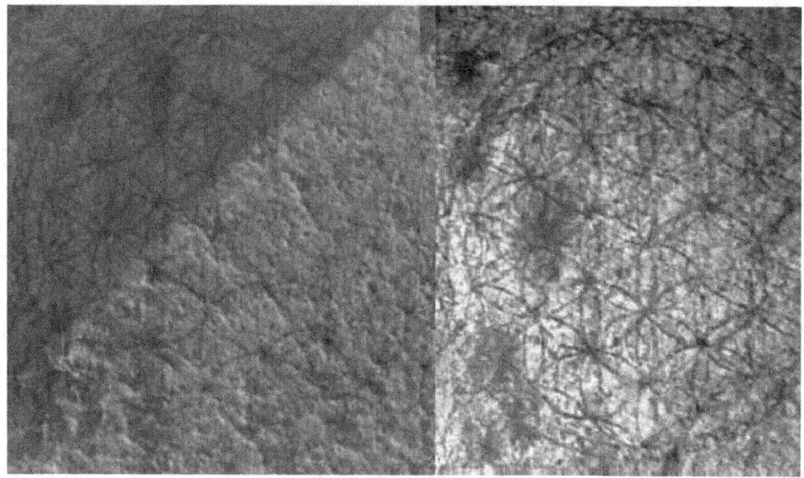

Flower of Life
Osirion Temple
Abydos, Egypt

Even Leonardo da Vinci studied the Flower of Life and made many drawings reflecting the various patterns and the mathematical properties of the geometric figures derived from this symbol. The most comprehensive work that I am aware of related to the Flower of Life has been completed by Drunvalo Melchizedek. He has written books on this subject and teaches seminars detailed on his website: http://www.floweroflife.org/index.htm.

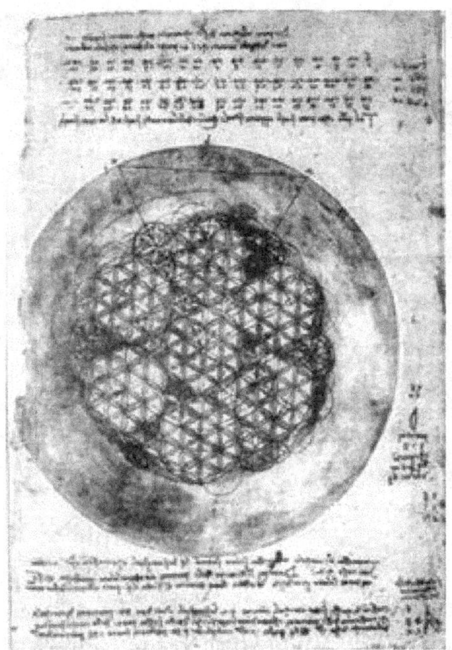

Flower of Life
Leonardo da Vinci

By using Gematria and studying some of the phrases out of both the Old and New Testaments, a total paradigm shift takes place in most people related to the number 666 as seen in the following phrases:

666 = *Let there be light* (Genesis 1:14)
666 = *Jehovah God that created the heavens* (Isaiah 42:5)
666 = *His secret place, his covering* (Psalms 18:11)
666 = *Your great and fearful name* (Psalms 99:30)
666 = *The head stone of the corner* (Psalms 118:22)

666 = *He hath made the Earth* (Jeremiah 6:12)

It is interesting to note that the number 666 can be reduced to one digit, the number 9 (6 + 6 + 6 = 18 and 1 + 8 = 9). We will learn in Chapter 5 that the number nine not only represents wholeness and completeness, but is often referred to as a "magic" number.

According to John Michell, "the meaning of 666 is apparent from its Gematria. It is that which comes from above, from God and it is translated in Liddell and Scott's Lexicon as "the heart, mind, understanding, reason"—the intellectual and rational part of the mind" (Michell 2001, 187).

Another discussion on the number 666 can be found in E.W. Bullinger's book *Number in Scripture* on pages 282-287. According to 1Kings 10:14, **666** was the number of talents of gold weight that Solomon received in one year.

Now the weight of gold that came to Solomon in one year was six hundred threescore and six talents of gold
1Kings 10:14

The number six was also important in ancient China. In the eleventh century B.C., King Wen of the ancient Chinese dynasty used the *I Ching* or *Book of Changes* as a means to help gain clarity about challenges. The Chinese believed that the spirits communicated to them through hexagrams that represented their present situation and their future outlook. These hexagrams were six lines of information or a code about life.

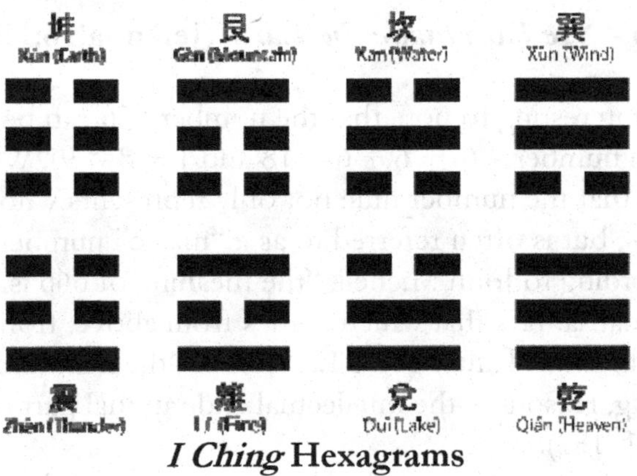

I Ching Hexagrams

The Greeks called the number six the Hexad and said it defined structure, function, and order and was called "The Perfection of Parts". They also said that six was the number to represent both the Earth and man. The Hexagon (six-sided) is the ideal structure that the bees use to build their hives. Drawings of bee hives were a very prominent symbol in ancient art. Of course, six is the current bases of time (60 seconds = 1 minute, 60 minutes = 1 hour). The number six will be meaningful when we discuss sacred geometry and the "cube" in Chapter 3.

Zero (0) was not yet known or a symbol. As a symbol of the void for the Hindus, zero was introduced by the Arabs into mathematics to represent a place holder and having no value which made calculations much simpler to perform. Originally the dot was used to represent zero which developed into a small circle. The Romans called zero "cipher".

There is documentation that zero was invented in the fourth century B.C. by the Babylonians from a tablet unearthed in Kish on which Bêl-bân-aplu, a scribe wrote his zeros with three hooks. In

Gematria, a zero can be dropped or added and not affect the outcome of a comparison or relationship.

In 976, Abu Abdallāh Muhammad ibn Mūsā al-Khwārizmī wrote in his book, *Keys of the Sciences*, "in a calculation, if no number appears in the place of tens, a little circle should be used 'to keep the rows'". He is considered the founder of algebra which is derived from the word *al-jabr*, one of the two operations he used to solve mathematical equations. The word "algorithm" also stems from his name through the Latin translation.

In Arabic, the circle was called *"sifr"* meaning "it was empty" or "nothing". The Greeks referred to zero as *"zephyrus"* and were confused how a number referred to as "nothing" could be "something". Zephyrus was also the term used by Fibonacci who will be introduced and discussed in Chapter 3.

Today we have the World Wide Web and behind all the computer programs and communications that make this possible are numbers. Anyone studying computer programming will learn very quickly that the root behind all programs is the binary code.

Whatever language the computer program (software) is written in, it is converted to numbers and those numbers are converted to the binary code, which are two digits: zero and one. In computer speak; it is either "on" or "off". In writing computer programs, the zero is often slashed "Ø", or "∅" to distinguish it from the alphabetic "o". You will see in Chapter 3 how this resembles the Greek symbol for Phi implying the first division of unity and why it was called "The Golden Mean".

In 1974, a binary coded message containing 1679 digits was sent into space from Arecibo, Puerto Rico. Known as the "Arecibo Message", the digits were arranged in a 23 by 73 matrix uniquely identifying the prime numbers of 23 and 73. When converted to a graphic, this message depicted numbers, chemical elements, DNA's double helix, a human stick figure, and Earth's location in the Solar system. An internet search will give you the details identifying each portion of the Arecibo message.

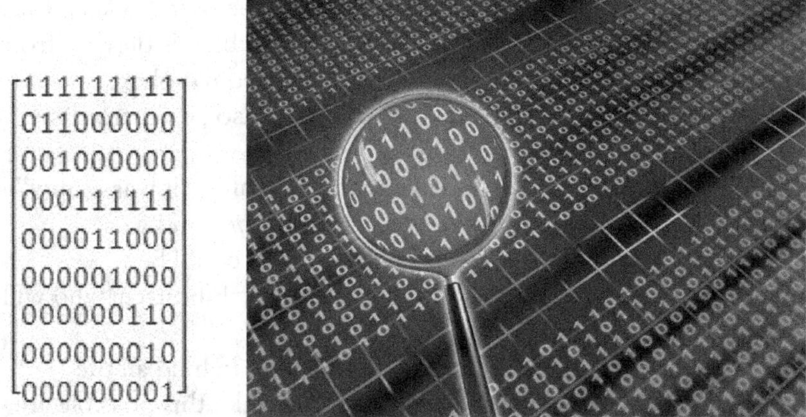

Binary Code in Computer Software

I find it fascinating that complex computer programs that can rocket astronauts into space can be reduced to two digits. It also reminds me how we live in a polarized world of "positive vs. negative", "dark vs. light", or "on vs. off".

We take our modern technology and our ability to access information and knowledge for granted. Scientific discovery has advanced in a geometric progression. What once took decades to create, now only takes years. Today, our youth are growing up with computers and high tech toys with everyone wanting the latest and greatest products. The ancients were denied these conveniences, but lived longer to study. Unfortunately, those seeking knowledge had to remain "underground" so to speak to avoid being punished or killed.

Secrets of the Divine

Since we can now grasp words and number values, an important one at the heart of this work is the word "key". In Hebrew, the Gematria value of the word "the key" is equal to 528 which is the same as the Hebrew phrase ***"the day of his coming"*** in Malachi 3:2, the very last book of the Old Testament. Is this a key to our *What If* foundation?

SACRED GEOMETRY AND NUMBERS

Plato, "God ever geometries"
Pythagoras, "Numbers are the language of the universe"
Galileo, "Mathematics is the language with which God has written the universe"

God Measuring the Universe
Bible Mortalisee (French)
13th Century–National Library, Vienna

The Shekhinah is Coming

This is the math part that most people dislike, but don't be concerned as you won't have to memorize anything or pass a test and you will always have this chapter to refer back to. In addition, I will provide drawings where possible to aid in the visualization of the concepts discussed. Sacred geometry is just another way to look at the world around us and the building blocks of creation.

Since I love discussing sacred geometry and numbers, I have probably spent too much time here. But, for me, it is evident of the "One", Divine Mind. I tend to agree with Sir James Jeans (1877–1946), a noted British astronomer and physicists, who once said, "The universe appears to have been designed by a pure mathematician".

Sacred Geometry is the bases of all natural laws of the universe and transcends time and space. It becomes a special kind of language and seen as a reflection of the "Oneness" in all of creation and the harmony between the Creator and the created. This discussion will delineate the fundamentals behind all of creation and how the language of numbers allows us to probe and understand the universe.

The etymology of the word "sacred" comes from the Latin word *"sacrum"* which referred to the gods or anything in their power. The Latin word *"sanctum"* meant to "set apart or consecrate". Often times translated as "holy" as referenced in Exodus 3:5 ***"...Put off thy shoes from off thy feet, for the place where on thou standest is holy ground."*** Jesus repeats this in Acts 7:33, ***"...Put off thy shoes from thy feet for the place where thou standest is holy ground."*** The gematria value for the phrases "holy ground" and "praise God" both equal 26 the same gematria number for YHVH, the Hebrew name of God.

Pythagoras (ca. 570–495 B.C.), an ancient Greek philosopher, taught that numbers were the ultimate elements and language of the universe and believed that there was a mysterious connection between God and numbers. "He coined the word *philosopher*, which he defined as *one who is attempting to find out*" (Hall 1923, 193). The word philosopher replaced the prior word used for wise men which was sage.

Pythagoras stated, "That all things are arranged and defined by number. Number represents a celestial power working in the divine sphere, a veritable blueprint of creation. Consequently, number is itself Divine and associated with the divinities" (Fideler 1993, 25).

"Pythagoras taught his students that "one" is not a number, but the principle of Unity, out of which all numbers emerge" (Gaunt 1995, 48). Gaunt also stated "Human reproduction, like all biological reproduction is, at the cellular level, growth by division called mitosis" (ibid, 61). "One is Unity and Unity creates by dividing itself. The prophet Zechariah said in the Bible, 'His name will be called One'. He used the Hebrew word meaning Unity. The number one equals unity which means all-inclusive. Unity as a symbol of the creator, divides itself from within, creating a multiplicity. Two is not the result of putting two ones together. It is the dividing of unity. Creation came from within the creator" (Gaunt 1995, 48).

In considering the number One, which Pythagoras referred to as the "monad", we can exam some examples of gematria words or phrases in scriptures showing that number "one" represents God or God phrases:

1000—Lord
100—Jehovah has founded
100—The Most High

Remember, zero is a place holder and has no impact on the results. Thus 100 and 1000 are both the same, equaling one (1) when using the gematria technique.

According to Gregg Braden, "For over ten thousand years, the ancient and mystic science of Sacred Geometry has preserved and provided the knowledge of the relationship between our bodies and the crystalline forms of creation; patterns that are constant, predictable and repeatable" (Braden 1993, 135).

These geometric forms are basic in all created matter. DNA, which determines our biological makeup, is one of these consistent patterns along with common salt, which crystallizes into a cube and the snowflake, which has six points. So, scared geometry begins to reveal the deep mysteries of the "One".

I think it is fitting here to quote Galileo. Galileo wrote, "Philosophy (i.e., physics) is written in this grand book—I mean the universe—which stands continually open to our gaze, but it cannot be understood unless one first learns to comprehend the language and interpret the characters in which it is written. It is written in the language of mathematics, and its characters are **triangles, circles, and other geometrical figures**, without which it is humanly impossible to understand a single word of it; without these, one is wandering around in a dark labyrinth" (Galileo Galilei, *Il Saggiatore—The Assayer* 1623, 232). (Bold and underlining is my emphasis).

The etymology of the word "Geometry" comes from the Greek word "*γεωμετρί*" (geometria) meaning "earth-measuring", where "geo" means "earth" and "metria" means "measurement". It relates to shape and size and is symbolically represented in the basic and simple forms of the circle, the square and the triangle. In the third century B.C., Euclid formalized geometry in writing which makes Euclidean geometry one of the oldest sciences. His book *Elements* is still widely used today.

The "One" is often represented as a "circle point". The point expands into the line and the line into the triangle. Out of these three basic symbols come two other distinct symbols, the vesica piscis and the hexahedron. The point ("one") exists in no dimension, the line is the "one" becoming "two", and the triangle is the further expansion of the "one" into "three".

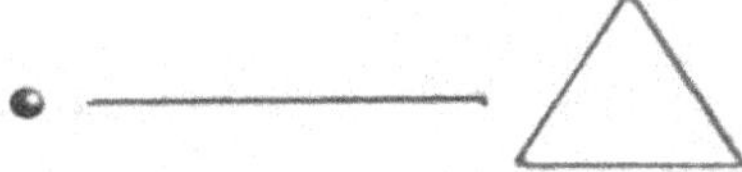

According to Manly P. Hall, "The dot is the sign of spirit, gold, the Sun, or the germ of life. If the dot be moved before itself it becomes a line. This motion of the dot is the first motion. The beginning and end of every line is a dot. The circle is the second motion and the most perfect of all lines. Out of it are formed all figures and bodies imaginable. It is the outpouring of the upper and spiritual life into manifestation" (Hall 2003, 470).

In the *Tao-te Ching,* a verse states "that out of the transcendent comes one. Out of one comes two, out of two comes three, and out of three comes all others." This Chinese text is said to be written by Lao-tzu, meaning old master, a 6th century B.C. sage and record keeper at the Zhou Dynasty. The text title, *Tao-te Ching,* translates to "Tao—way", "Te—virtue", and "Ching—canon or great book". Most people simply say, "Tao is the way".

The circle has no beginning and no end and represents eternity and wholeness. The circle was the first recognizable natural shape as it was viewed in the Sun, Moon, and the eyes of man. Throughout history, circles have related to divinity in the form of nimbus or halos around ancient masters and angelic beings in paintings and frescoes. As a symbol of wholeness, it represents oneness or unity and therefore, God or the male energy principle.

Empedocles (ca. 490–430 B.C.), a Greek philosopher, wrote in his treatise, *On Nature,* ***"God is a circle, of which the center is everywhere and the circumference nowhere".*** In Greek, the numeric value of the word "circle" is 740 which is the same value for the Greek word "creation" and the Hebrew words for "foundation", "circular", and "everlasting". Hence, creation begins with the circle representing "one" or "unit".

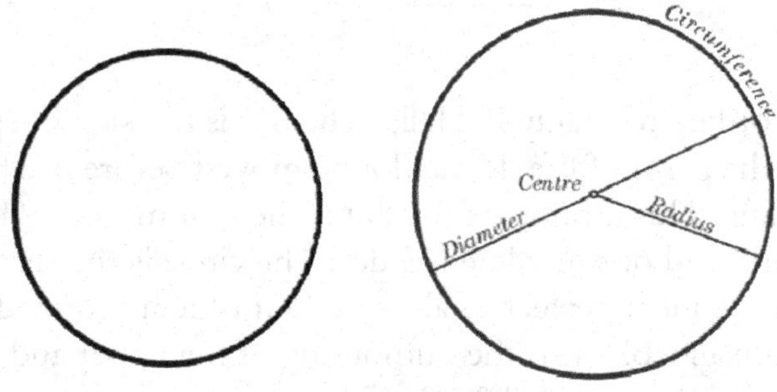

In Hebrew, "unity" is spelled *"AChD" (ached)* and has a gematria value of 13. Another Hebrew word with the value of 13 is *"AHBH" (ahebah)* which means "love". Here is our "sign", in Gematria, that "Unity" and "Love" would be related or have the same meaning, because they have the same value. In Aramaic, Jesus' native tongue, the word *"Alaha"* meant "Divine" which further means "unity". In the Gospel of Thomas, Jesus uses this word to mean "sacred unity".

Plotinus (ca. A.D. 204–270), a major Greek philosopher, taught that "there is a supreme, totally transcendent 'One', containing no division, multiplicity, or distinction; likewise it is beyond all categories of being and non-being. The concept of 'being' is derived by us from the objects of human experience called the 'dyad', and is an attribute of such objects, but the infinite, transcendent 'One' is beyond all such objects, and therefore is beyond the concepts that we derive from them. The 'One' cannot be any existing thing and cannot be merely the sum of all such things, but is prior to all existents. Thus no attributes can be assigned to the One. We can only identify it with the Good and the principle of Beauty" (Wikipedia–Plotinus' Theory of One).

The vesica piscis is formed when two circles of equal size are drawn so that they intersect and cross through each other's centers. The egg shape form created in the middle of the intersected circles is the vesica piscis. As the probable origin of the "cosmic egg", this almond shape is also the shape of the human eye known as "the window to the soul".

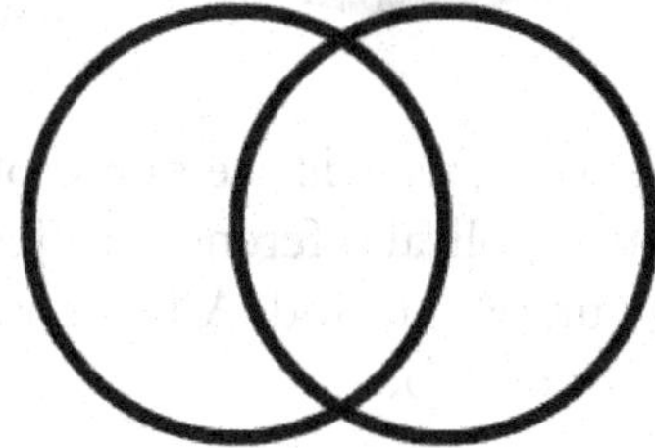

Since we have learned that the circle represents oneness and unity and now we have two circles, the second circle being the image of the first, we can see that unity divided to become two or dual. In the development of the human baby, the cells divide by what is referred to as "mitosis" and continues until a complete child is formed. The ancients would say that this is how the EL became the ELOHIM. Further in this chapter, you will see how this concept resembles the Golden Mean represented by the Greek symbol Phi.

The image of the invisible God, the firstborn of every creature
Colossians 1:15

The Shekhinah is Coming

When turned on its side, the vesica piscis is where the Christian fish symbol originates. In Greek, the word for "fish" is *"Icthus"*. In Saint Augustine's book, *The City of God,* he states that "Icthus" was an acronym for "Jesus Christ, Son of God, Savior", another cipher or code. The Hebrew word for "fish" is *"Nun"* with a numeric value of 8.

Throughout this work, we will see numerous examples of "8" (eight) being used in many biblical references to Jesus and the number "1" (One) representing "unity" or God. A few combined Hebrew examples of "1" and "8" would be:

18 = Majesty
18 = Life (Chai)
108 = Divide (two parts)—remember the El becoming the Elohim
1008 = the work of thy fingers

In many ancient paintings, you will see Jesus setting within the vesica piscis and oftentimes, the title of the work will include the word "majesty" as well as the four creatures from Ezekiel's vision (human, eagle, ox, and lion). As time progresses, these four creatures are displayed as the four evangelists of the gospels as discussed in Chapter 1 and in the book of Revelations they become the four beasts.

Secrets of the Divine

Christ in Majesty with the Four Creatures
Badische Landesbibliothek
Manuscript
Karlsruhe, Germany

Medieval Ivory
Hotel de Cluny
Paris, France

Christ in the Vesica Piscis surrounded by creatures from Ezekiel's vision
The Royal Portal–Chartres Cathedral
Chartres, France

Known as the "mystical almond" and originating with the pagans, the vesica piscis was adopted by the Christians to symbolize purity and virginity. The Virgin Mary can also be found within the vesica piscis in various art forms.

The square represents a foundation and is unique because it can be divided exactly in half in any direction, which yields two. It is a symbol for the Earth in astrology and therefore the material world and solid matter. As an Earth symbol, it represents the feminine energy principle and the opposite of the circle.

The square can be expanded into a cube or Hexahedron. The hexahedron has six sides and six angles and is formed by dividing the circumference of a circle by its radius and connecting the points on the circumference by straight lines. It is a self contained object with the six dimensions of above and below, front and back, and right and left. This platonic solid contains within it two more platonic solids, the tetrahedron and the octahedron. As we learned in Chapter 2, it is the "cube" that comes from the basic form of the Flower of Life.

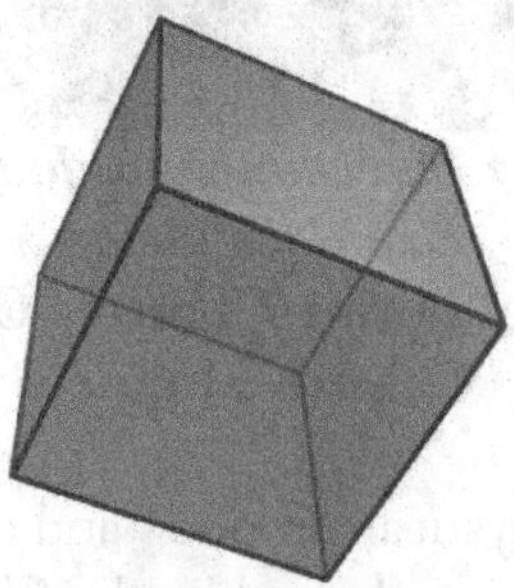

In Solomon's Temple, the Holy of Holies was in the form of a cube. Today, an excellent example of a cube-shaped building is the Kaaba in Mecca, Saudi Arabia adjacent to the Red Sea. The Kaaba sits within the courtyard of the Great Mosque in Makkah where tradition holds that it was the first house built for the worship of Allah.

First sanctuary appointed for mankind
Qur'an 3:96

The Kaaba

It is the most sacred site in Islam since the time of Muhammad (570–632). Said to be originally built by Abraham and his son Ishmael, all Muslims face the Kaaba, during their prayers, five times a day. The Muslims honor Abraham as a model of pious human behavior and consider him neither Jew nor Christian. The name Ishmael means "God hears".

The Kaaba's four corners are aligned with the four cardinal directions and it is believed that one of the corners encases a meteorite believed to be sent from Allah adding to its sacredness. The Kaaba is covered by a black silk and gold curtain which contains text from the Qur'an written upon it. The black covering is called the Kiswah and represents a sign of humility and respect. One should not gaze upon the Kaaba as it is equal to gazing upon Allah which is forbidden. This parallels the biblical text where Christians believe that no man can gaze upon God and live (Exodus 33:20).

Interestingly, the Kaaba is believed to be in line with the Pole Star, Polaris thus connecting Heaven and Earth. We will learn more about this star in Chapter 8.

If you were to unfold the cube, it would produce the Christian "cross". Remember as stated earlier, the number six (6) is the first perfect number. Here the number six is involved with one of the platonic solids, "the cube", the "Muslim Kaaba" and the "Christian cross".

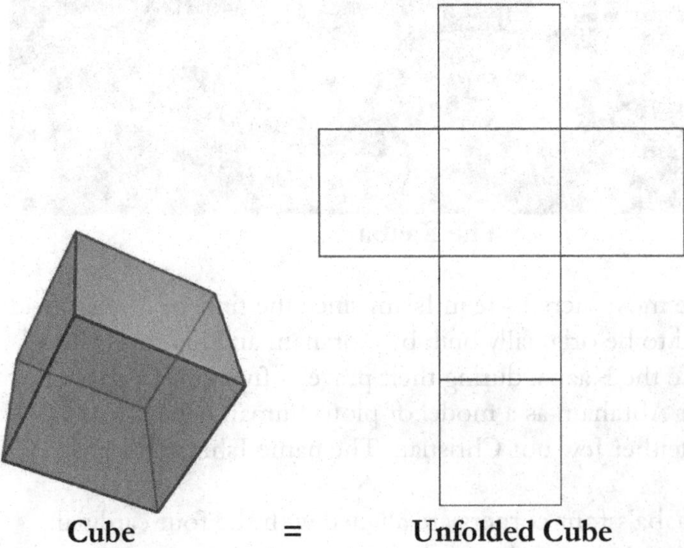

Cube = **Unfolded Cube**

The unfolded cube is also the traditional layout of many churches. This church architect is known as the "cruciform".

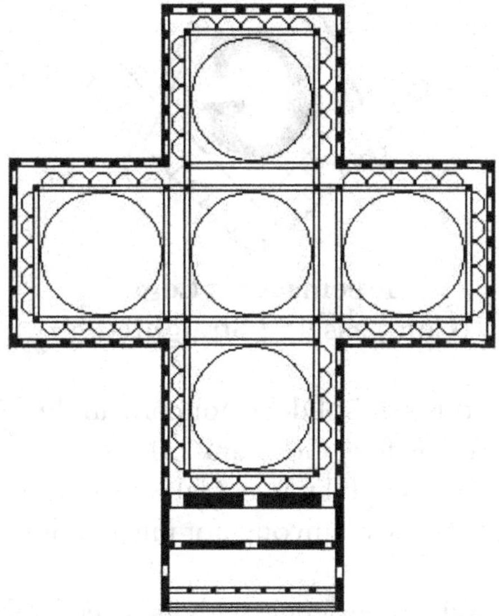

Apostoleion, Konstantino I-aren mausoleoa. Oinplanoa.

Church of the Holy Apostles in Constantinople
Mausoleum of Emperor Constantine I

Throughout time there have been several forms of the cross which are illustrated and described in Appendix G.

It is said that with a compass and a straightedge, one can create the entire universe. This statement is interesting when you consider that the compass and the square are combined in the symbolic logo of the Freemasons. The Freemasons were known for their beautiful architecture and built so many of the remarkable cathedrals that span the globe.

Freemason's Logo
(Compass and Straightedge)

Many times this symbol does not contain the "G" in the center. Some say the "G" stands for "God" and others say it stands for "galaxy" to distinguish the Milky Way Galaxy from others. The true meaning is really a mystery to anyone not initiated into this organization.

For Christianity, the triangle with its three straight lines represents the holy trinity. In addition, an equilateral triangle, where all three sides are of equal length, is used to symbolize the element fire when pointing upwards and the element water when pointing downwards. This makes sense when you consider that fire tends to rise and water tends naturally to flow down. Triangles were also some of the symbols used by the ancient alchemist. The equilateral triangle is anciently known as the "Delta of Enoch" and further discussed in Chapter 4.

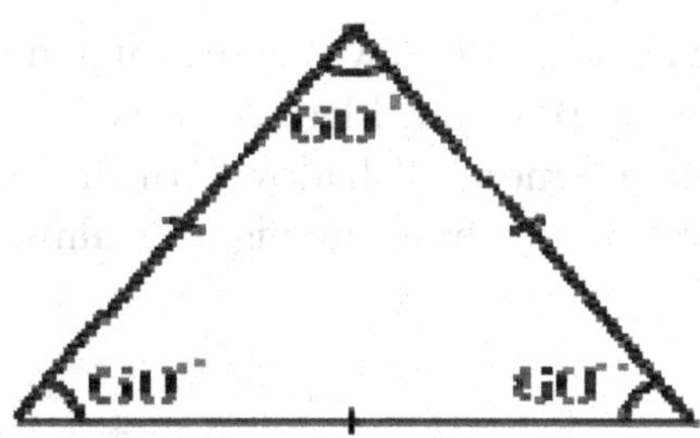

It is also this triangle overlaid with another triangle that forms the commonly known Star of David or the Seal of Solomon. It has become the symbol of Israel and appears on their State flag. Originally known as the Magen David (Shield of David) it is legendary to Jewish, Christian, and Islamic traditions. It was the symbol on Solomon's ring which gave him unknown powers with the interlocking triangles sealing the opposing forces of fire and water. It is displayed in the Leningrad Codex which is the oldest, authoritative manuscript of the Hebrew Bible and reproduced in *Biblia Hiebraica.* The Jewish scholars that edited the Codex are known as the Masoretic.

The symmetry of the symbol identifies it with balance and harmony and the phrase "As Above, So Below", an ancient axiom linking Spirit with the material world. This concept was beautifully expressed in the Emerald Tablets:

Look they above or look thee below, the same shall ye find. For all is but part of the Oneness that is at the Source of the Law. The consciousness below thee is part thine own as we are a part of thine.

Tablet XI

(Doreal 1939, 64)

The Shekhinah is Coming

This concept is what Plato was expressing in the "Allegory of the Cave" from *Republic*. Basically, Plato conveyed that what we perceive in this world are merely "shadows" of the ideal form or the archetype counterpart of a form in the higher realms.

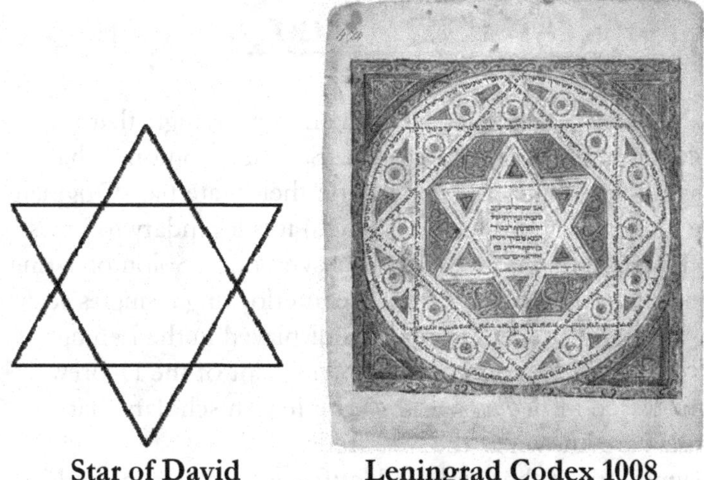

Star of David **Leningrad Codex 1008 St. Petersburg, Russia**

When the symbol for fire is overlaid with the symbol of water and spinning, it creates the body's energy field. This energy field was known as the Mer-Ka-Ba by the Egyptians. The term means light (Mer), spirit (Ka), and soul (Ba). The process was a means to transport the body and spirit from one world to another through increased vibrations. In modern thought, it would be a time-travel machine.

The Mer-Ka-Ba is also known as the "Star Tetrahedron", the structure that is the beginning of the DNA coding that is contained in every cell of the human body. Mer-Ka-Ba in Hebrew (Markava) means "chariot" and was the vehicle seen in the vision of Ezekiel 1:4–26.

Similarly, the same "chariot" was used by Elijah to ascend into heaven (2Kings 2:11).

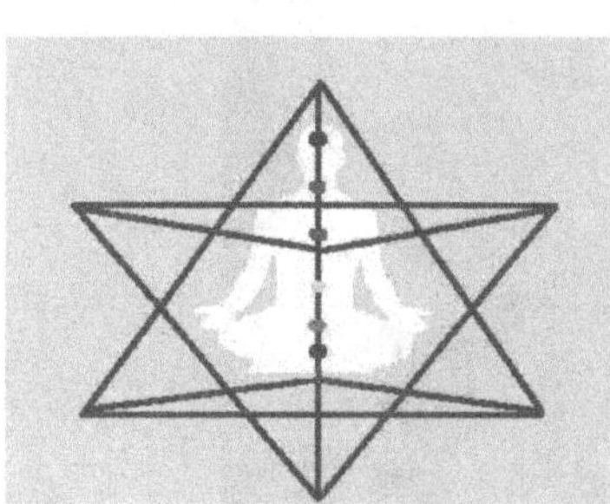

MER-KA-BA

Ezekiel's Vision of Mer-Ka-Ba
Icones Biblicae
Matthaeus Merian

Plato (ca. 427–347 B.C.) founded the Academy in Athens, the first institution of higher learning in the Western World. Plato was a student of the great Socrates (ca. 469–399 B.C.). Over the entrance of the Academy were the words, "Let none ignorant of geometry enter here". Plato's greatest student was Aristotle, whom he referred to as "the mind of the school". Eventually, Aristotle had his own school called the Lyceum. Plato's Academy was operational until A.D. 529 when Justinian I of Byzantium had it closed, because he feared that it was threatening Christianity.

Plato and Aristotle
The School of Athens Fresco
Raphael
Vatican Museums and Galleries
Vatican City, Italy

Secrets of the Divine

Plato wrote thirty-six philosophical dialogues including *Timaeus, Critias, Laws,* and the *Republic.* Many times using Socrates as his voice, these dialogues were his way to cure the ills of society by creating the ideal city based upon the Divine forms and patterns. While Socrates (469–399 B.C.) is considered the father of western philosophy, nothing has ever been found that he wrote. Most of what we know about Socrates comes from his student, Plato who followed Socrates' method of questioning knowledge to obtain truth. Unfortunately, Socrates upset those in control and he was prosecuted, condemned to death, and forced to drink hemlock. Plato never seemed to recover from this tragic event that extinguished Socrates' bright light.

The Death of Socrates
Jacques-Louis David–1787
Metropolitan Museum of Art
New York City

The Shekhinah is Coming

In the *Timaeus*, written around 350 B.C., Plato describes the creation of the universe by a Divine creator using the platonic solids. Plato was often criticized by the ancients for revealing too much information related to the mysteries in his writings, but for Plato, it was numbers that bound everything together. Plato traveled widely and many believe that he received vast information from the Egyptians and the Pythagoras doctrines.

The Platonic Solids are the five known bodies of sacred geometry that define the basic patterns or geometric codes of creation. Plato believed that these forms were the way that the Divine essence was projected into matter and crystallized, like a blueprint. The names of the five Platonic Solids are the Tetrahedron, the Hexahedron, the Octahedron, the Dodecahedron, and the Icosahedron. The name of each solid is derived from its number of faces being 4, 6, 8, 12, and 20 respectively. They are further described by their surface space, the lengths of the surfaces, and the value of all the interior angles defining the corners.

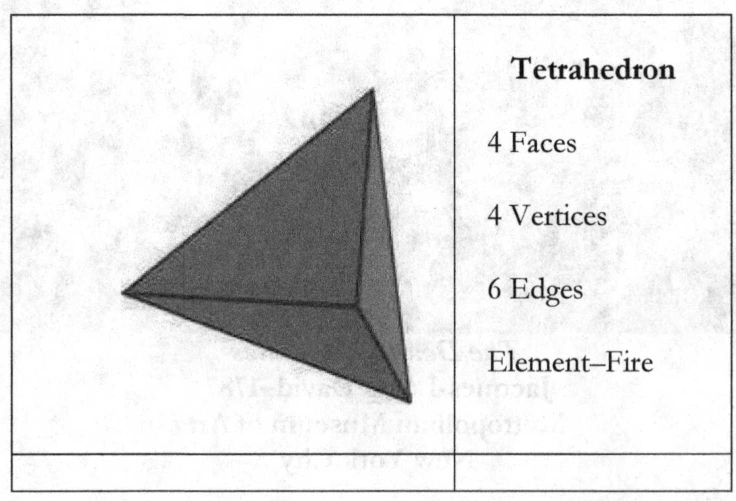	**Tetrahedron** 4 Faces 4 Vertices 6 Edges Element–Fire

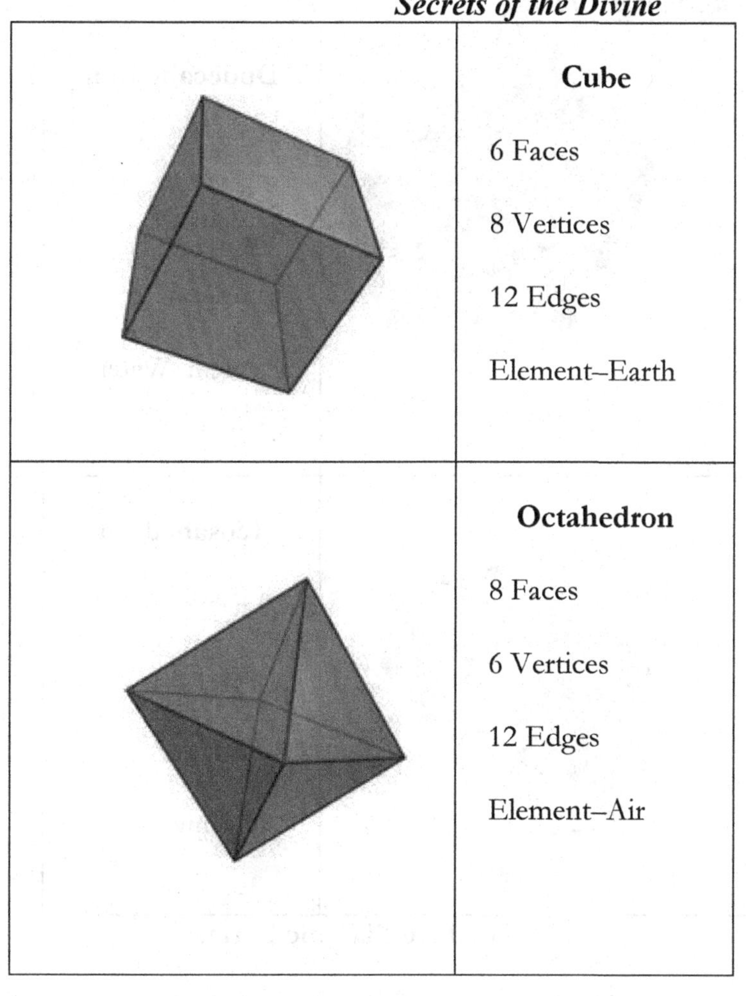

	Cube 6 Faces 8 Vertices 12 Edges Element–Earth
	Octahedron 8 Faces 6 Vertices 12 Edges Element–Air

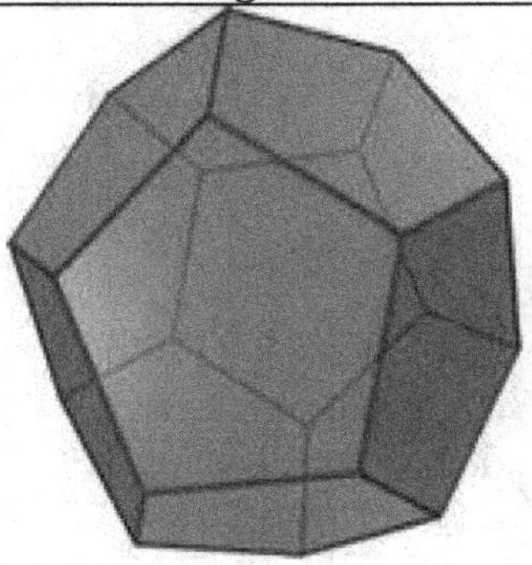	**Dodecahedron** 2 Faces 20 Vertices 30 Edges Element–Water
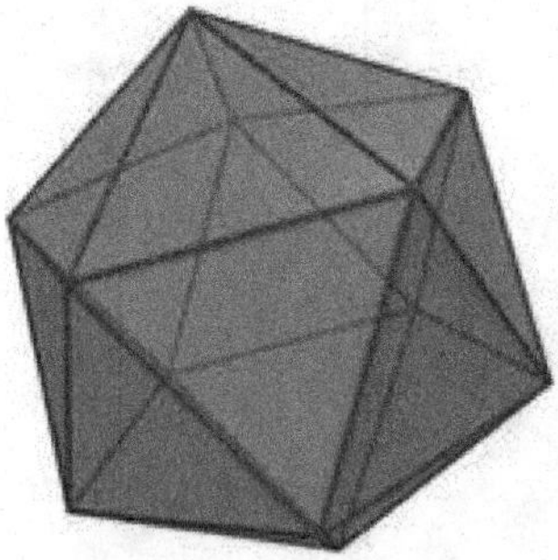	**Icosahedron** 20 Faces 12 Vertices 30 Edges The Universe

The Five Platonic Forms

"Platonic forms are aspects of ideal reality that give shape to material things and enable people to understand them. They are perfect and unchanging and influence human morality as well as the natural world" (Stevenson 1999, 256).

The Greeks taught that these five solids were the core patterns of physical creation. Four of the solids were seen as the archetypal patterns behind the four elements (earth, air, fire, and water). The fifth element was held to be the pattern behind the life force itself which the Greeks called "ether". This fifth solid, the dodecahedron, was in fact kept a closely guarded secret in the Greek school of Pythagoras as they feared that this pattern could cause tremendous destruction if misused.

Even more remarkable are the models found in modern physics. Robert Moon, the late physics professor emeritus at the University of Chicago, developed a model of the entire Periodic Table of Elements showing the Platonic Solids as the pattern of the neutrons and protons in the nucleus of each element. Moon stated "Given that the Greeks taught that these forms held the patterns of creation of the physical world, it is quite significant to find the same forms now appearing in physics as the possible basis of the Periodic Table of Elements, which is modern science's list of all the substances that literally make up the physical world. Furthermore, it could be said that the essence of creation is geometry: Change the number of the parts of the atom, and its resulting configured shape changes as academically a different element arises." Article by Robert J. Gilbert from www.sacred-geometry.com

All matter is composed of chemical elements and identified by their "atomic number" which is the number of protons in the nucleus. All known elements are listed in the Periodic Table originally published in 1869 by Russian chemist Dmitri Mendeleev, but the table changes as new elements are discovered. Today, the table contains 117 elements and is shown in Appendix H along with the lyrics to a song written by Tom Leher in 1960 which was used by students for the recall of the elements.

...By you ordered everything by measure and number and weight

The Wisdom of Solomon 11:20

In the *Timaeus*, Plato also discussed the Golden Mean as "the most binding of all mathematical relations and the key to the physics of the cosmos." It is the relationship of "unity to creation" or "one to diversity". The Golden Mean is numerically equal to 1.6180339 and is also known as the Golden Section, the Divine Ratio, or the Fibonacci Series. It is a mathematical ratio known as Phi, displayed as the Greek symbol Φ and is a concept that has been honored throughout history. The phrase from Zechariah 14:9, ***"the Lord shall be king over all the Earth"*** has a numeric value of 618, which matches the first three decimals of Phi's numeric value.

If you remember at the end of Chapter 2, we discussed the binary code and how the zero was often slashed by programmers. Does not the symbol for Phi look like the slashed zero? In the beginning of this chapter, we discuss how the "One" or "unity" divided to produce "two" through mitosis. Does your mind see the Phi symbol—the circle being cut in half? Can you begin to grasp the importance of symbols?

According to the Greeks, the golden ratio is the ideal proportion for the sides of a rectangle that the eye finds the most pleasing. This is why the Parthenon, the temple dedicated to the Athena, the goddess of wisdom, is so appealing to gaze upon. The rectangular face on the front of the Parthenon has sides whose ratio is the golden mean.

The Parthenon
447–432 B.C.
Acropolis, Athens, Greece

Inside the Parthenon stood a huge statue of Athena with her shield and Nike, the winged goddess of victory. Athena was the goddess of war, strength, and wisdom and often accompanied the Greek heroes on their quest including Hercules and Jason. In Greek mythology, Athena burst from Zeus' forehead fully dressed and armed with weapons. The Greek city of Athens was named in honor of Athena and her Roman counterpart was called Minerva.

Athena Parthenos with Nike
Austria Parliament
Vienna, Austria

Secrets of the Divine

There is an exact full-scale replica of the original Parthenon in Nashville, Tennessee as Nashville is often referred to as the "Athens of the South". It includes the gold-gilded figure of Athena Parthenos holding Nike in her hand. Built in 1897 for Tennessee's Centennial Exposition it is located in Centennial Park. Having visited the ancient Greek Parthenon ruins, it is amazing to view its complete majesty in Nashville.

The Nashville Parthenon
Centennial Park

Athena Parthenos with Nike
The Nashville Parthenon
Centennial Park

Mathematically, the golden mean (1.6180339) is the relationship of a measurable length divided into two parts, one smaller and one larger. "The ratio of the whole line to the longer piece equals the ratio of the longer piece to the shorter" (Devlin 1994, 108).

For example, a measure of "C" (a + b) is divided into "a" and "b" with "a" being larger. The phi ratio 1.6180339 is: C/a equals a/b, where "/" means "divided by".

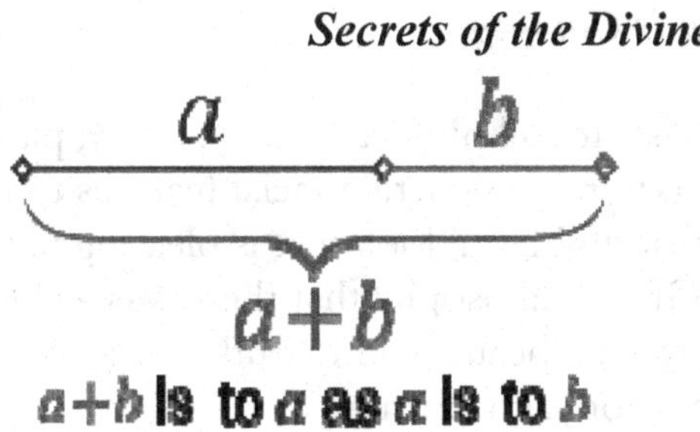

This can also be seen if you write out the Hebrew alphabet in a line and place a mark between the three "Mother" letters of Aleph, Mem, and Shin. The markings would yield the golden mean ratio. Interestingly, these three mothers parallel the elements where Aleph is breath or air, Mem is water, and Shin is fire.

Reading from Right to Left:

א ב ג ד ה ו ז ח ט י כ ל מ נ ס ע פ צ ק ר ש ת

Shin **Mem** **Aleph**

The golden mean is also clearly seen when you examine the ratio and proportions of the bones in the human body. The length of the human fingers to the hand and the hand to the arm (up to the elbow) is this same Divine ratio.

The ancient standard of measurement was known as the "cubit". The measurement represented the length between the elbow and the extreme end of the index finger which was approximately eighteen inches.

As the basis for all physical beauty, today, plastic surgeons are utilizing this ratio in reconstructing facial features to facilitate a more appealing and beautiful facial look that is pleasing to the eye. This aligns with the Greek philosophy that there was a close association in mathematics between "beauty" and "truth" and that beauty involved symmetry, proportion, and harmony.

So God created man in His own image, in the image of God created He him; male and female created He them
Genesis 1:27

As stated, the Golden mean is also known as the Fibonacci series after Leonardo Pisano Bogollo (ca. 1170–1250) known as Leonardo of Pisa, who introduced this sequence of numbers in his book *Liber Abaci*. However, this number sequence was already well known in ancient India and described in *Aryabhatiya*, a book written in A.D. 499.

Numerically, this series is represented by 1, 1, 2, 3, 5, 8, 13, 21, 34…infinity. Each subsequent number is the sum of the preceding two numbers and goes on ad infinitum. Although the shape increases in size as it progressives, it maintains the spiral form.

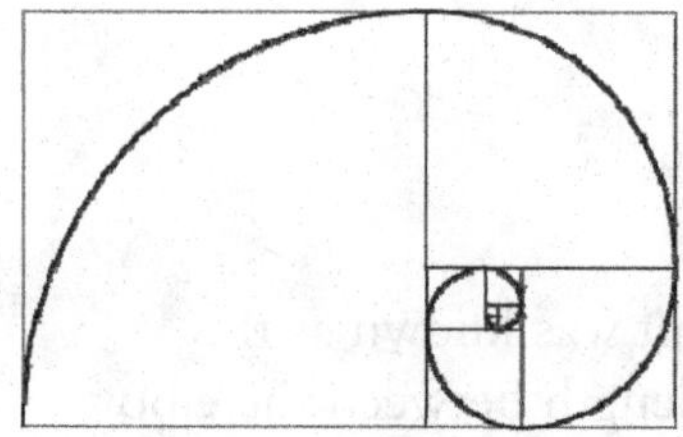

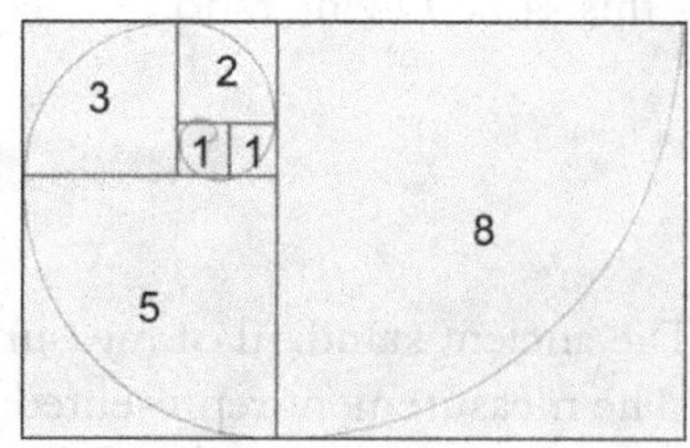

Secrets of the Divine

The Fibonacci series is the spiral of growth seen in the hair swirl on a baby's head and the human ear which is as unique as a fingerprint. It is also seen in the structure of many living organisms including, leaves, sunflowers, snowflakes, shellfish, tree branches, and plants demonstrating that numbers were involved in creation and evolution.

Sunflower

Snowflake **Pineapple**

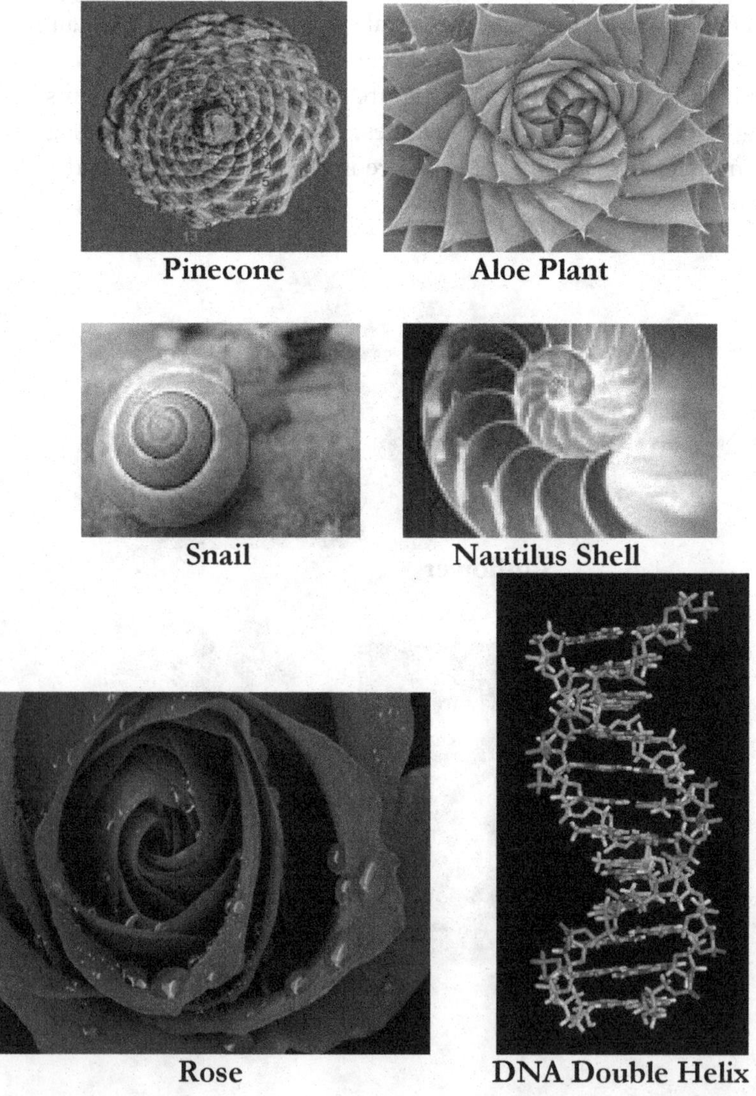

Pinecone

Aloe Plant

Snail

Nautilus Shell

Rose

DNA Double Helix

Isn't it interesting that the mathematical word "matrix" meaning an "array of numbers" comes from the Latin word *"mater"* which means "mother, pregnant animal, or womb"? And doesn't the human embryo begin to grow and look like the Fibonacci spiral of growth? Again, this aligns with the ancient's theory of numbers involved with creation.

When discussing the Fibonacci sequence, one must also look at the Pentagram or the five pointed star. Known to date back to 4000 B.C., the pentagram has been found in caves and on temple walls. According to Knight, "the pentagram was the Egyptian symbol for knowledge" (Knight 199, 102).

Pythagoras defined the pentagram as a symbol of the human body representing the limbs and the head as the five points. As another symbol found in nature, if you cut an apple across the core, it will picture a five pointed star. Today, this symbol is seen all over the world from stars on flags to military uniforms and law enforcement shields. If you look at the pentagram, where the lines intersect as they cross yields the golden ratio.

"As a time honored symbol, the pentagram represents the five senses of man, the five elements of nature, and the five extremities of the human body" (Hall 1928, 326).

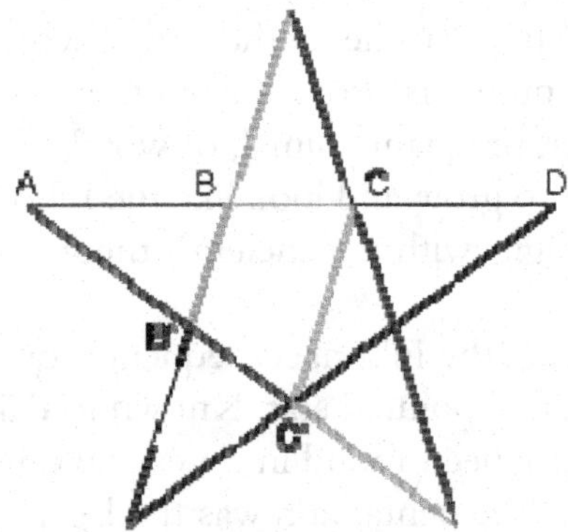

Personally, I love the Fibonacci Series. When I am not writing, studying ancient wisdom, or visiting sacred sites, I trade the foreign currency exchange and the stock market. When analyzing the charts for entries and exits of the market, I plot the Fibonacci retracements to see the values of those potential levels. It is amazing how the market will stop on a dime when it hits one of these levels. Different analyst will tell you that these are psychological levels that everyone monitors so that is why these levels are so predictable. But, the foreign currency exchange is a **Trillion** dollar a day industry many times larger than all of the world's stock exchanges, so I doubt that a few retail traders like myself can have that kind of drastic impact on these markets.

The Fibonacci levels are predictable and accurate. Outside the box, the bigger picture is that since we are part of the grand creation, it makes sense that we would resonate with these levels since it begins in our DNA. The sequence is represented in us as well as in all of nature where we co-exist in harmony.

For those who are more scientific in belief, the Fibonacci sequence actually supports the "Big Bang" theory as it demonstrates the ever expanding universe that was set forth by Edwin Hubble in 1929 and known as Hubble's Law.

Secrets of the Divine

The Qur'an also supports the "Big Bang" theory when it states:

Have the unbelievers not ever considered that the heavens and the earth were one piece and that We tore them apart from one another. From water We have created all living things. Will they then have no faith?
Qur'an 21:30

To the ancients, the "Big Bang" was known as the *"Tzimtzum"*, the "self-constriction of God's Light". According to the *Bahir*, "God first 'withdrew' His Light, forming a vacated space, in which all creation would take place. In order for His creative power to be in that space, He drew into it a 'thread' of His Light. It was through this thread that all creation took place. Tzimtzum did not take place in God's essence, but in His Light" (Kaplan 1979, 21).

Here's some Hebrew phrase with the gematria value of 618:

618 = El, the God of Israel (Genesis 33:20)
618 = To seal up vision and prophecy (Daniel 9:24)
618 = I am the first (Isaiah 48:12)

This discussion of Fibonacci leads directly into a discussion of Leonardo da Vinci (1452–1519) and his Vitruvian Man drawing which is just another example of sacred geometry within the human form.

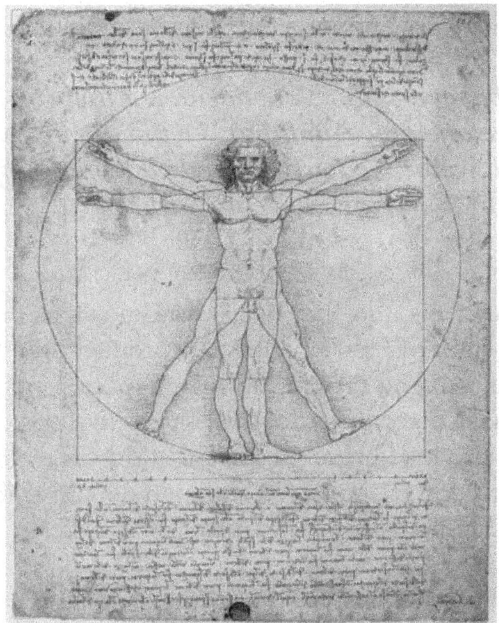

Vitruvian Man
Leonardo da Vinci

While Leonardo is most renowned for his *Mona Lisa* and *The Last Supper* paintings, he was also a great mathematician, astronomer, inventor, and philosopher. His drawings and sketches of the human form are so precise that it appears he studied anatomy in great detail to display such proportion.

The Vitruvian Man displays two superimposed male figures. The male figure with straight arms and legs, representing the square, is divided in half at the reproductive organs and the second male figure with outstretched arms and legs', representing the circle, is divided in half at the navel.

Why is this important? Many people confuse this drawing with "the squaring of the circle" which uses the "pi ratio of 3.1416" instead of the "golden ratio of 1.618". Like the golden ratio, Pi is also an irrational number represented by the Greek letter π or as the ratio 22/7 and is sometimes called the Archimedes Constant. It is the ratio of a circle's circumference to its diameter and was known to the Babylonians and Hindus. Most famously, the Pi symbol is built into the Great Pyramid at Giza to be forever memorialized.

In fact, the oldest known mathematical document is called the Ahmes Papyrus or Rhind Papyrus found at Thebes by Henry Rhind which currently resides at the British Museum. This papyrus contains the Pi ratio and Egyptologist believes that the papyrus dates to 1650 B.C., but is a copy of an earlier work dating between 2000 and 1800 B.C. Ahmes is the name of the scribe who copied the document which contains eighty-four mathematical problems and their solutions. Ahmes states that the papyrus contains "knowledge of all things, mysteries...all secrets" (Gillings 1972, 89).

Biblically, the Old Testament references the Pi ratio in several places, but the main reference relates to Solomon's molten sea.

And he made a molten sea, ten cubits from the one brim to the other: it was round all about, and his height was five cubits: and a line of thirty cubits did compass it round about
1Kings 7:23

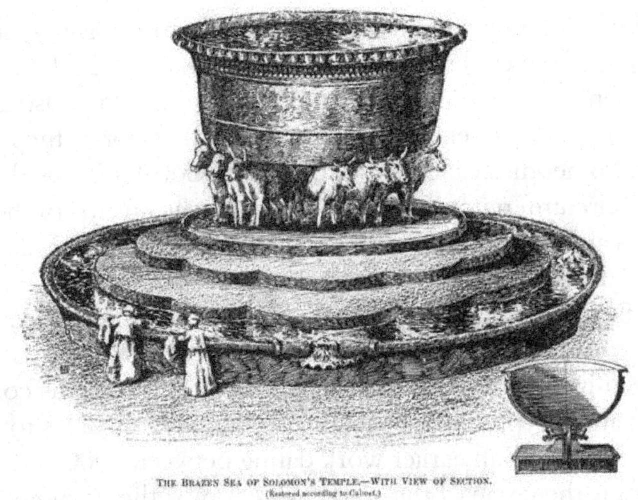

THE BRAZEN SEA OF SOLOMON'S TEMPLE.—WITH VIEW OF SECTION.
(Restored according to Calmet.)

The Moulton Sea

We will learn in Chapter 5 that where we live on Earth is an ideal location for "life" and through numerology it represents "wholeness" or "completeness" identified by the number nine (9). The number nine is derived from reducing the earth's diameter of 7,920 miles to a single digit (7 + 9 + 2 + 0 = 18 = 1 + 8 = 9).

By using the "squaring of the circle" related to the Earth, we arrive at some key biblically numbers as many believe that it represents the marriage of heaven and earth as spirit descends into matter. Previously, we learned that the circle represented male energy while the square represented female energy. Here we have the opposing energies joined.

Earth's diameter = 7,920 miles
Earth's radius = 3,960 miles
Square around Earth (perimeter) = 31,680 miles

Earth's diameter is 7,920 miles. If you drop the zero, the number 792 would equal the following words and phrases:

792 = Salvation in Hebrew which is also the meaning of Yeshua
792 = God Jehovah, creating the heavens and stretching them out
792 = creating the heaven

Look at the square (perimeter) around the earth. If you drop the zero, the number 3,168 equals Lord Jesus Christ in Greek, but so does the following biblical verse equal 3,168:

The Shekhinah is Coming

Thus saith God the Lord, He that created the heavens, and stretched them out; He that spread forth the Earth, and that which cometh out of it; He that giveth breath unto the people upon it, and spirit to them that walk therein
Isaiah 42:5

So the whole world belongs to only one person, Yeshua, who was called Lord Jesus Christ. Dropping the zero from the square around the Earth, you have the same number. This is what Paul is referring to in Acts 17:28, "***For in Him we live, and move, and have our being***" and discussed more in Chapter 6.

YESHUA	GREEK SPELLING	GEMATRIA
Lord	Κυριος	800
Jesus	Ἰησοῦς	888
Christ	Χριστός	1480
	TOTAL	**3168**

According to John Michell, "the value 1008 is the diameter of a circle with a circumference of 3,168 inches (Michell 2001, 172). Here is the alpha and omega, or the "one" and the "eight". We saw earlier in this chapter how the "one" and "eight" are combined in some significant words and phrases. The Greek phrases "first and last" and "true God" have a gematria value of 1332 which reduces to the single digit "9" (1 + 3 + 3 + 2 = 9) as does the "one" and the "eight" (1 + 8 = 9).

All things were made by Him; and without Him was not anything made that was made
John 1:3

Secrets of the Divine

By opening our minds to sacred geometry and numbers, we can begin to see that the Divine patterns are revealed in all things and numbers become the basic laws of creation and the building blocks of the Universe. Numbers become a common denominator for all nations and a language that communicates beyond time and space. Mathematics is undisputed, universally accepted, and totally objective. The ancients believed that mathematics was a way to represent ideas that had taken form as Plato had stated in the *Republic.*

As we leave this chapter, I hope you can begin to see the importance of comparing Biblical phrases using numbers rendering a much deeper and richer meaning of the written word. It can truly open the mind allowing one to step outside the box. Through numbers we can begin to understand the Divine essence that created our world and allow the scientist and faithful to walk the same path.

If nothing else, this chapter has demonstrated that there is not only design and patterns all around us, but there are signs for us to follow. If not, why does the Bible contain so many precise measurements?

WHO IS ENOCH, THE PROPHET?

If you were looking in the Bible to understand exactly who the Prophet Enoch was, you would find only three major references and two minor references.

The first major reference occurs in several verses of Genesis 5 where the descendents of Adam are delineated. Enoch was the seventh generation of patriarchs by way of Seth. Seth was the son born to Adam after Cain had slain Abel and would take up the mantel that Abel was denied. The lineage is Adam, Seth, Enos, Cainan, Mahalaleel, Jared and then Enoch (Genesis 5:18). The next three generations after Enoch would be Methuselah, who was Enoch's son, Lamech, and Noah.

Genesis 5:22 goes on to say, ***"And Enoch walked with God after he begat Methuselah three hundred years, and begat sons and daughters."***

Genesis 5:24 states ***"And Enoch walked with God: and he was not; for God took him."*** Enoch was 365 years old when he was taken (Genesis 5:23). The verb used here is "to take" which connotes "carried off". Enoch was carried off by God without experiencing death. In other words, he ascended into heaven, body and soul.

According to the Bible, only one other person walked with God and that was Noah (Genesis 6:9), who was Enoch's great grandson. But no other person mentioned in the Bible was "taken" by God, which made Enoch the first immortal man having knowledge considered to be super human. Enoch observed and recorded all the secrets related to heaven and Earth.

The two minor references to Enoch include Chronicles 1:1 which begins with the descendents of Adam and list Enoch. There is another brief mention in Luke 3:37, where Enoch is named in the retracing of Jesus' genealogy.

The second major reference is Hebrews 11:5, where St. Paul says, ***"By faith Enoch was translated that he should not see death; and was not found, because God had translated him; for before his translation he had this testimony, that he pleased God."*** The word "translated" here means ascended without death.

The third major reference is Jude 1:14, ***"And Enoch also, the seventh from Adam, prophesied of these, saying, 'Behold, the Lord cometh with ten thousands of his saints.'"*** It is this reference that is cited most often.

Although Enoch is not mentioned by name in Revelation 11:3, he is believed to be one of the ***"two witnesses"*** who will appear at the end of the world. The other witness is believed to be Elijah who ascended to heaven in a "whirlwind" (2Kings 2:11).

In Hebrew, Enoch is spelled *Henoch.* It is a masculine name meaning consecrated, dedicated, or teacher. Other ancient texts spell Enoch as *"ChNVK"* meaning "initiate" with a gematria value of 84. This number will be important in Chapter 6.

As history began to be recorded in written form, many prominent Church Fathers referenced the Book of Enoch in their writings. These included Irenaeus and Clement of Alexandria, both second century Christians as well as Origen of Alexandria, a theologian and philosopher in A.D. 254.

Josephus Flavius (A.D. 37–ca. 100) was a first century Jewish historian as well as a member of the priesthood who wrote two major works namely, *The Jewish War (ca. A.D. 75)* and *Antiquities of the Jews (ca. A.D. 94).* Josephus wrote about the destruction of the Temple in A.D. 70, but also stated that Enoch was "taken by God" clearly teaching the doctrine of immortality (*Antiquities 9:2:2*). The Septuagint states that Enoch was "taken by or returned to the deity."

The first century historian, Tertullian (A.D.160–220) felt that the Book of Enoch was not received by the Christians as it was not included in the Hebrew canon. Yet, the Church Fathers were deeply influenced by Enoch and wrote about the Book of Enoch as being divinely inspired.

It cannot be denied that the Book of Enoch was a known document that had existed for some time, but it was not included in the canon that became the accepted biblical document that was established by the Council of Nicea in A.D. 325. By A.D. 500, the Book of Enoch vanished from all Christian references. It is hard to understand why this happened unless one can understand what the Book of Enoch contains.

As stated, in 1947–48, the first of the Dead Sea Scrolls were discovered in Qumran located at the northern end of the Dead Sea near the border. The manuscripts related to Enoch were found in Qumran Cave 4 in Jordan around 1952.

However, in 1773, a Scottish explorer named James Bruce discovered the complete Enoch text in Abyssinia, now Ethiopia. The Book of Enoch was part of the Ethiopian Bible and still is today. Within the Ethiopian Bible, the book of Enoch is located just prior to the book of Job. James Bruce returned home with a copy of the Ethiopic version and in 1821 it was translated into English by Richard Laurence. It was translated again in 1912 by R.H. Charles.

It is believed that this ancient text was written in the second or first century B.C. in Hebrew or Aramaic. It was later translated into Greek, Ethiopic, and Latin. Only Greek and Latin fragments have been found, but a complete Ethiopic version—*1 Enoch* has been found which is believed to be a later translation.

The Shekhinah is Coming

The Book of Enoch describes how Enoch journeys through the seven levels of heaven with his angelic guide Uriel. Each level has its own special secrets and Enoch is taught the workings of the universe and the relationship between heaven and earth with the Sun, Moon, and stars. It also includes the legend of the two hundred "watchers" and their future fate as well as Enoch's direct interaction with the face of God in the seventh heaven.

Many scholars tend to describe the Book of Enoch as being comprised of five different books differentiated as *1 Enoch, 2 Enoch, 3 Enoch, 4 Enoch, and 5 Enoch.*

In *1 Enoch*, Enoch is aware of the "watchers—the fallen ones", who have interfered with humankind and with whom God is very angry. The watchers, led by the Angel Semyaza, ask that Enoch intercede on their behalf asking God to pardon their bad deeds. Enoch agrees, but is unsuccessful in obtaining a pardon for the watchers as they were regarded as introducing evil into the world. The watchers are said to have taught man how to make swords, knives, shields, and breastplates as well as how to observe the stars and signs along with the other secrets of heaven.

Our current Bible briefly mentions how the ***"sons of God"*** mated with the ***"daughters of men"*** **(Genesis 6:2)** and that there were ***"giants in the earth"*** **(Genesis 6:4)**. These "giants" were the offspring of the "watchers" mating with humankind and known as the Nephilim.

2 Enoch contains further discussion of condemning the watchers and the future coming of the Messiah to judge all and resurrect the righteous. Here we have the teachings of the pre-existence of the "son of man", who "from the beginning existed in secret", and whose "name was invoked in the presence of the Lord of spirits, before the Sun and the signs were created" (Chapter XLVII: 3). Enoch is also shown the fate of mankind and the coming flood.

3 Enoch is very scientific and explains the harmony and order of the universe, especially the luminaries of heaven. It goes on to state that in the end times, this order will not exist. It is interesting that the largest collection of *3 Enoch* can be found in the Vatican archives in Rome.

4 Enoch is a dream vision where Enoch sees the future that is akin to the Book of Revelations. Enoch's prophetic dream covers the history of man from the flood including the building of Solomon's temple, its subsequent destruction, and the exile of the Hebrew people.

5 Enoch is apocalyptic discussing the history and future of man and the new eternal Earth and heaven that is to come.

As Enoch leaves heaven, he is instructed to write down everything he learns and upon his return to Earth, he is to instruct his son Methuselah on everything so that the information can be passed from generation to generation. Enoch is given one year to complete this instruction before the angelic being returns to take Enoch to abode in heaven forever. Prior to the prophesied flood, the 365 books written by Enoch are taken by Noah into the ark to be preserved for future generations.

Even the Qur'an lists their twenty-five prominent prophets where Enoch is second only to Adam whom they believed to be the first prophet. In Islam, Enoch is referred to as Idris, which in Arabic means "the instructor". Muslim tradition credits Idris with inventing astronomy, writing, and arithmetic and considered him a man of truth and regarded him as righteous. Enoch (Idris) is mentioned twice in the Qur'an in 19:56–57 and 21:85–86. The story of Enoch also parallels the experience of Muhammad in the Islamic tradition.

It appears that Enoch was greater than Abraham whom we refer to as the "Father of All Nations" as God made a covenant with Abraham ***"in thy seed shall all the nations of the earth be blessed; because thou hast obeyed my voice"*** **(Genesis 23:18)**. Even the

Muslim faith stems from Abraham through his son Ishmael. The mother of Ishmael was Hagar who was Sarai's Egyptian handmaiden (Genesis 16:3).

In addition, Abraham did not prophesy nor did he see God's face as he was instructed to ***"walk before Him"*** **(Genesis 17:1).** The New Testament affirms the inability of people to see the face of God when John states ***"no man has seen God at any time"*** **(John 1:18)** and Paul states ***"no man has ever seen or can see God"*** **(1Timothy 6:16)**. Abraham was the twenty-eighth generation from Adam which puts Enoch four hundred years before Abraham and much closer to the original knowledge.

And obviously, the creation story as told by Moses comes from the records and instructions that Enoch had given to Methuselah to pass on to future generations. It should be noted that Methuselah lived longer than anyone and died at the age of nine hundred sixty-nine years which was certainly plenty of time to teach Enoch's information.

Moses was born the fifty generation after Adam. While Moses received the Ten Commandments from God, he was not allowed to see his face, but only his back (Exodus 33:20–23). And while Moses led the people in exile for forty years, he was not allowed to cross into the Promised Land as he had struck the rock twice with his staff against God's command to speak unto the rock (Numbers 20:8–12). Moses died in the land of Moab where he was buried and remains unto this day (Deuteronomy 34:4–6).

By all references and indications, Enoch was the forerunner to Jesus and an extraordinary man. Clearly, Enoch carried a mantle of greatness for his devoutness and faith. So, how is it that the Book of Enoch is not included in the present day Hebrew or Christian Bible? I think the answer lies in what the Book of Enoch contains. I will now reference some excerpts from the Richard Laurence translation.

In Chapter III: 1–2, "All who are in the heavens know what is transacted there. They know that the heavenly luminaries change not their paths; that each rises and set regularly, everyone at its proper period, without transgressing the commands which they have received. They behold the Earth, and understand what is there transacted, from the beginning to the end of it."

In Chapter XXXIL: 2–4, "To the East I perceived the extremities of the Earth, where heaven ceased. The gates of heaven stood open, and I beheld the celestial stars come forth. I numbered them as they proceeded out of the gate, and wrote them all down, as they came out one by one according to their number. I wrote down their names altogether, their times and their seasons, as the angel Uriel, who was with me, pointed them out to me. He showed them all to me, and wrote down an account of them. He also wrote down for me their names, their regulations, and their operations."

He determines the number of the stars and calls them each by name
Psalms 147:4

In Chapter LXXI:1 it states, "The book of the revolutions of the luminaries of heaven, according to their respective classes, their respective names, the places where they commence their progress, and their respective months, which Uriel, the holy angel who was with me, explained to me; he who conducts them. The whole account of them, according to every year of the world forever, until a new work shall be effected, which will be eternal."

After this, Enoch is informed of the laws of the Sun and the Moon. There is detail to the cycles of each luminary and the paths that they take including a discussion of the winter and summer solstices along with the spring and autumn equinox. I will define these terms in Chapter 5.

It further discusses the order and harmony of the universe and how the Sun, Moon, and stars are placed in the heavens for signs and seasons. They are revered for how they perform their designated tasks. "Of heaven in heaven, and in the world; that they might rule in the face of the sky, and appearing over the Earth, become conductors of the days and nights: the Sun, the Moon, the stars, and all the ministers of heaven, which make their circuit with all the chariots of heaven" (Chapter LXXIV: 8–9).

I blessed the Lord of glory, who had made those great and splendid signs, that they might display the magnificence of His works to angels and to the souls of men; and that these might glorify all His works and operations; might see the effect of His power; might glorify the great labor of His hands; and bless Him forever

Enoch 35:3

Hebrew legend states that Adam was given a book by the Angel Rezial upon his expulsion from the Garden of Eden which contained all the celestial and earthly knowledge to aid mankind. Made of sapphire and written by the hand of God, this wisdom was passed on to his son Seth who kept the book hidden away in the cleft of a rock. The location of the hidden book was given to Enoch in a dream. Even Josephus states in the *Jewish Antiquities* that Adam and his son Seth knew "this sort of wisdom which is concerned with the heavenly bodies and their order."

Many may not accept the Book of Enoch as being "divinely inspired", but taking the time to read this text, you will discover the origin of many of the "images" used to describe God like those viewed in the Sistine Chapel. The Book of Enoch also uses phrases like "sons of the God" which meant angels or messengers coming down from heaven. You will find many references that exist in the current day Bible including the son of man, the flood, and many more. It also speaks of the same "coming kingdom" that is referenced by Jesus during his ministry.

The Book of Enoch is similar to the Book of Revelation, except it is not a vision according to the early Church Fathers and Josephus. Enoch was actually taken into the heavenly realms to interact with the Divine.

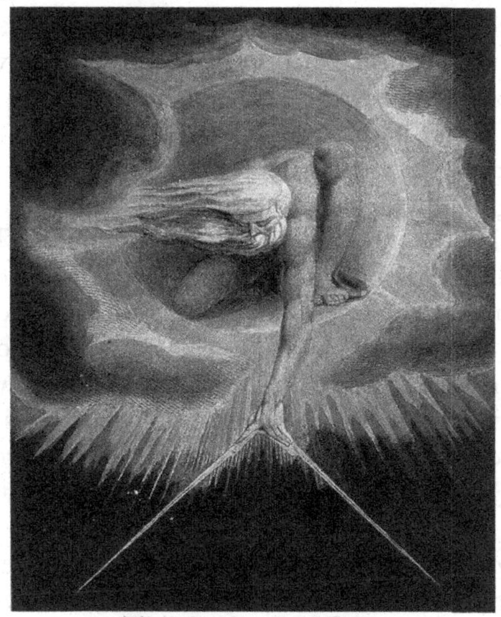

The Ancient of Days
William Blake–18th Century
Whitworth Art Gallery
University of Manchester, UK

The Shekhinah is Coming

He stretcheth out the north over the empty place, and hangeth the Earth upon nothing
Job 26:7

Lord, I have loved the habitation of thy house, and the place where thine honour dwelleth
Psalms 26:8

Some will say that Enoch visited an advanced civilization in the North and not really heaven. In ancient times, the North was often referred to as the "abode of the gods." These civilizations were referred to as gods, because they possessed a greater knowledge than most people. So, was it heaven or not, you be your own judge depending on if you're in or out of the box.

The word for heaven in Hebrew is "*Shamayim*". It actually means "the heights" and begins with the letter "shin". Later in this chapter, you will understand the significance of "shin". The Bible refers to three different heavens: above the Earth where clouds and birds exist, the area occupied by the planets and stars, and the area occupied by the high and lofty One. Even Paul spoke about a third heaven in 2Corinthians 12:2–6. Heaven is beyond the physical world as it is a spiritual dimension where vibration, light, and sound originate.

As stated in Chapter 3, the equilateral triangle is referred to as "The Delta of Enoch" and comes from the Masonic Testament.

In this vision Enoch saw a mountain and a golden triangle showing the rays of the Sun. From that time this device became known as the Delta of Enoch
Enoch 2:2

NOTE: The Masonic Testament is historical research gathered together by Dr. Robert Lomas and maintained at the University of Bradford. The information is also discussed in Dr. Lomas' book, *The Hiram Key*.

Enoch was very devout with a great love of God. In his vision, the golden triangle is God like the burning bush of Moses. God says, "Enoch, thou hast longed to know my true name. Arise and follow me, and thou shalt know it."

Enoch went in search of the mountain he saw in his vision. He found it in the land of Canaan and excavated nine levels of earth one above the other and built a temple above the top one. As in the vision, Enoch created a gold triangle upon which he inscribed the ineffable name of God and attached it to a cube of Agate crystal. The stone was then enclosed in a great ring of iron and placed on the bottom level.

Knowing of the impending flood, Enoch then erected two great columns so that the wisdom given to him by God would not be lost. One column, upon which a description of the nine levels was written in hieroglyphics, was made out of granite to resist fire. The other column, upon which the wisdom teachings were written, was made out of brass to resist water damage. The granite column was lost in the Flood and so was the true name of God, but the brass column was found by Noah after the Flood waters dissipated.

The name of God remained lost until it was given to Moses who also inscribed the name on a gold triangle and placed it in the Ark of the Covenant. The name was only given to the High Priest, first to Aaron and then his successor Eleazar. Unfortunately, the sacred name has been lost again and the Bible does not reference it.

According to the Bible, the Ark of the Covenant contained only three items identified in the book of Hebrews 9:4:

1. Two Tables of the law
2. A Golden Pot containing an omer of manna
3. Aaron's Rod that budded

The Qur'an 2:248 confirms what was contained in the Ark of the Covenant. It is a belief in Islam that the Ark of the Covenant will be found near the end of times.

J. James Tissot. Copyright by de Brunoff, 1904.

THE ARK OF THE COVENANT. Ex. xxv. 10.

"And they shall make an ark *of* shittim wood."

The Ark of the Covenant

Since we have already discussed Sacred Geometry, it should be noted that the Ark of the Covenant was built utilizing the Golden Mean in its dimensions (Exodus 25:10–16). It is these same dimensions that were used in the design of Solomon's Temple.

Legend holds that Enoch's temple was discovered by Solomon who built the Temple of Justice upon the site. Solomon constructed his temple, known as the First Temple upon Mount Moriah in 960 B.C. which contained secret vaults below on nine different levels.

During Enoch's time there was no reference to the "trinity" of the Godhead as this came much later as Christianity was being formed and delineated in the Nicene Creed which was discussed in Chapter 1.

Secrets of the Divine

Is it possible that the "Delta of Enoch", symbolized as an equilateral triangle, is the genesis for the concept of the trinity? Many ancient pictures that refer to the ***"Ancient of Days"***, described in Daniel 7:9 shows the equilateral triangle behind the head of the God figure. This is much different than the halos displayed behind Christ and the Saints in other pictures. I'm sure you have also seen images with an "eye" in the middle of an equilateral triangle. This is the same image on the back of the American dollar bill shown in the apex of the pyramid.

Ancient of Days
Russia
19th Century

The Shekhinah is Coming

A possible related topic to the "Delta of Enoch" is what is known as the "Priestly Blessing" commanded by the Lord unto Aaron. In Hebrew, the priestly blessing is known as the *Birkat Kohanim* or *Nesi'at Kapayim* which means the "lifting of the hands". It states:

יברכך יהוה וישמרך:
יאר יהוה פניו אליך ויחנך:
ישא יהוה פניו אליך וישם לך שלום:

And the Lord spake unto Moses, saying, Speak unto Aaron and unto his sons, saying, on this wise ye shall bless the children of Israel, saying unto them, The Lord bless thee, and keep thee: The Lord make his face shine upon thee, and be gracious unto thee: The Lord Lift up his countenance upon thee, and give thee peace. And they shall put My name upon the children of Israel; and I will bless them
Numbers 6:22–27

The Israel Museum is in possession of a twenty-seven hundred year old parchment that contains this blessing that originated during the First Temple built by King Solomon. It is written in the ancient Semitic script which preceded the Aramaic language spoken by Jesus and the current day Hebrew language.

It is not so much the words that are said, but the way in which the High Priest holds his hands while saying the prayer, especially since we know that the name of God was placed on a triangle. Notice the formation of the triangle within the hand gesture used by the High Priest as they place the sacred name upon the children of Israel during the blessing. The priest hands should be precisely level with the mouth as they speak (vibrate) the words and the Divine blessings flow.

According to the Talmud, this forms the lattice through which God peers as referenced in Song of Songs 2:9.

According to scripture, when God interacts directly with the physical world, especially when it relates to creation, it is said He uses his hands and fingers.

Mine hand also hath laid the foundation of the Earth, and My right hand hath spanned the heavens: when I call unto them, they stand up together
Isaiah 48:13

Birkat Kohanim: The Priestly Blessing
Zely Smekhov

The Shekhinah is Coming

In recent history, we have witnessed half of this gesture in the Vulcan Hand Salute given by Mr. Spock on the hit television series *Star Trek*. Mr. Spock, played by Leonard Nimoy, would raise his hand in this gesture and say, "Live Long and Prosper." It was his Vulcan blessing.

Leonard Nimoy as Mr. Spock

Many think that this gesture resembles the Hebrew letter "shin–ש" which begins the word "Shaddai" another name for God as a protector. It also begins the word Shabbat, the Jewish Sabbath and sacred time of rest. In the Sefer Yetzirah, it states that the letter Shin is "King over Fire" and the symbol representing the letter "shin" certainly does appear as a flame.

The letter "shin" is also inscribed on the "mezuzah" a vessel which contains a prayer and placed on the door frames of homes as directed in Deuteronomy 6:9. The prayer states:

Hear, O Israel: The Lord our God is one Lord: And thou shalt love the Lord thy God with all thine heart, and with all thy soul,

and with all thy might. And these words, which I command thee this day, shall be in thine heart
Deuteronomy 6:4–6

Mezuzah

If you have ever witnessed someone performing the ancient healing art of Reiki, you will see a similar hand position used over the face and the chest of the one receiving the healing as the energies are channeled to them. The healer is the conduit for the energies to flow from Spirit as is needed by the person during a Reiki healing session. It is done by the "laying on of hands". Reiki is similar to tuning your radio to the right frequency to hear a particular station. The frequency always exists whether your radio is turned on or off.

Is Reiki similar to Einstein's theory of Energy or $E=mc^2$? This mathematical formula means (E) energy equals mass or matter (m) times the speed of light (c) squared (2). It is the process where matter is infused with energy. To the ancients this was the "Azoth" or universal medicine. It was the "One" that was in all things.

According to the *Bahir*, "It is written in Habakkuk 3:4, ***"He has rays from His hand, and His hidden force is there"***. This is the light that was stored away and hidden as it is written in Psalms 31:20" (Kaplan 1979, 54).

This energy charge is the same type of energy that Moses used when he named Joshua to succeed him. When Moses was one hundred twenty years old, the Lord informed him that he would die and not cross over the Jordan River into Canaan. The leadership was passed to Joshua after he received a "**charge**" from Moses. Moses did this by laying his hands on Joshua.

Moses lays his hands upon Joshua
Gerard Hoet–1728
Bizzell Bible Collection
University of Oklahoma Libraries

And the Lord said unto Moses, behold, thy days approach that thou must die. Call Joshua and present yourselves in the tabernacle of the congregation that I may give him a charge
Deuteronomy 31:14

The Shekhinah is Coming

And he gave Joshua, the son of Nun a charge, and said, be strong and of good courage for thou shalt bring the children of Israel into the land which I swear unto them and I will be with thee
Deuteronomy 31:23

Could this be the same hand gesture that Jesus and the disciples used when they healed others?

UNDERSTANDING COSMOLOGY THE DIVINE SCIENCE

And God said, Let there be lights in the firmament of the heaven to divide the day from the night; and let them be for signs, and for seasons, and for days, and years: And let them be for lights in the firmament of the heaven to give light upon the Earth: and it was so

Genesis 1:14–15

According to Webster's Dictionary, the word "sign" comes from the Latin word *"signum"* meaning "a mark" and defines it as:

- That by which anything is shown, made known, or represent; something that indicates a fact, quality, etc.; a mark; a token; an indication
- A motion, action, or gesture by which a thought is expressed
- Any symbol or emblem which prefigures, typifies, or represents an idea
- A mark or symbol having an accepted and specific meaning

In Hebrew, "a sign" is called *"AVTH" (תוא)* and means "prophetic mark" which is a very appropriate definition in view of what I am proposing in this book.

It is simply something selected to represent something else. Signs are arbitrary but agreed upon by all. For example, the letters of the alphabet are "signs" for sounds. Numbers are "signs" for quantity. From the very beginning of our lives, we are taught various "signs" which are usually clues for making choices. We use "signs" on the road when we drive to signal a certain condition. When you travel to various countries, you need to learn their signs to navigate your visit. But, there are also so called universal signs as one thinks of the Red Cross or the Handicapped images. How many people identify the manufacturer of a car just by seeing the car's logo or emblem? And let's not forget about the sign of the most famous "golden arches" of McDonalds now a worldwide phenomenon.

Towers were signs and existed in all ancient cultures as a means to connect heaven and Earth and were usually connected to the temples. In Islam, the minaret or tower above the mosque comes from the Arabic word *"manara"*, which means "giving off light". From the minaret the faithful are called to prayer and the towers are a constant reminder of Allah's presence. The Babylonians had ziggurats which were known as "peaks of the gods" and were built in a stair step fashion with each step related to one of the planets in the solar system.

For me when I see the word "light", I immediately pause and pay attention. Is the word something luminous or a code word to enlightenment? As I am always looking for clues to the bigger picture, for me, the word "light" means more than just something that shines as it is more about wisdom and knowledge.

I believe that the Divine mind placed wisdom in the stars and that we need to find what the wisdom is telling us. Don't we always think of God in heaven as being above us (Psalms 103:11)? Who isn't amazed at the magnificent view of the heavens on a clear, dark night?

The last thing I do at night prior to locking up the house is to take my dogs out. While they are doing what comes naturally to them, I take the opportunity to view the night sky. It's my way of saying goodnight to the Divine and being humbled by what I see. It certainly puts my petty little issues into perspective before going to sleep at night. I don't even have the vocabulary to explain the awesomeness of what we view each and every night in the sky.

Secrets of the Divine

Let me pause here and put some perspective on where we live as seen from the celestial heavens down to Earth including some explanations to understand a more complete picture of the workings of our solar system. Remember, we are building a foundation for *What If?*

First, we live in a Universe filled with galaxies. Our home galaxy is called the Milky Way Galaxy and is filled with billions of stars and star systems. Our star system, known as the Solar System, is located on the Orion spur of the Milky Way Galaxy which when viewed from above gives the appearance of spiral arms coming out from a central point. To me it looks like an expanding Fibonacci spiral.

If viewed from the side, the Milky Way Galaxy appears as a blanket with a hump in the middle. That hump is the fertile central point that is continuously giving birth to new stars. It is a process that continually takes place whether we are aware of it or not. From Earth, the Milky Way appears as a snowy belt, about four to twenty degrees in width and stretches over the sky from southwest to northeast cutting across the ecliptic. It is best viewed from below the Earth's equator in the Southern Hemisphere of the planet.

The ancient Egyptians referred to the Milky Way as the River Styx and many of their temple hieroglyphs contained boats for the deceased to travel in on their return to the stars. The Egyptians saw the Nile River as the terrestrial Milky Way following the ancient axiom "As Above, So Below."

Milton refers to the Milky Way as:

A broad and ample road, whose dust is gold, and pavements stars,—as stars to thee appear seen in the galaxy, that Milky Way, which nightly as a circling zone thou seest powder'd with stars.
Milton, Paradise Lost: Book vii–Line 577.

The Shekhinah is Coming

Many ancient poets and philosophers called it "the way" as the path which their deities used in the heavens and claimed that it led directly to "the throne and the Thunderer's abode" as Ovid wrote in *Metamorphoses*, a narrative poem that described the creation and history of the world (Translation by Sir Samuel Garth in 1717–lines 1:220–1:222).

As you can see from the picture, our location (the Sun with arrow) is a mere "speck" of light in relationship to the whole universe. In Greek, the word "universe" has a gematria value of 63 as does the Greek word "Theos" meaning God.

Our system has a central Sun with 7 primary planets, 85 asteroids, 21 satellite moons, and several hundred comets. The planet Pluto was dethroned in 2006 and classified as a dwarf planet when a new definition for planet was established by the IAU (International Astronomical Union). I find the dethroning of Pluto fascinating, because as you will discover later in this chapter, the number nine has magical abilities and is also known as the number for wholeness and completeness. Our solar system is now short one planet for completeness. Does this decision make room for the much debated Planet X? What does NASA know?

The Universe is dynamic with everything moving. All ancients documented how certain lights moved across the sky. From the Greeks, they were known as *"planetes asters" ('πλάνητες ἀστέρες')* meaning "wandering stars" as they were continually changing their place in the heavens. Today, we simply call them planets.

The ancients referred to the planets as the "seven great gods". Many legends from all ancient cultures abound about these gods identified with the celestial orbs which some say began with the Sumerians around 3500–3000 B.C. Both the Greeks and the Romans assigned gods and goddesses to the planets as well as symbolic meanings. It is the same planets that we know today as their names have not changed. They include the Sun, Moon, Mercury, Venus, Mars, Jupiter, and Saturn. The planet names also became the names for the days in the week:

Sunday—Sun
Monday—Moon
Tuesday—Mars
Wednesday—Mercury
Thursday—Jupiter
Friday—Venus
Saturday—Saturn

The Shekhinah is Coming

All ancient cultures have the same name for the days of the week including the same sequence. They differ only in which day begins the week as each of the three major religions have a different holy day. The holy day for Islam is Friday, Jewish is Saturday, and Christian is Sunday.

The Sun, our star, is located ninety-three million miles from Earth providing the perfect climate for life as its rays reach the Earth in eight minutes and nineteen seconds. If the Earth was 1,000 miles closer or further away from the Sun, life would not exist as we know it or not at all. Yet another 1,000 miles would only be a .00001075268 (1/10,000) percent of change.

Therefore, the Sun, a gaseous ball of plasma and composed of 73% hydrogen, becomes the life-giving force of our solar system without which we could not exist. The ancients viewed the Sun as their supreme deity and the vital principle in nature as it provided Life, Light, and Heat. This was the main reason that the temples of worship faced the East where the Sun rises. To the Egyptians, the Sun related to immortality and the gods. In Greek, the word for "brightness" has a gematria value of 930 as does the Greek word for "love" and the phrase "to save life". Interestingly, this number is the same as the distance between the Sun and Earth when dropping the zeros. You can begin to see why the Sol Invictus was so important to respect as Christianity was being formed.

Anyone who has taken a high school biology class has probably studied Photosynthesis. Simply, it is the interaction of the Sun's life-giving force with all plant life. It is the process where plants convert the carbon dioxide released by human breathing into oxygen. This oxygen is then available for the human being to breathe in again. This is the cycle of life on Earth as both mankind and plants could not grow if it weren't for the Sun's energy and this process. Photosynthesis comes from the Greek word "phos" which means "light" and the word "synthesis" which means "putting together" or "composition".

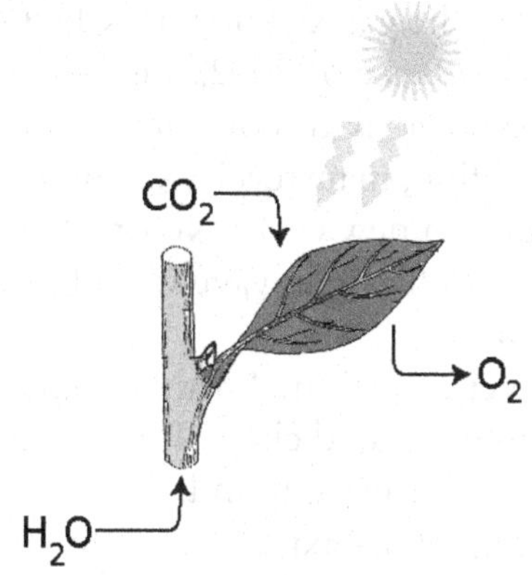

The Process of Photosynthesis

Interestingly, the atomic weight for oxygen as shown on the Table of Periodic Elements discussed in Chapter 3 is equal to eight which is the same number for Jesus in gematria. In addition, the Sun, composed primarily of Hydrogen which carries the atomic weight of one, the lightest of elements, is equal to Lord in gematria as seen in Chapter 3. So, you have the Sun (One) providing oxygen (eight) to the Earth which we have identified as the Alpha and Omega concept. In essence, it is our life line and becomes more apparent if you look at some more gematria. The word "Sun" in Greek is equal to 318 as is the Hebrew phrase "The God of gods and Lord of lords" from Deuteronomy 10:17.

Their line is gone out through all the Earth and their words to the end of the world. In them He set a tabernacle for the Sun
Psalms 19:4

The Shekhinah is Coming

The Earth turns on its axis as does the Sun and all the other planets. As I stated, nothing is static in the Universe, everything is moving. The Earth revolves around the Sun and the Sun revolves around a central point in the galaxy known as the Galactic Center. As we approach the winter solstice of 2012, this central "Sun" will become extremely important to the activities of Earth as many celestial bodies will align with it. In addition, many cycles within our galaxy will be completing and beginning a new cycle. No one knows for sure what will transpire, but any galactic superwave would certainly disrupt the magnetic fields of Earth.

The yearly movement of the Earth around the Sun is in the form of an ecliptic—an elongated circle. It is in this path that the constellations in the zodiac can be found. As the Earth moves around the Sun, it is also rotating on its axis at a twenty-three degree tilt. It is this tilt that creates the seasons on Earth and relates to the solstices and the equinoxes. To the ancients, the solstices and equinoxes were a time of rituals and celebrations and marked the four creatures that represented the zodiac signs we discussed in Chapter 1. As time has shifted, these zodiac signs have changed and no longer apply. Today we have the Christian celebration of Easter and Christmas marking two of these times.

If you imagine that the Earth's equator is extended out into the heavens, it will cross the ecliptic path at two points. These intersections are termed the Vernal Equinox and the Autumnal Equinox. It is from the Latin word meaning "equal night". The equinox is the midpoint between the two extremes of the Sun, when night and day become of equal length, twelve hours each. The Vernal Equinox, known as the "Rite of Spring" occurs around March 21 and the Autumnal Equinox occurs around September 21 each year. In ancient times, these would have been the zodiac signs Taurus the Bull and Scorpio the Eagle respectfully, but due to the precession of the equinox, they have changed.

The precession of the equinox moves the Sun backward (retrogrades) along the path of the ecliptic about one degree every seventy-two years. Every 2160 years, the Sun passes into the zone of the preceding zodiacal sign. This phenomenon is due to the tilt of Earth's axis and the slow wobble of its rotation. Thus the Sun remains in each sign of the zodiac for 2160 years and the complete circuit would take 25,920 years (12 x 2160 = 25,920). This is known as the Grand Celestial Year or the Platonic Year and is usually rounded to 26,000. It is the Sun's rotation around the central sun of our galaxy that will complete this Grand cycle in 2012.

Each year the Sun reaches two extreme points in its travels. These points are called the solstices from the Latin words meaning "sol" for "Sun" and "sistere" for "to stand still". When the Sun reaches its most northerly position, known as the Winter Solstice on December 21, daylight is the shortest time of the year. The Sun then appears to stop and reverse directions until it reaches the most southerly position, known as the Summer Solstice on June 21, where daylight is the longest time of the year. The ancients called the solstices the "gates of the soul" and these would have been the zodiac signs Aquarius the Waterman and Leo the Lion.

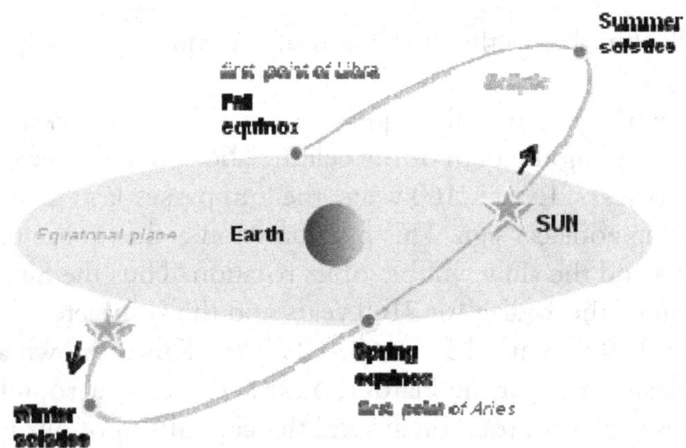

Celestial Equator–Horizontal disk
(the imaginary extension of Earth's equator)
Solstices and Equinoxes along
The Sun Path–Diagonal Ecliptic

To maintain the importance of the two solstices (winter and summer), they were marked by the two free standing bronze pillars (Boaz and Jachin) of Solomon's temple as shown in Appendix I. During Solomon's long reign of 40 years, he was the "supreme light" as his name identifies: SOL–OM–ON and his kingdom the highest in the land. Remember, Sol meant "Sun".

Are you beginning to understand why there was so much Sun worship by the ancients? Many of the ancient sites around the world have huge stone temples dedicated to the Sun and their legends include many gods and goddess that hail from the Sun, our star, as they believed that is where life originated. They were absolutely right as the Sun provides the perfect environment for life to exist.

Let's briefly discuss the Moon. Scientists are now confirming that the Moon was once part of the Earth before it collided with a large object. This information had been maintained in the Babylonian myth of Marduk and Tiamat, but it wasn't until the astronauts brought rock samples back from the Moon that the collision was confirmed. The Earth is very indebted to the Moon which helps maintain the Earth's tilt that provides the seasons. However, each year the Moon moves further away from Earth and eventually will not be caught in Earth's gravity and voyage into space. Knowing the Moon's diameter of 2,160 miles some interesting gematria comparisons can be made:

2160 = Diameter of the Moon
2160 = Number of years that the Sun spends in each zodiac sign
216 = All nations shall serve him
216 = Breath
216 = He shall speak
216 = Lion
216 = Power

The Greek Astronomer, Hipparchus (ca. 190–120 B.C.), is credited with the discovery of the precession of the equinox, which Ptolemy then mentions in his work the *Almagest,* but many believe that the Egyptians were well aware of this phenomenon prior to that time. Hipparchus cataloged eight hundred fixed stars and is considered the greatest ancient astronomer of antiquity. He is also credited with developing trigonometry.

Claudius Ptolemy (ca. 90–168) was a Greek mathematician and astronomer living in Alexandria, Egypt in the second century A.D. who studied Babylonian astronomy and the arithmetical techniques for calculating astronomical phenomena regarding the motion of the stars and planets. His first authoritative work called the *Almagest: "The Great Treatise"* contains a star catalogue similar to Hipparchus that is still in use today. It is the only surviving comprehensive ancient work on astronomy.

Ptolemy promoted the "Geocentric" model for calculating celestial motions which places the Earth fixed at the center of the Universe. Ptolemy believed that everything revolved around the Earth rather than the Sun. Ptolemy documented astrology in his third book known sometimes as *Apotelesmatika* or more commonly *Tetrabiblos, "Four books"*. This work also had great influence on the Islamic world.

Ptolemy's Earth Centered Universe
The Celestial Atlas
Andreas Cellarius
British Library–London, UK

In 1543 just before his death, Nicolaus Copernicus (1473–1543), a Polish man, published his book, *De Revolutionibus Orbium Coelestrium* which promoted the theory that the Earth was also a planet and that it revolved around the Sun fixed at the center of the Universe. This differed from the accepted Ptolemaic model and was called the "Heliocentric" model coming from the Greek word *"helios"* meaning "Sun" and *"centric"* meaning "near the center".

Copernicus' Sun Centered Universe
The Celestial Atlas
Andreas Cellarius
British Library–London, UK

The Shekhinah is Coming

Galileo Galilei (1564–1642) who observed the Universe through some of the first telescopes promoted the Copernicus theory and published his work in the *Sidereus Nuncius* meaning Starry Messenger. These teachings were highly frowned upon by the Church as dangerous to the faith. The Church felt his theories contradicted passages in scripture, namely 1Chronicles 16:30, Psalms 93:1, Psalms 96:10, Psalms 104:5, and Ecclesiastes 1:5.

In 1633, Galileo was charged with heresy and brought to trial in Rome "for holding as true the false doctrine taught by some that the Sun is the center of the world". The process, known as the "Galileo Affair" (Il Processo Galileano) ended after fourteen years with Galileo guilty and under permanent house arrest. Galileo was forced to deny the Copernicus theory on his knees before the Pope. Galileo contributed much to the scientific community with his work eventually being honored and used to further the understanding of the Universe. Galileo was certainly more fortunate than his predecessor Giordano Bruno (1548–1600) an Italian Dominican friar, who was burned at the stake for the same beliefs as he was found guilty of heresy by the Roman Inquisition.

Galileo before the Holy Office
Joseph-Nicolas Robert-Fleury
19th Century

Johannes Kepler (1571–1630) was a German contemporary to Galileo and defended the Copernican system. Kepler designed a platonic solid model of the solar system which was included in his astronomical work, *Mysterium Cosmographicam.* Within this model, you can view the five platonic solids we discussed in Chapter 3. Kepler's greatest contribution was his three laws of planetary motion contained in his work called *Epitome.* These laws came from his study of the Music of the Spheres which originated with Pythagoras and documented by Aristotle. We will discuss the Music of the Spheres a little later in this Chapter.

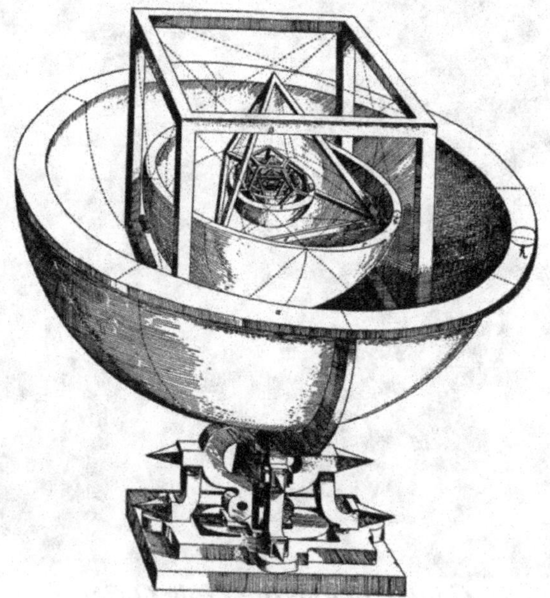

Platonic Solid Model of the Solar System
Johannes Kepler

On the heels of Galileo and Kepler came Sir Isaac Newton (1643–1727) whose published book *Principia* in 1687 literally changed the scientific community. Known as the Father of Physics, Newton believed that the planets were interrelated and that there were secret codes hidden in the Bible. Newton spent his later years in the study of these hidden Bible codes. Writing over four hundred fifty books, Newton extensively studied ancient wisdom especially the proportions of Solomon's temple including an entire chapter in his book *The Chronology of Ancient Kingdoms*. In 1675, Newton wrote, "God made Solomon the Greatest philosopher in the world" in an annotated copy of *Manna—a disquisition of the nature of alchemy*.

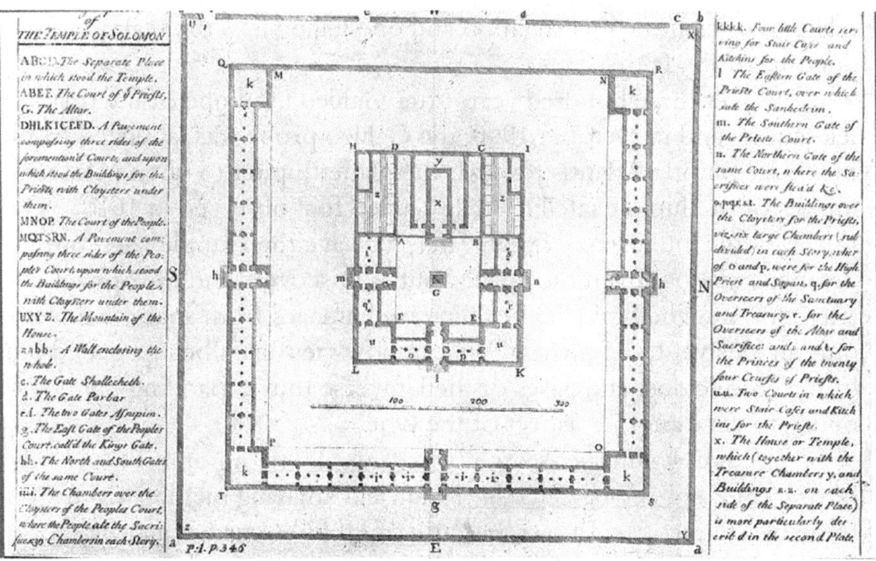

Newton's diagram of the Temple of Solomon
The Chronology of Ancient Kingdoms–Plate 1
Published London, 1728

Today, as we increase our knowledge, many of these visionaries are being praised for what they believed in and tried to prove, but meant with resistance and narrow thinking as many were killed for their beliefs. It is interesting how time allows history to right itself and let the truth finally surface. What was once considered outside the box is now scientifically proved.

According to the Columbia Encyclopedia, "Pope John Paul II asked that the 1633 conviction of Galileo be annulled. The Pope concluded that while seventeenth century theologians based their decision on the knowledge available to them at the time, they had wronged Galileo by not recognizing the difference between a question relating to scientific investigation and one falling into the realm of doctrine of the faith".

Over three hundred years after Galileo used one of the first telescopes, and in October 1990, the Galileo probe was launched from the Space Shuttle Atlantis towards the planet Jupiter to obtain closer images of the Jupiter satellites that Galileo first observed in 1610.

Now, hundreds of years later, we have the Hubble telescope deployed in 1990 from the Space Shuttle Discovery and the Spitzer telescope launched in 2003 beaming back images from space that were only an idea yet to be proven. We can now view stars being created out of the cosmic dust and gases of the Universe thus expanding our minds to view another aspect of the One.

A simple internet search (www.hubblesite.org or http://www.spitzer.caltech.edu/) will yield amazing pictures from these two telescopes. In fact, because of Hubble, current astronomers believe that the edge of the Universe can be determined. I personally use the picture of the Nebula NGC 3603 on my desktop computer to remind me of the vastness of the Universe, the awesomeness of the One Divine Mind, the birth of new stars born in this nebula, and our continual evolution.

The advent of these high level telescopes has also allowed scientists to discover different forms of light in the Universe including Gamma waves, X-rays, Ultraviolet, Infrared, and Microwaves. This is because everything is moving in the Universe which means vibrating. If something is vibrating, it is creating waves that produce both sound and color. It is the speed of these waves that produce the various colors, well beyond those of the seven in the rainbow and known as Newton's sevenfold:

Red, Orange, Yellow, Green, Blue, Indigo, and Violet
(Where red is the outer arc and violet is the inner arc)

Secrets of the Divine

The rainbow was extremely important to the ancients as it was the first covenant that God made with Noah after the flood. It was the "sign" created by light to reunite the faithful and reconnect God to Earth. Appearing as a half-circle, the rainbow symbolizes God's potential taking form. The gematria value for the Hebrew word "YHVH" (God) when multiplied will equal 1500. This is the same value for the Greek words meaning "light" and "power" demonstrating the importance of God's promise. Noah is also one of the Islamic prophets and referenced twenty-nine times in the one hundred fourteen suras of the Qur'an.

And God said this is the token of the covenant which I make between Me and you and every living creature that is with you, for perpetual generations: I do set my BOW in the cloud, and it shall be for a token of a covenant between Me and the Earth
Genesis 9:12–13

Noah's Thanks Offering
Joseph Anton Koch
19th Century

Newton was the first in 1672 to publish that "white light" alone was responsible for color from his experiments with a glass prism. Newton also found that color was determined by the length of the light wave which is used to measure each color. From this, Newton established a color wheel which painters then adopted to separate the primary colors of red, yellow, and blue from their complementary colors of green, violet, and orange.

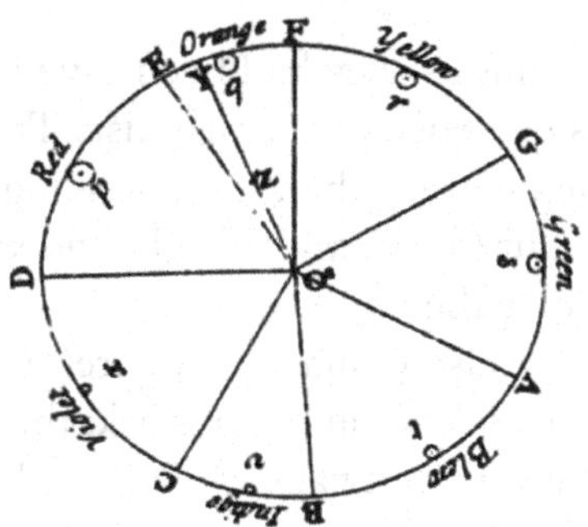

Newton's Color Wheel
Opticks—1704

According to Bonnie Gaunt, "Each of the colors of white light are determined by the length of the light wave. The units commonly used for this measurement are the millimicron, which equals one millionth of a millimeter; and the Angstrom unit (A.U.), which is one ten millionth of a millimeter. In the table below I have converted these into inches. These numbers are derived from the center of each color range, giving the truest color" (Gaunt 1995, 85).

COLOR	MILLIMICRON	A.U.	INCH
RED	710	7100	.00000284
ORANGE	620	6200	.00000248
YELLOW	570	5700	.00000228
GREEN	520	5200	.00000208
BLUE	470	4700	.00000188
VIOLET	410	4100	.00000164
		AGGREGATE	**.00001320**

The number 132 is equal to "white" in Hebrew and "made whole" in Greek. This speaks directly to the covenant that God had with Noah and his family as they had been saved from the flood. The rainbow was Noah's evidence of the promise. The number 132 is the gematria value of the Hebrew phrases "The Kingdom is the Lord's", "Jehovah (YHVH) your God", and "God divided" meaning that white light divided to produce the rainbow.

The flood story also contains many references to the number eight. There were eight people in Noah's ark; the Hebrew word for bow or bending has a gematria value of 800, and the value of the Hebrew word YHVH (26) can be reduced to 8. All references to Jesus.

In 1878, Edwin D. Babbitt wrote, "Light reveals the glories of the external world and yet is the most glorious of them all. It gives beauty, reveals beauty and is itself most beautiful. It is the analyzer, the truth-teller and the exposer of shams, for it shows things as they are. Its infinite streams measure off the universe and flow into our telescopes from stars which are quintillions of miles distant" (Babbitt 1878, 1).

In Greek mythology, the rainbow was the path between heaven and Earth that the angels took or the messengers of God. In India's mythology, the rainbow was known as the God of love called Kama. In the *Epic of Gilgamesh* (Tablet 11), the rainbow is the "jeweled necklace of the Great Mother Ishtar."

The "rainbow bridge" or "rainbow body" is oftentimes shown in art as a symbol of transition or transformation. They are bodies of pure light. The Tibetans call this mystical state *Dzogchen* which means "Great Perfection" and their path to enlightenment. In many last judgement images of Christianity, Christ is shown sitting on a rainbow above the Earth.

Vajrasattva

Tibetan Mastery State of Dzogchen

Tibetan Mastery State of Dzogchen

Clearly there is harmony in the Divine design that is revealed when you look at the Universe and the numbers related to the created masses. Using gematria, the phrase "In the beginning God" in Hebrew reduces to "9". The diameters of the Sun, Earth, and Moon taken individually are also each equal to "9". Numerology identifies "9" as representing "wholeness" or "complete" so you have the location of where we live on Earth as being the completeness and wholeness of the Divine beginning.

"In the Beginning God" = 9
Sun's diameter—864,000 miles = 9
Earth's diameter—7920 miles = 9
Moon's diameter—2160 miles = 9
(Adding each number and reducing to one digit)

Let's take a few minutes and look at the magic related to the number nine (9). If you were to multiply nine "ones" times nine "ones", you would get the number:

111111111 x 111111111 = 12345678 <u>**9**</u> 87654321

This number is known as a "palindrome" from the Greek roots *"palin"* meaning "again" and *"dromos"* meaning "way or direction". Palindromes can be traced back to A.D. 79 and can be words, phrases, or numbers that can be read the same way in either direction.

Another interesting palindrome is the comparison of the name "Moses" to "I AM". In Hebrew, Moses is spelled *"MShH or Mosheh"* and has a gematria value of 345. When Moses ask God what name to use with the children of Israel, He replied "I AM" hath sent me (Exodus 3:12–14). The Hebrew "I AM" is written *"Eheyeh Asher Eheyeh"* and has a gematria value of 543. Thus, Moses (345) is the image of I AM (543), a reflection of the "One".

I AM = 543 / 345 = Moses

An God said moreover unto Moses, thus shalt thou say unto the children of Israel, The Lord God of your fathers, the God of Abraham, the God of Isaac, and the God of Jacob, hath sent me unto you: this is 'my name forever', and this is my 'memorial' unto all generations
Exodus 3:15

In this verse, the word "forever" in Hebrew is *"olahm"* which means "for eternity" or "for all that exist". Another interesting palindrome is the Hebrew value for the words 'truth" and 'eternity" which both reduce to the number "9".

Truth = 441 / 144 = Eternity

According to Del Washburn, "God put the theomatic structure together in such a manner that every portion of a phrase is bringing out some clear aspect of truth" (Washburn 1994, 112).

Since we are discussing images or reflections, let's look specifically at the word "image" to see what relationships exist. The word "image" has a gematria value of 425 in Greek as does the words "man" and "created". The number 425 can be reduced to 2 (4 + 2 + 5 = 11 and 1 + 1 = 2). We learned in Chapter 3 that "The One" divided to become two which appears as the Greek symbol (image) Phi. Do you see how infinite the levels of understanding are? It's like peeling the thin layers of the onion skins.

The Greeks used the word *"ennead"* when referring to the number nine and it was known as "the horizon". Pythagoras recognized the ennead as the first square of an odd number (3 times 3 = 9). The number nine is the only number when multiplied by any other number will always resolve back to nine. For example, nine times three equals twenty-seven which can be reduced to nine (9 x 3 = 27 = 2 + 7 = 9). Regardless of the numbers multiplied, this always happens. For the Hindus, nine was the number for their creator, Lord Brahma.

Returning to the Bible we find the following words or phrases are equal to or reduce to "nine":

99 = Amen—the last word of the Bible—meaning "faithfulness"
90 = Perfection
99 = The garden of the Lord
999 = In the beginning

According to 1Corinthians 12:8–10, there are nine ***"Gifts of the Spirit"*** which include: The word of wisdom, the word of knowledge, faith, healing, the working of miracles, prophecy, discerning of spirits, divers kinds of tongues, and the interpretation of tongues.

The ***"Fruit of the Spirit"*** also comprises nine graces detailed in Galatians 5:22–23 including: love, joy, peace, longsuffering, gentleness, goodness, faith, meekness, and temperance.

Nine was considered a number that represented completion because after the number nine, the numbers begin again only a set higher much like the musical octave.

This gives raise to the subject of Harmonics or Music which the ancients considered part of the "Quadrivium", the four subjects that were taught in the academies. In Latin, the word Quadrivium means "the four ways" or "the four roads" and included arithmetic, geometry, music, and astronomy. The ancients felt that harmony was nothing more than numbers in time. In the *Laws*, Plato states that it was the Egyptian priests who possessed the canon of proportions and harmonies which had maintained their civilized standards for over thousands of years.

Pythagoras was the first to hear *"Musica universalis"* or the "Music of the Spheres" an ancient concept of harmony regarding the movement of the celestial bodies through ratios or proportions. A ratio is the comparison of two different numbers. Pythagoras discovered that the most pleasing tones were called: Octave—1:2, Fifth—2:3, and Fourth—3:4.

To the Greeks, harmony was beauty and "the key to harmonic ratios is hidden in the famous Pythagorean 'Tetractys', or pyramid of dots" (Hall 1928, 251).

The Tetractys was a symbol for the four elements of earth, air, fire, and water representing the harmony of the spheres and the cosmos as it was made up of the first four numbers (1, 2, 3, and 4). This also created ten dots and appears within an equilateral triangle. The Tetractys is sometimes called the Decad meaning ten and reduces to "One".

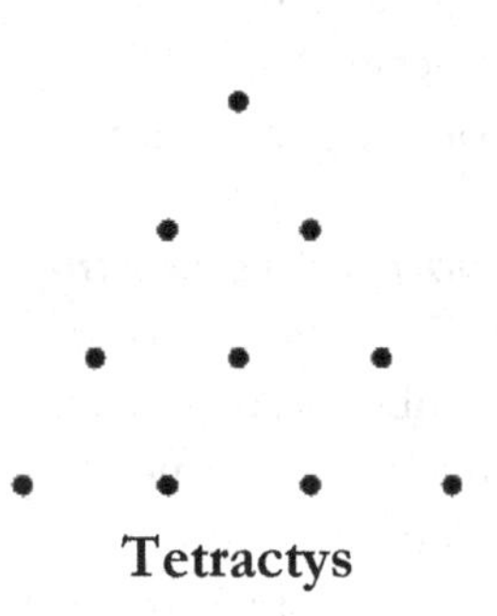

Tetractys

Coat of Arms
Cardinal Ratzinger
Pope Benedictus XVI
(See the Tetractys on each side?)

According to Wikipedia, "A prayer of the Pythagoreans shows the importance of the Tetractys (sometimes called the 'Mystic Tetrad'), as the prayer was addressed to it":

"Bless us, divine number, thou who generated gods and men! O holy, holy Tetractys, thou that containest the root and source of the eternally flowing creation! For the divine number begins with the profound, pure unity until it comes to the holy four; then it begets the mother of all, the all-comprising, all-bounding, the first-born, the never-swerving, the never-tiring holy ten, the key holder of all"

In the *Timaeus*, Plato wrote: "The circles of heaven subdivided according to the musical ratios." He called it the "Law of Proportion" as he believed that creation began with sound and vibration. To the ancients, the Universe sang to us as the sound descended down from heaven in a set of vibrations that our brain translates to sound. There is also documentation that different colors were assigned to musical notes. Interesting, the Hebrew letter *"nun"* which means "fish", the Christian symbol of "faith" begins the Hebrew word *"niggun"* with means "melody" or "tune".

In Job 38:7, we are told that ***"when the morning stars sang together, all the sons of God shouted with joy."*** The gematria value of "the morning stars" is equal to 360 the same number of degrees in a circle representing the "One". Jesus is also referenced as the "morning star" in several biblical verses, two of which are 2Peter 1:19 and Revelation 22:16. We will learn more about this reference in Chapter 9.

If harmony is numbers in time expressed in ratios, can we not say that music is the dance of numbers? As we have seen, those numbers can be expressed in circles and triangles or the magic of sacred geometry.

AUM or OM is the Hindu sacred sound or intonation of the original vibration that creates and sustains the cosmos from the void. In Sanskrit it means "to sound out loudly" or "praise". It is specific in both the Vedas and the Upanishads representing the three stages of life—birth, life, and death. To many spiritualists, OM is a mantra used in meditation to align one's energies with the cosmic vibration. As a sacred symbol, OM (AUM) is found in all Hindu temples.

The Mandukya Upanishad states, "AUM is the one eternal syllable of which all that exists is but the development. The past, the present, and the future are all included in this one sound, and all that exists beyond the three forms of time is also implied in it." Dating to 900 B.C., this is the shortest of the Upanishads which means "sitting near a teacher" and consists of the three letters (matras) of "a", "u", and "m". The letter "a" stands for the state of wakefulness, where we experience externally through our mind and the five sense organs. The "u" stands for the dream state, in which inward experiences are available and the "m" is for the deep sleep where no desires exist. There is also a fourth state that is transcendent where the individual is unaware called "*turiya avastha*" or the state of silence. Jesus would tell you that this is the "kingdom of heaven within".

Around A.D. 1000, an Italian Benedictine monk named Guido d'Arezzo recognized the difficulty that other monks were having with the Gregorian Chants and devised the "solfeggio" or staff-notation to help with the memorization. It was a way to assign syllables to the musical scale and was first done on the ancient Latin hymn *Ut Queant Laxis,* dedicated to St. John the Baptist.

The first stanza is: ***Ut** queant laxis, **re**sonare fibris, **Mi**ra gestorum **fa**muli tuorum, **Sol**ve polluti **la**bii reatum, **s**ancta **I**ohannes.*

The translation in English is: *O Saint John, loose the sinfulness of our polluted lips, that they servants may be able to sing thy wondrous deeds with free voices.*

Or: *So that your servants may, with loosened voices, resound the wonders of your deeds, clean the guilt from our stained lips, O Saint John.*

Guido d'Arezzo's work has become the standard for today's music and known as the DO, RE, MI made popular with the movie *"Sound of Music"*:

DOminus—Lord—Absolute (the Beginner)
SIder—Stars—All galaxies
LAatea—Milk—Earth's Galaxy, the Milky Way
Sol—Sun—Sun
Fata—Fate—The Planets
MIcrocosmos—Small Universe—The Earth
REgina Coeli—Queen of the Heavens—Moon
DOminus—Lord—Absolute (the New Beginner)

Jim Bumgardner, a computer programmer, has designed a computer program using satellite information to hear the "Music of the Spheres" from his Whitney Music Box. You can hear this on his web site: http://wheelof.com/whitney/

According to Manly P. Hall, "Pythagoras discovered that music had great therapeutic power and he prepared special harmonics for various diseases. He apparently experimented also with color, attaining considerable success. One of his unique curative processes resulted from his discovery of the healing value of certain verses from the *Odyssey* and the *Iliad* of Homer" (Hall 1928, 197).

Today, extensive work has been done with the use of sound for healing various diseases and altering one's consciousness. Knowing that everything is made of energy, vibrating at different frequencies, sound is used for balancing those frequencies that leads to healing. Many times these sound techniques include light and color as they are also vibrating frequencies.

Studies by neurologist have shown that when certain people are shown "letters" or "numbers", they will actually see colors. The colors vary depending on which letter or number they are shown. This involuntary and automatic process is called Synesthesia and comes from the Greek word meaning "combined sensations".

It has also been documented that sounds will stimulate a person to see colors. According to Steven Halpern, "...vibrations at 1000 cycles per second are easily audible. If you double the vibrations to 2000 cycles per second, that is one octave higher. If you double it again to 4000 cycles per second, that is another octave. A normal piano spans a bit more than seven octaves. If, hypothetically, we could extend the piano keyboard another 35 to 50 octaves higher, the keys at the higher end would produce colors, rather than audible sounds, when played" (Halpern 1985, 182–183).

When attending school, you may have been shown sand placed on vibrating sound boxes. As the vibrating continues, the sand takes on geometric shapes and forms resembling the platonic solids discussed in Chapter 3. This field of study was called Cymatics by Hans Jenny, a Swiss medical doctor. The word Cymatics comes from the

Greek word meaning "wave". Many have also seen how opera singers can break crystal glasses with the pitch of their voice demonstrating how sound waves pass through objects.

I believe the future to healing all diseases is in advancing these techniques that include sound, color, and light. Some of the most extensive sound work has been done by Jonathan Goldman and can be reviewed at his web site: http://www.healingsounds.com/.

Interestingly, in Hebrew the gematria value of the word "sound" and the phrase "to make perfect" both equal 80. Isn't that what healing is all about? Here again we see the importance of the number eight.

We are also told in Psalms 33:6, Hebrews 11:3, and 2Peter 3:5 that it was God's word that formed the heavens and the Earth. When someone speaks "words" are they not making sound creating a wave of energy? Can you begin to see the importance of sound techniques in creating order and harmony? Is this how we will heal the Earth and return her to her original beauty? Is this why songs (sound) are included in many church services?

Within the grand scheme created by the "One" Divine Mind or Master Architect of the Universe we have glimpsed at our location and the order in the Universe. Our tour has identified our solar make-up along with the relationships of light, color, and sound.

So, who out there thinks that they can set up such a workable model to sustain life or develop a working concept like Photosynthesis to maintain life? Is music the key to opening spiritual gateways and illumination?

THE CONSTELLATIONS AND THE STARS

When I consider thy heavens, the work of thy fingers, the moon and the stars, which thou hast ordained
Psalms 8:3

Researchers will agree that the star's names and groupings are older than any known writings and Arab astronomy will tell you that they are as old as Adam's time and that he past them onto Seth. As we have seen, the Book of Enoch confirms the origin of the star names from the beginning of creation. While historians believe that the cradle of civilization began in Sumer (modern day Iraq) around the sixth millennium B.C., it is the Babylonians who inherited and documented the Sumerian constellations and stars.

The Babylonian *MulApin Tablets* is a star catalogue listing the names of sixty-six stars and constellations. Scholars believe that this text originated around 1000 B.C. even though the constellations were known much earlier and most likely comes from the list of *Three Stars Each* (twelfth century B.C.), which identified the northern path of Enlil, the equatorial path of Anu, and the southern path of Ea. These were the three great gods of the Sumerians.

Additional clay tables have been found called *Enuma Anu Enlil*, meaning "when the gods Anu and Enlil" or "in the days of Anu and Enlil" that related to Babylonian astrology. Approximately seventy tablets were found in the nineteenth century as part of the library of Assyrian King Ashurbanipal (668–626 B.C.) at Nineveh. The tablets date from around 650 B.C., but the contents are believed to date back as far as 1646 B.C. Tablets 1–22 describe the Moon, known as Sin and its various phases. Other tablets describe the stars and planets, especially Venus on the tablet of Ammisaduqa (#63). The Venus tablet is considered the oldest surviving planetary text, a seventh century B.C. copy, listing the motions of the planet Venus which was known as Ishtar to the Babylonians.

The tablets, written in cuneiform, also contained the well known eleventh century B.C. *Epic of Gilgamesh*, the legendary Sumerian king who was two-thirds god and one-third man. Gilgamesh and his friend Enkidu, a mortal human, journey together on several quests. Gilgamesh is seeking Utnapishtim, the survivor of the flood and the secret of his immortality. At least twelve tablets exist regarding Gilgamesh including the story of the Biblical Flood (Deluge) on Tablet 11. Some of these tablets can be viewed at the British Museum in London.

The Deluge (Flood) Tablet

Cuneiform writing, the oldest form of writing, is done on clay using a wedge-shaped stylus and was the predecessor to the Egyptian hieroglyphics. The word cuneiform comes from the Latin words *"cuneus"* meaning "wedge" and *"forma"* meaning "shape".

Cuneiform Writing
Sumerian: 26th century B.C.

What we do know, is that the age of many of the ancient sacred sites like Stonehenge and the Great Pyramid are aligned to certain constellations rising at certain times of the year mostly on the solstices. By using certain computer programs like Sky Globe, and inputting these alignments, dates are rendered that go back well beyond the accepted dates of most historians. For example, the Sphinx and the

Great Pyramid of Egypt are estimated to be over 10,000 years old using this method which might make one wonder about the information contained in our Western school's history books.

Each ancient civilization seems to share the same groupings, star names, and certain identifying figures or mythology. Of course the star names vary by language, but it is amazing how their meanings are similar if not the same. The mythologies may also have different names, but the story or legends are similar. In the Middle East, various deities were assigned to the different star groups. As the Greeks traveled to the Middle East, they applied their own legends to the star groupings. The same applied to the Romans who assigned many Latin names to the star groupings which only added more confusion.

There appears to be a common and universal language in the stars as can be seen in the different ancient maps and planispheres, which are celestial globes. One of the oldest pictorial drawings is on the Hathor temple ceiling in Dendera, Egypt. Hathor was the goddess of love, beauty, motherhood, and joy. She is pictured as the cow goddess with horns. As the celestial cow, Hathor provided the nourishment of milk spilled from the Milky Way.

Egyptian Goddess Hathor
(Headdress of Sun Disk and Cow Horns)

Temple of Hathor
Dendera, Egypt

Goddess Hathor
Atop the columns of the temple

The Shekhinah is Coming

Depicting the forty-eight ancient constellations, a copy of the Dendera zodiac was taken to France during Napoleon's campaign in Egypt (1798–1801) and in 1820 the zodiac relief was removed from the temple's ceiling. It is currently at the Louvre Museum in Paris. We will reference this as we discuss the star groups and the images presented in Chapter 8.

This first image of the Dendera Zodiac is the actual sandstone one in Paris. The second image gives a more detailed quality for viewing the signs of the zodiac.

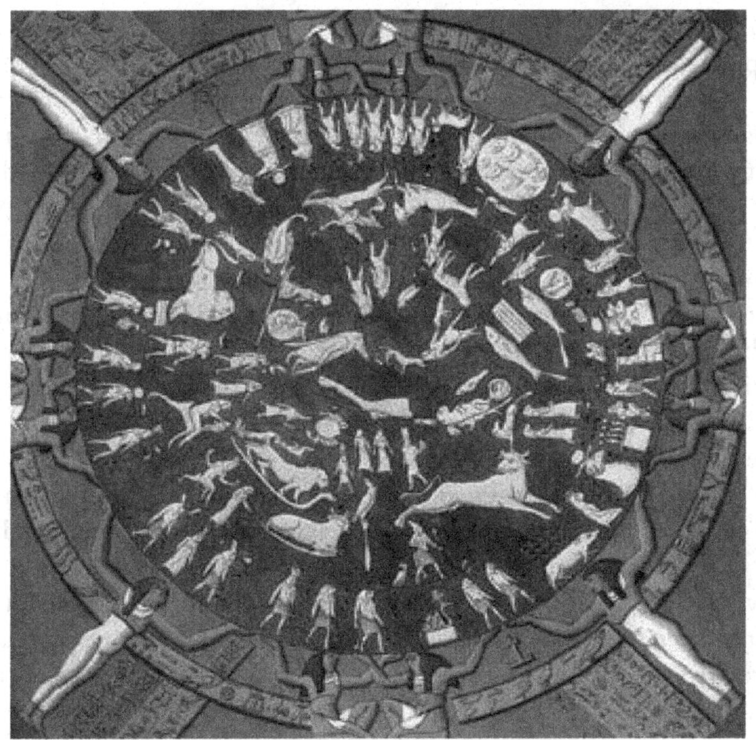

Dendera Zodiac
Ceiling of Temple of Hathor

Interestingly, the Dendera Zodiac is the only circular monument the ancient Egyptians dedicated to astronomy. The others are either squared or pyramided. A large picture of the Dendera Zodiac and the work done by Jim A. Cornwell can be found in Appendix J.

We will identify the ancient Egyptian names and meaning that have been left to us by the Persian astronomer, Mīrzā Muhammad Tāriq ibn Shāhrukh (ca. 1393–1449), commonly known by his moniker, Ulugh Beg which is somewhat translated as "great ruler". A complete table can be found in Appendix K.

What I find most amazing, is that many religions can differ in so many ways, yet the same cultures honor the universal language in the stars. These ancients certainly put more emphasis on the stars than what we do today.

The Book of Job, considered one of the oldest and most scientific books in the Bible, contains numerous references to the constellations and the stars. It should also be noted that Job lived prior to Abraham who is recorded as teaching Astronomy to the Egyptians. Isn't it interesting that the Book of Job follows the Book of Enoch in the Ethiopia Bible. I have provided the star references of Job in Appendix L.

Let's begin our discussion by looking at the whole and then the parts to gain an understanding before delving into the story at hand.

By now, we know that the Universe is all about circles. We know that the Earth travels around the Sun in the form of an ecliptic. Extending eight to nine degrees on either side of this ecliptic path is where the signs of the zodiac are found. This is the same path that the Moon takes and why the ancients venerated the Moon with goddess worship.

The word Zodiac comes from both the Greek word *"zodiakos"* and the Latin word *"zodiacus"* meaning "circle of animals". The Greek word *"zo-on"* means "an animal" and is the root word for "zoo". I have also read where the primitive root of the word Zodiac is *"zoad"* meaning "a walk, way, or going by steps". This makes sense if you think of the Sun walking or stepping through the zodiac. In Greek, the gematria value of the phrase "go in a circle" equals 999 as does the Hebrew phrase "in the beginning God". Here we have the magic 9's again.

The division of the zodiac is equal to twelve sections of thirty degrees each giving a complete circle of three hundred sixty degrees (12 x 30 = 360) making it the ideal form that Plato addressed and identifying the "One". Within the twelve sections of the zodiac are groupings of stars, called constellations, which form patterns or pictures of animals and human figures that appear to rotate around the Earth. In its annual course from west to east, the Sun passes through the twelve zodiac signs while during that same time, the Moon makes twelve complete revolutions around the Earth.

Each constellation has three associated minor constellations called decans, making thirty-six in total (12 x 3 = 36). The word decan comes from the Semitic word *"dek"* meaning "a part or piece". The Greeks called them *"dekanoi"* meaning "tenths" and here we have the full circle again (36 x 10 = 360). The Greeks called the three decans "tenths" because they divided the thirty degrees of each constellation evenly into ten degrees. These decans provide additional meaning to the zodiac signs to which they correspond.

In total we have forty-eight signs, the twelve constellations plus the thirty-six decans. While the current list consists of eighty-eight constellations recognized by the International Astronomical Union (IAU) since 1922, we are only going to discuss the ancient constellations. Our goal, in Chapter 8, is to be able to read the life of Jesus, not to learn astronomy. You might say that the constellations are the main plot of the story with the decans representing the sub-plots of the story providing greater detail.

To the Greeks, each constellation had a symbolic meaning and number value. In gematria, the Greek word for constellation *(Ελληνική)* equals 1071 = 9. It is the equivalent value to the Greek word for witness *(μαρτυρέω)*, 1071 = 9. Again, a relationship between the two words (constellation and witness) is a "sign".

The heavens declare the glory of God
Psalms 19:1–6

In Hebrew, this biblical statement has a gematria value of "888" which we have learned matches the name Jesus in Greek. Chapter 8 will clarify why the heavens and Jesus are related.

Hesiod, a Greek poet who lived in the eighth century B.C., codified the Greek myths in poetry, many of which dealt with the constellations with the most prominent writing being *The Theogony (Θεογονία)*, meaning "the birth of God(s)". It was about the creation of the Universe and the order of the gods, placing Zeus at the head of the pantheon.

The Greeks believed via Hesiod that from Chaos, the five original elements were produced:

Gaia—The Earth
Tartarus—The Underworld
Erebus—The Gloom of Tartarus
Eros—The Force of Love
Nyx—The Night and the Power of Darkness
(Littleton 2002, 136)

We will include the most typical myths in our discussion of the constellations and the story that they help to tell. Myths exist in all cultures and were verbally passed from generation to generation. The ancient myths held the parallel theme of explaining creation and how the world evolved from "chaos", the dark void of nothingness, yet, the potential for all things. Myths were considered a true rendition of the unexplainable phenomena of creation that resonate on an unconscious level.

Secrets of the Divine

And the Earth was without form, and void; and darkness was upon the face of the deep
Genesis 1:2

Eudoxus of Cnidus (ca. 410–347 B.C.) was a Greek astronomer and mathematician who studied under Plato. His work on astronomy has been lost, but his knowledge and one of his writings called *"Phaenomena"* comes to us by way of Aratus (ca.315–240 B.C.), a Greek poet. His famous poem, also called *"Phaenomena"* meaning "appearances" describes the constellations and the path of the Sun. His second work called *"Diosemeia"* meaning "forecasts" describes weather forecasts from astronomical phenomena. Hipparchus preserved fragments of Aratus' writings and Paul references Aratus' poem when he was spreading the gospel in Athens.

For in Him we live, and move, and have our being; as certain also of your own poets have said, for we are also His offspring
Acts 17:28

When looking at the zodiac signs, you will see stars labeled with Greek letters which identify the magnitude or brightness of a star. The letters begin with "alpha" and follow more or less in order of brightness. This traces back to Hipparchus who labeled a star's brightness on a scale of "1 to 6" with "1" being the brightest as viewed from the Earth.

In 1603, Johann Bayer established the "Bayer designation" in his star atlas *Uranometria*, which identified a star with a Greek letter followed by the Latin genitive form of the parent constellation's name. For example, Orion's brightest star Betelgeuse would be labeled "α Ori".

The Shekhinah is Coming

There is one glory of the Sun, and another glory of the Moon, and another glory of the stars; for one star differs from another star in glory
1Corinthians 15:41

In 1856, Norman Pogson defined the magnitudes further by stating that a second magnitude would be one hundred times less bright than a first magnitude. Today, the system isn't limited to Hipparchus' "1–6" scale as the brightest stars now have negative values. For example, Sirius, the brightest star, as seen from Earth, has a magnitude of minus 1.4 compared to the full Moon with a magnitude of minus12.6. A list of the brightest stars with their corresponding magnitude is provided in Appendix M.

If we were to list out the twelve constellations with their Hebrew name and number value and then added them together, we would arrive at a number equal to 2592. If we add the place holder "zero" to the end, we arrive at the Grand cycle of 25,920 years as discussed in Chapter 5 another fascinating revelation of the Divine design. We will see in Chapter 9 how the number 25,920 is meaningful to the city of Jerusalem which equals the Hebrew phrase "the heart of Jerusalem" (when multiplied) that Isaiah referenced.

CONSTELLATION NAME	HEBREW NAME	GEMATRIA VALUE
VIRGO	BETULAH	145
LIBRA	MOZNAYIM	56
SCORPIO	AKRAB	372
SAGITTARIUS	KASSHAT	171
CAPRICORNUS	GEDI	580
AQUARIUS	SHEVAT	180

PISCES	ADAR	12
ARIES	TALEH	41
TAURUS	SHOR	250
GEMINI	TEOMIM	441
CANCER	SARTON	261
LEO	ARI	83
	TOTAL	**2592**

As we will see in Chapter 8, these twelve constellations and their accompanying decans, tell the story of the salvation of man through the Lord Jesus Christ. Adding the numeric value of each constellation, we arrive back to the beginning and the length of time it takes the Sun to travel through each of these signs. It is the cycle of the Sun.

It becomes very evident that the constellations and their stars are Divine in origin and sacred in character as the word for "Star" in Hebrew equals 48 and the statement ***"the coming of the son of man"*** (Matthew 24:27) in Greek equals 4800. Dropping the zeros we have the "Son of Man" equal to the word "Star". Is this the new "Pistol" star discovered by NASA and discussed in Chapter 11?

...there shall come a Star out of Jacob
Numbers 24:17

In Chapter 5 we discussed the reflective nature of palindromes. Here is a very interesting one considering what we learned in Chapter 4 and the knowledge left by Enoch, but ignored by the Church.

Enoch = 84 / 48 = Star

The Shekhinah is Coming

Wasn't Enoch the forerunner of Jesus? Are we not studying the stars as "His life in lights"? I think you can see why numbers are considered the common denominator for this discussion.

AN OVERVIEW OF OUR STORY

As we begin our celestial story, it is important to keep in mind the centuries that have past, the number of translations that have occurred on the ancient documents, and the destruction of many documents. It is like telling a secret in a circle and when the secret returns to the original person, it is not always relayed with accuracy and if there are different languages involved, the secret will definitely change with the translations.

This will be the overview of our story to set the stage for the details that follow in the subsequent chapter. Our story is about a hero and contains three parts referenced throughout both the Old and New Testaments. The three parts include the hero's works, his ultimate humiliation, and his glory.

The first part of the story begins with the prophecy of the hero's coming incarnation, his attributes, and his characteristics. This information is given in both the Old Testament (Isaiah 7:14) and the New Testament.

Behold, a virgin shall be with child, and shall bring forth a son, and they shall call his name Immanuel, which being interpreted is, God with us
Matthew 1:23

The second part of our hero story deals with the results of his work and his second coming that is not only about glory but also about judgement. It is the promise of the prophecy that is set forth in the first part.

Of the increase of His government and peace there shall be no end, upon the throne of David, and upon his kingdom, to order it, and to establish it with judgement and with justice from henceforth even forever. The zeal of the Lord of hosts will perform this
Isaiah 9:7

He shall be great, and shall be called the Son of the Highest and the Lord God shall give unto Him the throne of His father David and He shall reign over the house of Jacob forever; and of His kingdom there shall be no end
Luke 1:32–33

Throughout both the first and the second parts is woven the third part of our hero story that relates to the enemy that our hero must subdue. This enemy has been condemned from the beginning, but has continued to terrorize.

And I will put enmity between thee and the woman, and between thy seed and her seed; it shall bruise thy head, and thou shalt bruise his heel
Genesis 3:15

As we begin our hero's story, it is important to keep all three parts of his story in our minds: the prophecy of the hero, the promises of the hero, and the enemy of the hero. As you will see, our hero will survive many test and trials on his journey to succeed and become one with God. The story is his mastery of life's journey and his soul's reconciliation with the One.

So, who is our hero and where does he come from? Our hero is none other than Jesus, the Christ. His Hebrew-Aramaic name was יְהוֹשֻׁעַ (*Yehošua*, Joshua), meaning "Yahweh delivers, saves, or rescues". While our hero's story is written through mythology and various characters, it doesn't change what should be gleaned much like the way that Jesus taught with parables.

The story ends with a triumphant conclusion of the prophecy and the promise to all who believe in our nightly bedtime story that is forever and always visible to mankind. The story is unending and unchanging. You need no one to interpret the story except your inner heart. The story has been there from the beginning and has remained throughout the rise and fall of many cultures and nations.

It is clear that our hero never gives up fighting the enemy no matter what form it takes. In our story the enemy comes in three forms: the serpent (deceiver), the sea monster, and the dragon (destroyer). And each time the enemy is defeated by our mighty hero, Jesus who will demonstrate a mastery of the soul and a union with the One. In the end, the prophecy and the promises come to pass and we are left with the knowingness of hope, salvation, and eternal life.

There is only one place to begin reading this story and that is with the hero's mother. The hero's mother is the beautiful young maiden Virgo. But why do we begin with the constellation Virgo as opposed to the modern day listing that begins with Aries? Let's take a minute and look at the explanation of why we begin with Virgo and what that has to do with the Sphinx of Egypt.

Regardless of the ancient civilization one is studying; each one has left some sort of a record in the form of a calendar, a monument, or written documents. While translations may have caused some confusion and changed some meanings, it cannot be denied that the ancients were preoccupied with the heavens and celestial occurrences.

The ancient Egyptian civilization has left profound records of information in their hieroglyphics and monuments. The pyramids and the sphinx, considered as one, is the only remaining "ancient wonder of the world" where the writings of the historian Herodotus (ca. 484–425 B.C.) listed seven as delineated in Appendix N.

The Sphinx is the largest and oldest monolith statue in the world measuring 241 feet long, 20 feet wide, and a little over 66 feet high. It was literally carved out of the bedrock of what is known as the Giza plateau and is an amazing site to view.

Secrets of the Divine

As an imaginary animal and the epitome of mystery and hidden secrets, the Sphinx has the head of a woman and the body of a lion. In many ancient cultures, Sphinxes oftentimes have wings as well and can be found in all cultures, old and new.

It is unclear where the word Sphinx comes from with some grammarians stating that it was derived from the Greek verb *"sphingein"* which means "to bind" or "to squeeze". Some say the word is derived from the Greek verb *"sphingo"* which means "combining form". The most logical root of the word comes from historian Susan Wise Bauer who states that the word sphinx was a Greek corruption of the Egyptian word *"shesep-ankh"* which means "living image" of Atum, the Egyptian deity of Heliopolis. Hesiod referred to the Sphinx as "Phix" in his *Theogony* writings.

There is a stele between the paws of the Sphinx that states it is an image of the Sun God, Hor-em-akhet (Horus of the Horizon). The stele is known as the "Dream Stele" from the story of Prince Tuthmosis, the son of Amenhotep II, and future King Tuthmosis IV. While resting against the Sphinx after a hunting expedition, the prince dreams that the Sphinx grants him kinghood if the prince removes the sand that covers its body.

Sphinx with Dream Stele

When the Greeks first view the Sphinx, it was buried up to its shoulders in sand. Over the years several attempts to unbury the Sphinx have transpired and we are blessed today to see the complete monument in its repose.

Bonaparte before the Sphinx
Jean-Leon Gerome
Hearst Castle
San Simeon, California, USA

The dating of the Sphinx has been a controversial issue with the Egyptologists wanting to stick to the history books dating it to Pharaoh Khafra's reign of 2520–2492 B.C., the recorded builder of the pyramids. The more advanced thinkers, who are looking beyond the box, place a much older date on the Sphinx. According to Wikipedia, the oldest known sphinx was found in Gobeki Tepe, Turkey and was dated to 9500 B.C. Some recent and interesting work on the Sphinx has been done by Robert Bauval and Graham Hancock documented in their two books: *The Message of the Sphinx* (1996) and *Fingerprints of the Gods* (1995).

In summary, their work with the aid of star-mapping computer programs, places the date of the Sphinx at 10,500 B.C. which would be in the processional era of Leo (10,900–8700 B.C.). This was substantiated by the work of John Anthony West suggesting that the weathering of the Sphinx by rainwater supports the 10,500 B.C. date.

Robert M. Schoch, a geologist has also contributed writings to these same weathering effects.

The date of 10,500 B.C. would mean that the Sun rose in Leo at the vernal equinox and identifies this with the "Zep Tepi" or "First Time" of an advanced civilization or "gods" that came to Earth and settled in the Nile Valley. Bauval and Hancock believe that this is documented in an ancient text called *Shat Ent Am Duat* meaning the *Book of What is in the Duat.* Documentation can also be found on the walls of the Temple of Edfu.

The image shown here is a relief from the Temple of Esneh showing the zodiac signs of Virgo and Leo with a definite break between the constellations along with the Sphinx looking toward Leo, the lion. The complete relief, located on the ceiling of the portico of the Edfu temple, contains all the zodiac signs much like the Dendera zodiac found at the Temple of Hathor.

Temple of Esneh
Jim A. Cornwell
http://www.mazzaroth.com/ChapterOne/TempleOfEsneh.htm#Esneh

The Sphinx was left to be our guide to the stars. I believe the original Sphinx was the image of an advance civilization and was left as a pointer facing East toward the stars representing Leo. It was over time that various rulers changed the Sphinx's face.

...set signs and wonders in the land of Egypt, even unto this day...
Jeremiah 32:20

The Shekhinah is Coming

The Virgo timeframe which falls in the month of September is also significant to the Jewish celebration of Rosh Hashanah and the Islamic celebration of Ramadan. In more esoteric circles this same timeframe is the beginning of the Universal Year. It makes me stop and ponder all the connections that exist with such a monument.

Among the many ancient historians that have documented what the Egyptians preserved in the stars include Diodorus Siculus (first century B.C.), a Greek who wrote forty books under the title of *Bibliotheca historica* and Manetho (third century B.C.), an Egyptian historian who wrote *Aegyptiaca (History of Egypt)*.

I personally believe that the 10,500 B.C. time frame can be substantiated with the most recent work of Gregg Braden in his book *Fractal Time*. Braden has traveled extensively to sacred sites around the world and has a vast understanding of ancient wisdom from both a scientific and spiritual perspective. In summary, his book discusses the "World Ages" that have passed and states that there have been four world ages and we are in the process of completing the fifth world age which began in 3114 B.C. and ends in A.D. 2012. In addition, Braden states that each world age is 5,125 years in length.

Therefore, we are completing a 5,125 year cycle which is basically all our recorded history. An additional prior cycle would land us right in the sign of Leo, which according to the Egyptian calendar dawned in 10,948 B.C.

The Sphinx then binds our story together with the two ends meeting to form the circle of heaven much like the symbol of the Ouroboros that the Gnostics used to symbolize the soul's eternity. The Christians used the Ouroboros to symbolize the limited confines of the material world and to the Alchemist, the Ouroboros was a purifying symbol.

This concept aligns with the meaning of the deity Atum's name which is believed to be derived from the word *"tem"* which means "to complete or finish" or "the creator of the world", viewing the circle as "The One".

For those who are more esoteric in their studies, this same information has been preserved in the Major Arcana Tarot Card # 8—Strength:

The connotation of this image is one of confidence and courage which are actually two prerequisites to a "spiritual path." The woman (Virgo) is demonstrating "spiritual strength" as she trusts embracing the lion (Leo) while the lion is demonstrating "animal strength" existing in the world. After all, the lion is "king of the animal kingdom." Is this the key to wisdom? Or, is this representative of the axiom "living in the world, but not being part of the world"? Give yourself a few minutes to think about this.

Notice the lemniscates ∞, or infinity symbol above her head. The word lemniscates comes from a Latin word meaning "ribbon" and in mathematics, the symbol denotes unbound space or infinity. We learned in Chapter 3 that the Hebrew word "everlasting" or "eternity" has a gematria value of 74 which is the same value as the Greek word "creation".

Some scholars say that the symbol is derived from the Greek letter "omega" which has a value of "800" or "8" and if you rotate the lemniscates one turn to the right or left, you see the number "8". From previous discussions we know that the number "8" represents Jesus. Here was another way to preserve the information known only to a few initiates.

There is obviously something sacred with the Sphinx as the ancient Greeks added it to their mythologies in "The Riddle of the Sphinx" which appeared on vases made around 470–460 B.C. While originally found in the writings of Apollodorus, second century B.C., it became part of Hesiod's *Theogony*.

Apollodorus states, "For Hera sent the Sphinx, whose mother was Echidna and her father Typhon; and she had the face of a woman, the breast, feet, and tail of a lion, and the wings of a bird. And having learned a riddle from the Muses, she sat on Mount Phicium, and propounded it to the Thebans." And the riddle was this:

"What is that which has one voice and yet becomes four-footed and two-footed and three-footed?"

Anyone unable to answer the question correctly was snatched away and devoured. The only person able to answer the question correctly was Oedipus.

His answer: "A Man"

"For as a babe, he is four-footed, going on four limbs, as an adult he is two-footed, and as an old man he gets besides a third support in a staff"

Upon the correct answer, the Sphinx threw herself from the citadel and died and Oedipus succeeded to the kingdom". (From the Library of Apollodorus, Book III, Chapter 5, verse 8)

Oedipus and the Sphinx

The Sphinx was definitely a guardian figure. To the Egyptians, the Sphinx was benevolent, but to the Greeks she was a nemesis as the riddle conveys.

Some scholars will tell you that the Sphinx is symbolic of the four creatures in Ezekiel's vision with the face representing man, the wings the eagle, the body the lion, and the feet the ox. Remember that these creatures represented the cardinal points on the compass and the elements found on Earth.

Clearly, the Egyptians weren't the only ones to have a Sphinx monument as they were also found in the Sumerian culture. Remember from Chapter 2 that Sargon built the palace walls to correspond to the value of his name. On the relief displayed, you can clearly see a winged sphinx with its face resembling the God next to him.

Why was it so important that the image of the God's become the face of the Sphinx? Does this relate to what we studied about the palindromes and the reflective images like the Moses and the "I AM" gematria value images that we discussed in Chapter 5? It sure makes me pause and ponder especially when we are told that man was created in the image of God (Genesis 1:26). According to Del Washburn, the Greek words for "God", "image", and "created" all have the same gematria value of 425 (Washburn 1994, 82).

This Assyrian guard that looks like a sphinx was called a "cherubim" which means "one who prays" or "one who intercedes" from the Akkadian translation. These cherubim were always placed at the entrance to temples and palaces representing the "spirit of protection."

Cherubims are the first angels listed in the Bible in Genesis 3:24 where they are placed at the gates of the Garden of Eden preventing Adam from returning. Cherubims were also the guardians of the Ark of the Covenant. Through Angelology, the study of angel hierarchy, the Cherubim angels occupy the second highest level out of the nine angel levels.

Stone Relief from Palace of Sargon II at Khorsabad, Iraq
Assyrian School–8th Century B.C.
Louvre Museum
Paris, France

Isn't it amazing that the Great pyramid and the Sphinx are the only remaining "wonder" of the ancient world? Do you think this is a coincidence?

I believe that science has advanced because of the stars. It was the stars in Virgo that Hipparchus discovered the precession of the equinox. It was also the stars in Virgo that Einstein discovered the speed of light reflected in his famous equation $E=mc^2$.

Now that we know why we begin with Virgo, let's take a look at the detail of mankind's oldest history book, ***The Stars: His Life in Lights***, which has remained true, unchanged, and untouched by anyone.

THE STARS: HIS LIFE IN LIGHTS

The heavens declare the glory of God; and the firmament sheweth his handiwork
Psalms 19:1

While the ancients may not have had a written "Bible", they did have a book that was open for all to read and that could never be destroyed by a conqueror or religion. It was and still remains free to all for viewing and will forever stand for "hope". The book's title is *THE STARS: HIS LIFE IN LIGHTS*. It is our daily nighttime story.

Celestial Map
Frederik de Wit
17th Century–Denmark

The Shekhinah is Coming

The story created by the constellations in the heavens unfolds like a book of visual pictures. It begins with the promise prophesied by the ancient prophets which is hope for salvation as referenced in the following verse:

Blessed be the Lord God of Israel. For He has visited and redeemed His people and has raised up the horn of salvation
Luke 1:67–70

And He shall send Jesus Christ, which before was preached unto you. Whom the heaven must receive until the times of restitution of all things, which God hath spoken by the mouth of all His holy prophets since the world began
Acts 3:20–21

The presentation that follows will give the names of the twelve constellations followed by the constellation's three decans. I will discuss the meaning behind the constellation's names as they appear in various languages, what some individual stars names mean, the related mythology, any meaningful gematria, and supportive biblical text. In previous chapters, I detailed the scientific information concerning the constellations so as not to bough down the flow of the story at hand.

As stated in the Chapter 7, there is only one place to begin reading this story and that is with the hero's mother. So, we begin with the constellation Virgo, the Virgin accompanied by the three decans named Coma, Centaurus, and Bootes.

VIRGO

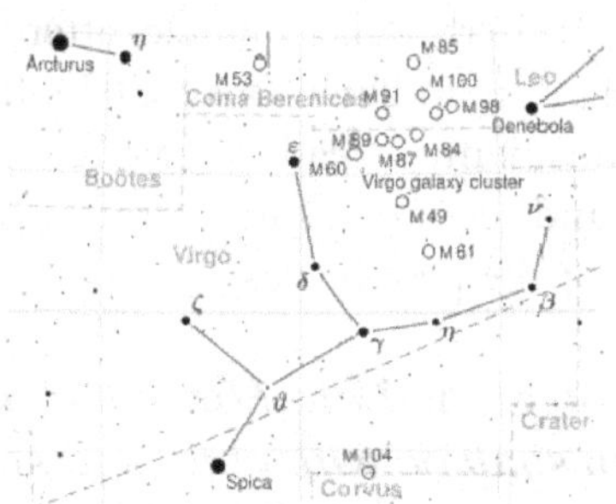

In all ancient cultures she is the goddess by different names with emphasizes on her virginity. The Egyptians referred to her as Aspolia, in Greece she is known as Athena, Astrea, Parthenos, or Demeter and the Romans called her Ceres meaning "goddess of grain or harvest". The Babylonians called her Ninmah meaning "mother goddess".

As Athena, she is the goddess of wisdom born from the head of Zeus fully dressed in her armor, a warrior for justice always accompanied by the goddess Nike. Her temple was the great Parthenon in Athens. She was the helper of many heroes including Jason and Heracles. She never had a lover which earned her the title of Athena Parthenos, meaning Athena the Virgin.

As Astrea she is the goddess of justice, peace and harmony. She is one of the last to leave the Earth and take her place among the stars as the Golden Age faded out. As Demeter and Ceres (the Latin name for Demeter) she is the goddess of grain and fertility as she taught mankind about producing food.

In Arabic, she carries two names, Aware and Sunbul which means "the pure virgin" and "an ear of corn" respectively. In Hebrew and Syriac, she is called Bethulah which means "the maiden", specifically a virgin.

Motherhood, a miracle, attends this virgin who is the holder and bringer of an illustrious SEED, far greater than herself that will bruise the enemy's head. So, we have a dual image here. One, she is a woman and secondly, she is a mother who will carry the seed (the branch) of the prophecies.

Therefore the Lord Himself shall give you a sign; Behold the virgin shall be with child and shall bring forth a son; and she shall call His name Immanuel
Isaiah 7:14

Immanuel means "God with us" with a Hebrew value of 197 and "God with us" has a Greek value of 1236. Matthew 1:18 informs us that this prophecy was fulfilled.

She is clutching a branch in her right hand and an ear of corn or wheat in her left hand to represent the two fold nature of her coming son. She lies prostrate waiting for her son to lift her up for salvation.

The brightest star in her right hand (clutching the branch) is called Al Mureddin, an Arabic word meaning "those who sent forth" or "who shall have dominion". In Latin, this star is known as Vindemiatrix meaning "the grape gatherer".

He shall have dominion also from sea to sea and from the river unto the ends of the Earth
Psalms 72:8

The brightest star in her left hand (an ear of corn or wheat) is called Spica, a Latin word meaning "ear of grain (wheat)". This star in

Arabic is called Azimach meaning "the branch or shoot". According to Wikipedia, Spica was believed to be the star that provided Hipparchus with the data which enabled him to discover the precession of the equinox discussed in Chapter 5.

Another bright star worth mentioning is Zavijava or Zavijaveh located in the maiden's hair. It is a Hebrew word meaning "gloriously beautiful". This was the star Einstein used during the solar eclipse of 21 September 1922 to determine the speed of light in space, as it was close to the Sun.

In that day shall the branch of the Lord be beautiful and glorious
Isaiah 4:2

The key word "branch" in Hebrew is "tsemach" with a number value of 138. It is the same number value of the Greek words, "the man" that Pilate used.

And Pilate saith unto them, Behold "the man"
John 19:5

Using gematria, we have further identification of the name of the man who is the branch from the prophet Zechariah.

Behold the man whose name is the branch; and he shall grow up out of his place, and he shall build the temple of the Lord
Zechariah 6:12

The value of this phrase is equal to 2368 which is the identical value of the name Jesus Christ in Greek, *Iesous Christos* where Iesous equals 888 and Christos equals 1480.

The Shekhinah is Coming

So, as the story begins, we are promised a "seed of dominion" out of which we will know "wisdom", "justice", and "peace". And through gematria, we are given the name of the SEED.

Verily, verily, I say unto you, except a corn of wheat fall into the ground and die, it abideth alone; but if it dies, it bringeth forth much fruit
John 12:24

Behold, the days come, saith the Lord, that I will raise unto David a righteous Branch, and a King shall reign and prosper, and shall execute judgement and justice in the earth
Jeremiah 23:5

VIRGO'S FIRST DECAN: COMA

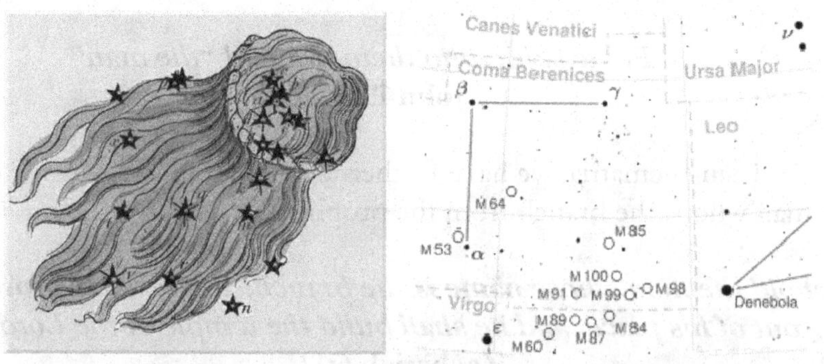

The first Decan of Virgo is called Coma. The ancient name for this constellation was Comash meaning "the desired" or "longed for". He is our hero, Jesus, the SEED of Virgo.

And I will shake all nations, and the desire of all nations shall come

Haggai 2:7

In the ancient Egyptian picture of Coma, a woman is sitting on a throne as she nourishes an infant, a boy named ShesNu meaning "the desired son". The infant is the seed of the virgin who the prophets described as "the desired one" or "the desire of all nations". The Arabs, Persians, Chaldeans, and the Egyptians taught that the infant boy had the Hebrew name of *Ihesu*, which in Greek is *Ieza* meaning Jesus.

The Shekhinah is Coming

It is documented that the Star of Bethlehem appeared in this constellation. In A.D. 69, in his epistle to the Ephesians, Ignatius, Bishop of Antioch stated, "At the appearance of the Lord, a star shone forth brighter than all the other stars". The ancients called this star the "Shekhinah".

Balaam prophesied, *There shall come a Star out of Jacob, and a Sceptre shall rise out of Israel*
Numbers 25:17

Even the ancient text of *Zend Avesta* stated that in the sign of the virgin, this new star was to appear. The Persian magi, Zoroaster, said that when they see a new star appear, it would notify the birth of a mysterious child who they were to adore.

And then shall appear the sign of His coming
Matthew 24:30

The sign is "His star" shinning down on Bethlehem, the "house of bread" for all to see. It is the place of our soul's nourishment. It was also the city of David's "beloved" birth and the location where he was crowned the King of Israel reigning from ca. 1010 B.C.–970 B.C. On the surface of the Earth, Bethlehem is located at 31.68 degrees longitude and the Greek spelling yields the magic number "99". This location is also equal to the gematria value of the Greek spelling of Jesus Christ, Ihesu giving more evidence of the Divine plan. The evidence is enhanced when you consider the numbers. The value of the phrases "the key" and "shall come the desire of nations" are both equal to 528 which identifies our hero.

To the Greeks this constellation was known as Berenice's Hair of golden color, because their word *"Come"* meant "hair" as they did not know how to translate Coma. The Latin's as well translated Coma to be "the hair of Berenice". This has led to the constellation being presented as a woman's wig rather than the "desired one" in the older planispheres.

The story of Berenice's Hair comes from her consecrating her hair to Venus. She did this by hanging her hair in the temple for her husband's safe return home from a dangerous expedition to Syria around 247 B.C. Her husband was Euergetes, king of Egypt in the third century B.C. who was also known as Ptolemy III. Upon the king's return, the hair was missing and it was declared that Jupiter had transferred the hair to the heavens.

VIRGO'S SECOND DECAN: CENTAURUS

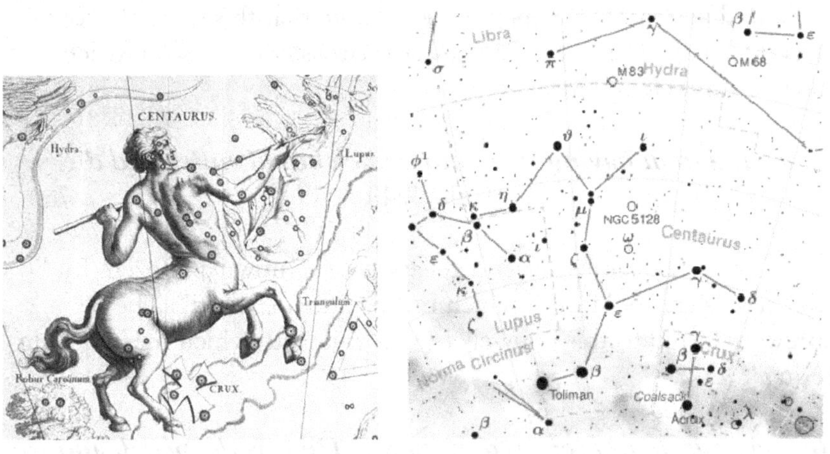

The second Decan of Virgo is called Centaurus. A Centaur is a mythological creature composed of half-man and half-horse. The man is represented from the head down to the torsal with the remainder of the body represented by a horse. Here our hero is displaying his two-fold nature as while he will be teaching wisdom and righteousness, he will also be hunting the enemy.

Centaurs were known to be great bull killers. While Centaurs are said to be heaven begotten, they are hated and abhorred by both gods and men. They were eventually driven to the mountains and exterminated.

The most famous centaur was named Chiron. Chiron was endowed with great wisdom and the art of prophecy. He was also known for his skill in hunting, medicine, and music. He was a friend of Hercules and the Argonauts. He was a teacher to many of the Greek heroes with one of his pupils being Achilles. In Hebrew, Chiron means "the pierced" and in Greek, Chiron means "the pierced", or "who pierces".

Here begins the appearance of man's two natures as was represented in Christ. It is interesting to note that this constellation is located immediately above the Southern Cross constellation which alludes to this statement:

That a man having two natures he should suffer and die
Luke 2:40

To the ancients, this constellation was known as Bezeh. In Arabic it was called Al Beze which means "the despised". The Hebrews referred to this constellation as Asmeath which means "a sin-offering".

He is despised and rejected of men....He was despised, and we esteemed Him not
Isaiah 53:3

There is an interesting star in this constellation located in the horse's fore foot that according to some astronomers is growing rapidly brighter. This star is named Toliman and has a root meaning of "prayer" or "the meditation". The name Toliman was used in the following verse:

I am Alpha and Omega, the beginning and the end, which is, and which was, and which is to come
Revelation 1:8

In mythology, during a struggle with the Erymanthean boar, Chiron was unintentionally wounded by one of Hercules' poisoned arrows. Although Chiron was immortal, he volunteered to die and transferred his immortality to Prometheus, whereupon he was placed amongst the stars. Prometheus was the one who gave "fire" to mankind against Zeus' wishes.

As we complete this constellation, we see that the child born of the virgin has grown strong both physically and in wisdom. This is very fitting of the Centaur's character. Even though the Centaurs were born from the heavens with great attributes, they were still despised like the "desired child" will encounter in adulthood.

VIRGO'S THIRD DECAN: BOOTES

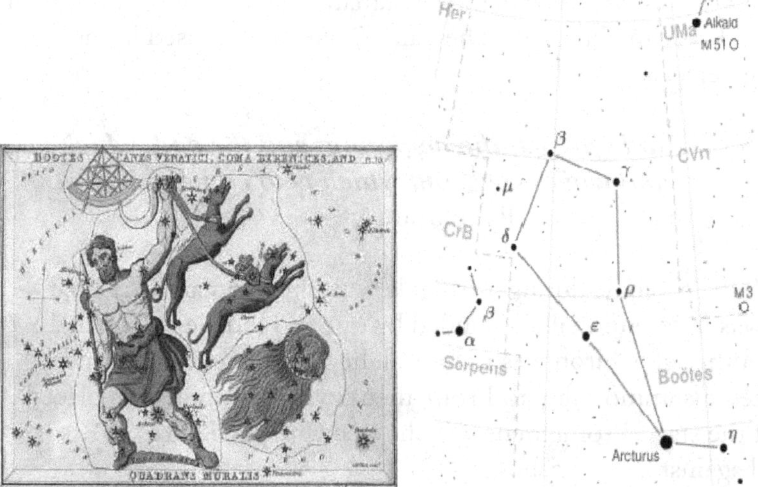

The third Decan of Virgo is called Bootes. This constellation is the picture of a strong man walking rapidly with a spear in his right hand and a sickle in his left hand. He is known as the "coming one" from the root "Bo" and in this role, he is referred to as "a shepherd". Our hero has come to protect his kin and subdue his enemy. Additionally, in his left hand, he holds the leash of the dogs named Asterion and Chara.

For He cometh to judge the Earth: He shall judge the world with righteousness and the people with His truth
Psalms 96:13

And I looked, and behold a white cloud, and upon the cloud one sat like unto the Son of man, having on his head a golden crown, and in His hand a sharp sickle
Revelation 14:14

The brightest star in this constellation is called Arcturus by the Greeks and located in his left knee. Arcturus means "he cometh" and was known as the guardian or keeper of Arktos. The ancients associated the word Arktos with the idea of an enclosure referring to a shepherd and his sheep. Known as the herdsman who invented the plough, Bootes appears to drive the oxen of Ursa Major as the dogs offer their help by barking at the Great Bear.

Bootes' ancient Egyptian name was Smat meaning "one who rules, subdues, and governs". A star located on his waist is called Mires meaning "the coming forth". A star located in Bootes' head is called Nekkar which in Arabic means "the pierced". This same star in Hebrew is called Merga which means "who bruises".

And I will pour upon the house of David, and upon the inhabitants of Jerusalem, the spirit of grace and of supplications: and they shall look upon me whom they have pierced
Zechariah 12:10

A star located in the spear head, in his right hand is called Al Katurops which in Arabic means "the branch" or "the rod". This is the image associated with the shepherd's crook or the staff carried by the Pope representing wisdom and understanding. In gematria, the words "shepherd" and "his flock" both equal 280.

In summary, the constellation Virgo with its three decans describes the virgin goddess that will bear the seed of prophecy as announced by the Star of Bethlehem. The infant grows into a strong man of great wisdom and righteousness known for his abilities to heal. While he is despised and wounded, he stays strong as a shepherd with his rod to gather his flock. His strength and resolve set the stage for what is to follow.

In Chapter 2, we discussed discovering the "keys of knowledge and the mysteries" that led to enlightenment. In this very first constellation, we see this unfolding. In gematria, the value of the Hebrew words, "the key" equals 528. The two phrases "the day of his coming" and "and shall come the desire of nations" have the same value as "the key". This is a confirmation that the constellation Virgo is the correct place to begin our study of *The Stars: His Life in Lights.*

LIBRA

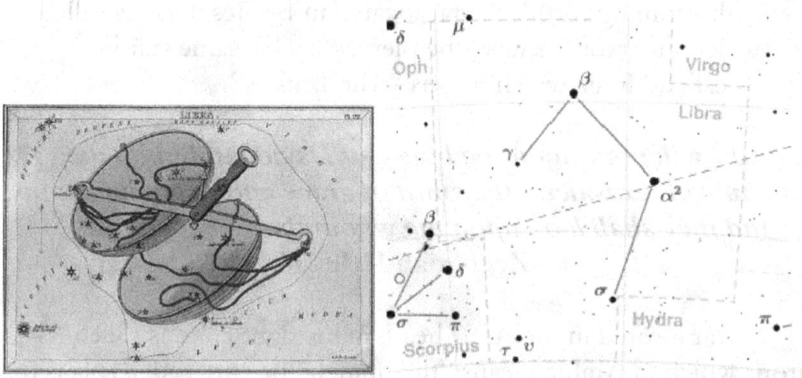

The story continues with the constellation Libra accompanied by the three decans named The Southern Cross, The Victim-Lupus, and The Northern Crown. While the hero was wounded, justice takes the stage as the balance of truth in resolving disputes, establishing order, and inflicting penalties.

The constellation Libra is the picture of scales used in weighing or balancing. The word Libra in Latin means "weighing" with balancing connoting equal weights. The Hebrew word for scales is "mozanim" which means "the scales weighing" and has a numeric value of 148. This is the same value for the word "blood" in Hebrew which matches the value of Christ (1480) in Greek, remembering that zero's can be dropped and not change the relationship between words.

Are made nigh by the blood of Christ
Ephesians 2:13

In Arabic, this constellation is called Al Zubena which means "purchase", "redemption", or "gain". A star in the lower scale is called Zuben Al Genubi in Arabic and means "the purchase or price which is deficient". In Greek, it is known as Zugos which is the crossbar that "yokes" two oxen together.

Thou art weighed in the balances, and art found wanting
Daniel 5:27

Additional stars include Al Gubi meaning "heaped up high" and Zuben Akrabi meaning "the price of the conflict". A star in the upper scale is called Zuben al Chemali in Arabic and means "the price which covers".

Ye are bought with a price; be not ye the servants of men
1Corinthians 7:23

In the Egyptian hieroglyphs, there are several images that relate to the "weighing of the soul" upon death. Anubis weighed the heart of the deceased against the feather of Maat. Maat was the Egyptian concept of Truth, Justice, Balance, and Order. If the heart was too heavily burdened and did not balance with Maat, it would be devoured by the crocodile.

Heart **Maat**

The Egyptian hieroglyph for the "soul" was called "Bau" (plural of "Ba"). It is the picture of a bird with a human head and often pictured in scenes related to death depicting the importance of the soul in the afterlife.

Ba
Egyptian Soul

In Christian iconography, the "weighing of the soul" morphed into the images of St. Michael performing this same task.

The Archangel Michael
Rogier van der Weyden
Hotel-Dieu de Beaune
Beaune, France
1446–1452

St. Michael Weighing the Souls
Juan de la Abadia
Catalunya, Barcelona
15th Century

Clearly, this sign relates to justice and redemption. It is the balancing of the scales with the blood of the strong man from Virgo. The goddess, Athena, who stood for justice in Virgo morphed into "lady justice" holding the scales in one hand and a sword in the other. Lady Justice can be seen adorning courthouses where issues are settled and justice prevails. Many times, she appears blindfolded to indicate fairness and objectivity in the decisions and settlements.

LIBRA'S FIRST DECAN: CRUX

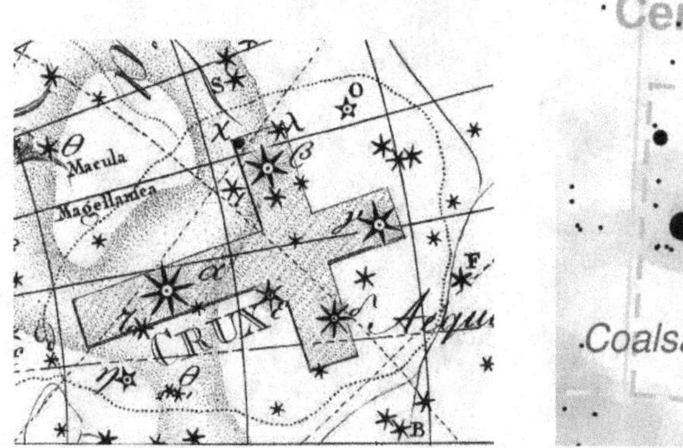

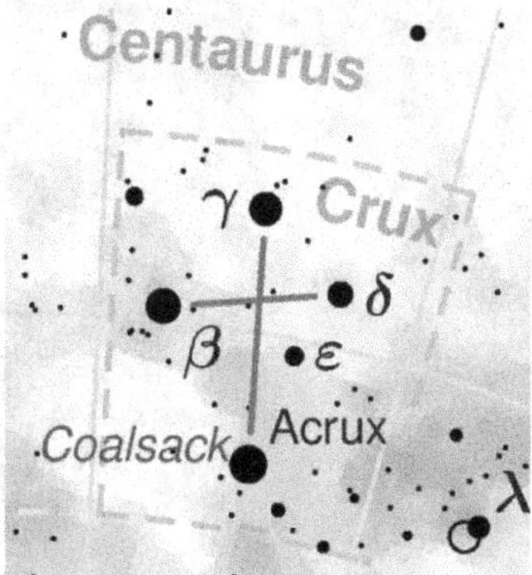

The first Decan of Libra is called Crux or The Southern Cross. The cross is the ultimate sign of faith and marks the crossroad or the intersection of two ways. While it is a burden for some, it is virtue and steadfastness for another. The location of this constellation is located very low in the darkest area of heaven. It is visible only near or south of the equator.

This constellation was originally seen in the Northern Hemisphere. It moved into the Southern Hemisphere around the time of the crucifixion in Jerusalem and could no longer be seen. It wasn't until the sixteenth century when visiting missionaries to the south saw the cross and proclaimed it magnificent. In Dante's *The Divine Comedy*, he states:

"To the right hand I turned, and fixed my mind upon the other pole, and saw four stars Ne'er seen before save by the primal people"
Purgatorio: Canto I

I was fortunate to travel to the sacred sites of Peru and view this constellation in the summer of 2001. I found it very hard to take my eyes off this amazing celestial configuration of stars. Every night during my trip, I would view this image.

The Hebrew name for this constellation is Tau, the last letter of the Hebrew alphabet. Tau means "mark" or "cross" and is written with the horizontal top resting on the vertical and perpendicular like a balancing apparatus and like the English "T", unlike the Christian cross. As a "mark" it also meant a "boundary" or a "limit". As the last letter in the Hebrew alphabet, it carries the connotation of final or finished. Tau also has a value of 800, the value of the Lord in Greek. It aligns with the last words spoken by Jesus in his earthly life.

It is finished
John 19:30

The Tau was found on ancient coins in the form of an "x" or "t". The "x" morphed into the saying "x marks the spot". It is also the mark that people make when they cannot sign their name.

Among all ancient cultures the cross is considered sacred and connected with deliverance and salvation. In Egypt, the cross is known as the "Ankh" and is the symbol of life and immortality. As the "key of life", the Ankh oftentimes appears before a person's mouth symbolizing the connection between "life" and "breath". You will also see the "ankh" carried by the Egyptian gods and pictured frequently on many temple walls. We will discuss the importance of this in Chapter 10.

Ankh Giving Life

The Ankh **The Cross**

Even Krishna known as the "god of deliverance" can be found pictured holding the ankh.

Interestingly, the cross has gone from the symbol of life and immortality for the Egyptians to the symbol of death for the Church. Why and how did this change come about?

Jesus, when He had cried again with a loud voice, yielded up the ghost
Matthew 27:50

Another ancient Hebrew name for this constellation is Adom which means "cutting off" as referenced by Daniel.

And after threescore and two weeks shall Messiah be cut off
Daniel 9:26

This was from a message delivered by the angel Gabriel. The value of "shall be cut off" is 630 and matches the word that Moses used for "prophet" when speaking with the Israelites.

The Lord thy God will raise up unto thee a Prophet from the midst of thee ...unto Him ye shall hearken
Deuteronomy 18:15

LIBRA'S SECOND DECAN: LUPUS–THE VICTIM

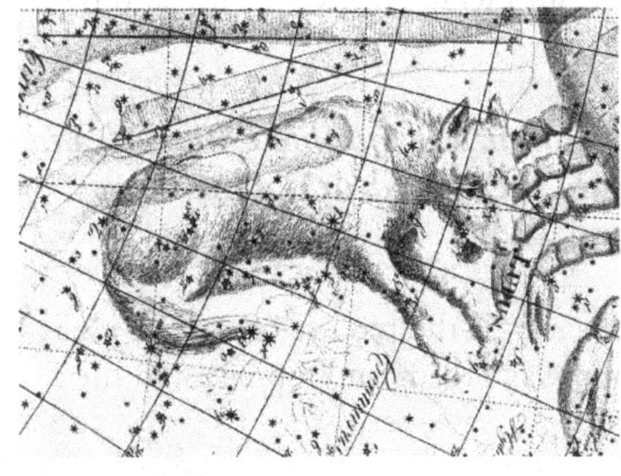

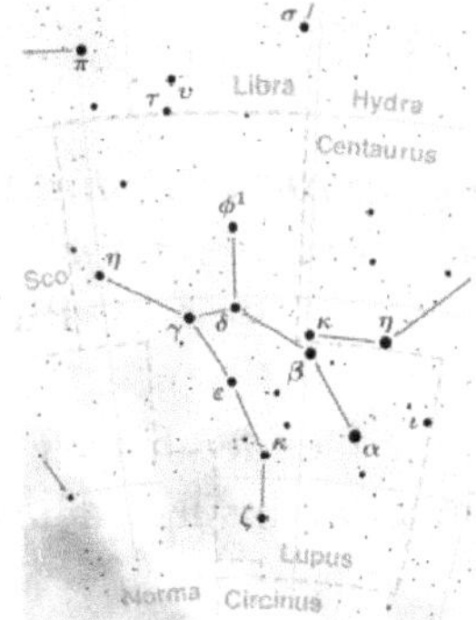

The Shekhinah is Coming

The second Decan of Libra is called Lupus or Victima. This constellation is known as the victim slain and is pictured like an animal that has been killed and falling down. Here, our hero has volunteered to submit to the ultimate punishment of death as he is killed by the Centaurus, but the Centaurus is really himself. He has made his choice and silently submits to the penalty.

Asedah is the ancient Hebrew name for this constellation which means "to be slain". The Arabic name is Asedaton, which means "to be slain". The Greeks had two names for this constellation. One is "Thera", which means "a beast" and the second name is "Lycos", which means "a wolf". In Latin the name for this constellation is Victima or Bestia, which meant "a great lesson".

The brightest star in this constellation is called Men meaning "the star of the future". Another star called Thusia means "the sacrifice".

…And I lay down my life for the sheep…..No man taketh it from me, but I lay it down of myself
John 10:15–18

This references the fact that Chiron is the adult Jesus who decides to make the choice to freely and willingly give his life and pass his immortality to Prometheus.

And being found in fashion as a man, He humbled himself, and became obedient unto death, even the death of the cross
Philippians 2:8

In the Denderah zodiac this sign is the picture of a small child with his finger on his lips. The child was Horus and represented the daily rising of the Sun. The Phoenicians, Greeks, and Romans called him Harpocrates who was the "god of silence".

Verily I say unto you, except ye be converted, and become as little children, ye shall not enter into the kingdom of heaven
Matthew 18:3

LIBRA'S THIRD DECAN: CORONA AUSTRALIS THE NORTHERN CROWN

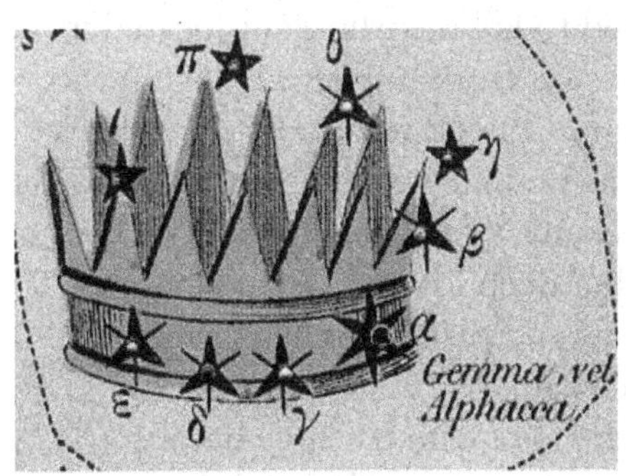

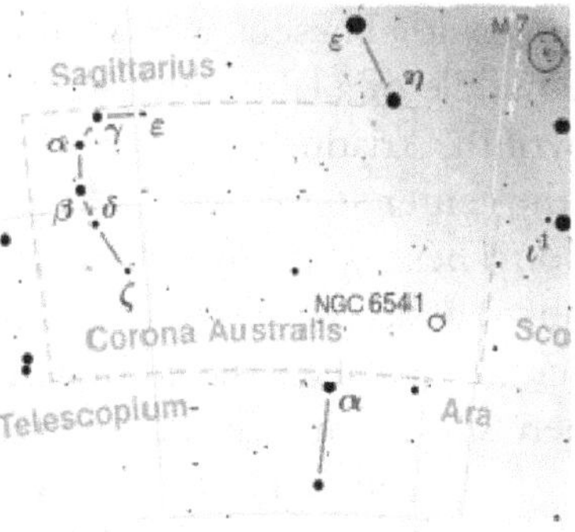

The third Decan of Libra is called Corona Australis and follows the first Decan, the Southern Cross. It is also known as the Northern Crown and pictured as a royal crown. While it appears that our hero has been slain, all is not in vain. Here we are shown the royal crown that will be worn in the second coming. The faithful are still full of hope.

In Hebrew, this constellation is called Atarah or Ataroth, which means "a royal crown" and has a numeric value of 284 which is equal to the Greek words "God" and "holy". In Arabic, it is known as Al

Iclil, which means "an ornament or a jewel". The brightest star in this constellation is called Al Phecca, which in Arabic means "the shinning".

The constellation is about a royal person's crown, much different from the crown of thorns that Jesus wore on the cross.

And they stripped Him and put on Him a scarlet robe. And when they had planted a crown of thorns…
Matthew 27:28–29

In Greek mythology, this crown was given to Ariadne, the daughter of King Minos of Crete, by Bacchus/Dionysus. Ariadne was in love with Theseus who volunteered to kill the Minotaur located in the middle of a labyrinth. To aid Theseus from not getting lost in the labyrinth, Ariadne gave him a ball of red thread to unroll as he traveled to the center so that he could use it to find his way out of the labyrinth. Upon Theseus triumphant return, he and Ariadne escaped to Naxos. Unhappy that Theseus didn't share her deep love, Ariadne attempts suicide when she is saved by Dionysus and placed in the heavens where she remains immortal in her crown.

In summary, the constellation Libra with its three decans describes the blood of the fallen victim found wanting and the balancing of justice with the final awarding of the crown from love.

SCORPIO

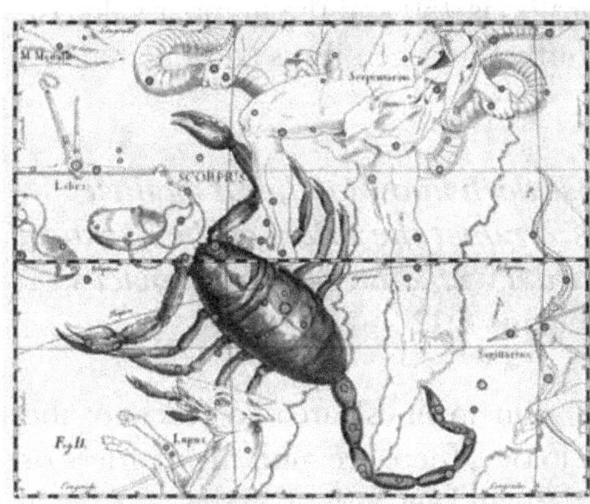

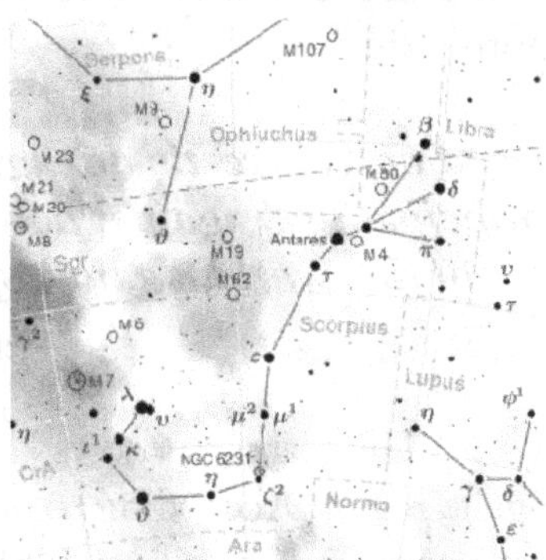

This constellation is the image of a gigantic scorpion with its uplifted lethal tail ready to strike the heel of a mighty man, Ophiuchus, struggling with a serpent. The conflict is not over as the scorpion is posed to inflict a fatal sting to prohibit the hero who is destined to obtain the royal crown. Scorpions look like small lobsters with a tail of poison that is often fatal to the victim being struck. It is reported to be the most intense pain inflicted upon a human, clearly a deadly and malignant enemy.

In Hebrew, the name of this constellation is Akrab, which means "the conflict" or "war". In Arabic, this constellation is called Al Akrab, which means "wounding him that cometh". In Coptic, this constellation is called Isidis which means "attack of the enemy".

Even the brightest star located in the heart of the scorpion, named Antares, shines with a red glow like the color of blood. In Arabic, Antares means "the wounding", "cutting", or "tearing".

The Shekhinah is Coming

Clearly, this constellation is about a conflict, but we're not sure who the conflict is between until we look at the number values. In Greek, the number value for scorpion is 750 and the number value of Lucifer in Hebrew is 75. It is a conflict between Jesus and Lucifer, another duality.

For we wrestle not against flesh and blood, but against principalities, against powers, against the rulers of the darkness of this world, against spiritual wickedness in high places
Ephesians 6:12

The terms "powers" and "principalities" are two orders of the angelic realm. According to Angelology, there are nine angel orders or levels and these two occupy the sixth and seventh positions respectfully. The number one position is the highest level of angels known as the "seraphim".

SCORPIO'S FIRST DECAN: SERPENS

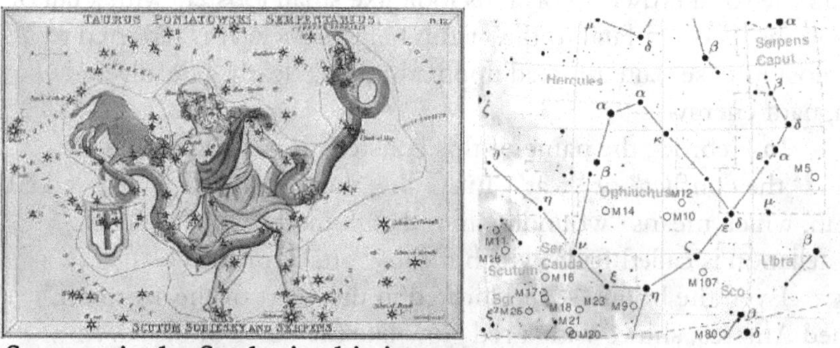

Serpens is the Snake in this image
Ophiuchus is the Man and discussed later

Secrets of the Divine

The first Decan of Scorpio is called Serpens. It is the picture of a serpent reaching for the Northern Crown, that crown of jewels, and the third decan of Libra which is located immediately over its head. The serpent is helping the scorpion to prevent the rightful heir destined to receive the royal crown. He must be restrained by the powerful grasp of Ophiuchus as the crown belongs to only one person.

It is a strength contest of who will have dominion over the crown. Ophiuchus has been wounded on his heel by the scorpion as he is in the process of crushing the scorpion's head with his other foot. Clearly, our hero has been wounded by the enemy as we were warned in Chapter 7 referencing the third part of our story (Genesis 3:15).

The brightest star located in the serpent's neck is called Alyah, which in Hebrew means "the accursed". In Arabic it is called Al Hay, which means "the reptile". This takes on a greater meaning when you consider the numbers involved. In Hebrew, Alyah has a value of 165 the same as the Greek words "that man" in Acts 17:31.

Because He hath appointed a day, in which He will judge the world in righteousness by "that man" whom He hath ordained
Acts 17:31

That man is Jesus and he will judge the enemy, the serpent who is attempting to take his crown.

SCORPIO'S SECOND DECAN: OPHIUCHUS

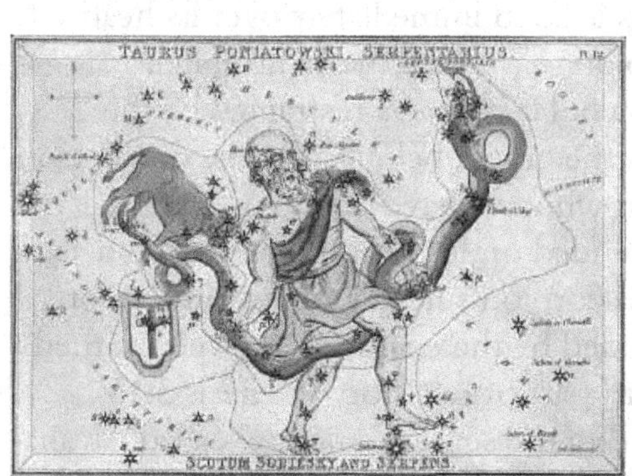

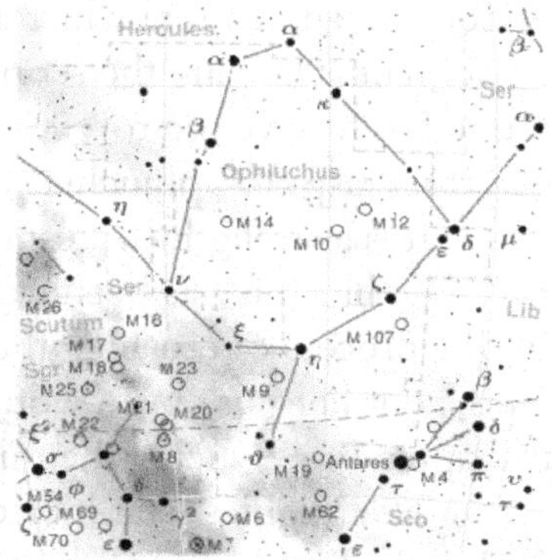

The second Decan of Scorpio is called Ophiuchus, a Greek name meaning "the serpent holder". In Hebrew, the name is Afeichus which means "the serpent held". In Latin he was referred to as Serpentarius meaning "snake holder". In the Dendera Zodiac, Ophiuchus is known as Api-bau, meaning "the chief who cometh".

This constellation is the picture of the strong man struggling with the serpent of the first decan. Ophiuchus stands on the heart of the scorpion as he holds the serpent in his two powerful hands. With Ophiuchus' superior power, the serpent is unable to reach the crown.

The brightest star located in the head of this constellation is called Ras al Hagus which in Arabic means "the head of him who holds". The star located in his foot is called Saiph which means "bruised".

This constellation was also called "The Great Physician" after Aesculapius, a physician skilled in ancient astronomy. He was known as the "god of health" who cured all and brought the dead back to life.

These actions angered Zeus who killed Aesculapius with one of his thunderbolts to prevent human immortality.

In Greek mythology, Aesculapius was the son of Apollo who, as an unborn child, was rescued from his dying mother and given to Chiron, the centaur to be raised. It was Chiron who instructed him in the art of medicine. Aesculapius means "to cut open" as he was cut from his mother's womb. He represents the character of the redeemer.

Seen as both a god and man, he was worshiped all over Greece. His temples were built on hills or near wells believed to have healing powers. The original Hippocratic Oath began with the invocation, "I swear by Aesculapius the physician". Serpents were connected to Aesculapius as they were believed to have the power to discover healing herbs.

As the Greek god of medicine and healing, the rod of Aesculapius was a snake entwined staff which morphed into the current medical symbol of the caduceus.

Aesculapius
God of Medicine
Pergamon Museum
Berlin, Germany

Rod of Aesculapius Caduceus

Azoth, from the Arabic word "al-zā'ūq" meaning "the mercury", was the universal medicine sought by the ancient alchemist. The symbol used for this universal medicine was the Caduceus. This can be likened to the "manna" that the Israelites ate during their Exodus to sustain life (Exodus 16:14–18). Manna is known as the "food of the angels" and in Hebrew the word means "What is this?" as the Israelites had never seen it before.

Scholars believe that manna is a form of a dew drop that hardens into grains and can be ground into flour for making bread. It is believed that Elijah was given manna by an angel when he sojourned for forty days in the wilderness detailed in 1Kings 19:5.

Manna Reigning From Heaven on the Israelites
Maciejowski Bible
ca. 1250

The Shekhinah is Coming

In the books of Exodus and Numbers, we are told of three separate occasions where Moses is instructed to use his rod and turn it into a serpent. This process was not only used to demonstrate to the Pharaoh that Moses was a prophet for God, but also as a means of healing when the Israelites were in the desert (Exodus 4:2–4, 7:10 and Numbers 21:8–9).

Make thee a fiery serpent, and set it upon a pole and it shall come to pass, that every one that is bitten, when he looketh upon it shall live
Numbers 21:8

The term "fiery serpent" was translated from the Hebrew word "seraph", which is the highest order in the angel hierarchy. Isaiah 6:3 describes God's throne surrounded by seraphim who continually chant in Hebrew, *"Kadosh, Kadosh, Kadosh"*, which translates to "Holy, Holy, Holy".

Moses and the Brazen Serpent
James Joseph Jacques Tissot

King Hezekiah destroyed Moses' highly treasured bronze serpent which was protested by the Hebrews as an attack upon their heritage. It was memorialized in the stars with Serpens representing Moses' bronze serpent and Ophiuchus representing Hezekiah.

The Shekhinah is Coming

This is the same device that Archangel Gabriel uses when he imparts the Holy Spirit onto Mary at "the annunciation". In many pictures related to the annunciation, the caduceus becomes a stock of flowers appearing as lilies.

In other pictures of Archangel Gabriel, his caduceus becomes his trumpet. It is the trumpet sound that will announce the coming of Judgment Day. Interestingly, the number value for the words "trumpet" and "sign" in Hebrew are both equal to 576.

And I saw the seven angels which stood before God; and to them were given seven trumpets
Revelation 8:2

The Annunciation
Gerald David

The Annunciation
Francesco Granacci

SCORPIO'S THIRD DECAN: HERCULES

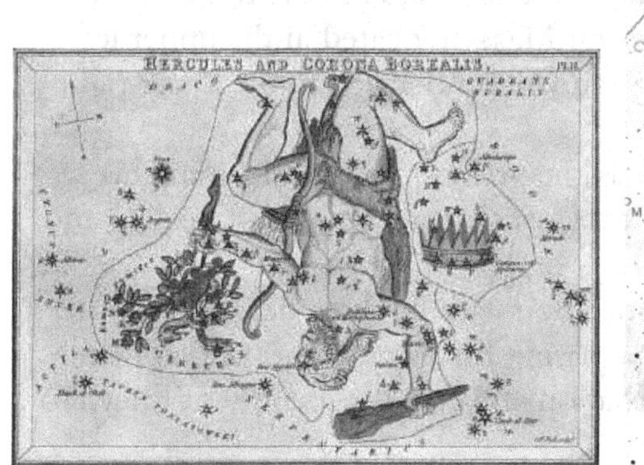

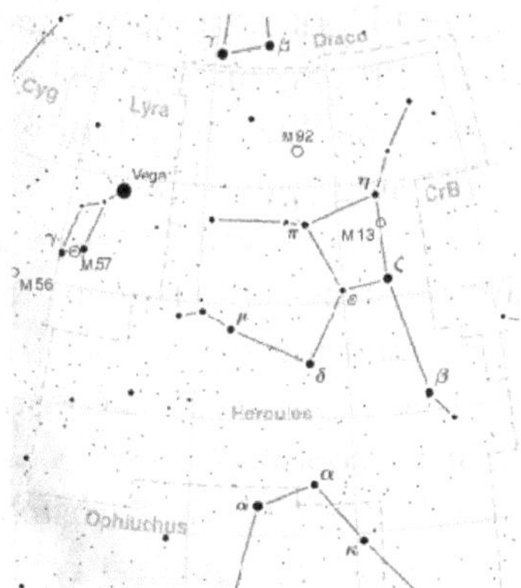

The third Decan of Scorpio is called Hercules. Ancient mythology abounds about Hercules and his amazing feats known as the twelve great labors (Appendix O). All of these labors were related to vanquishing great evil powers. Hercules was known as "the mighty one" or "the mighty vanquisher". In Arabic, Hercules was called Al Giscale which means "the strong one".

This constellation is the picture of a mighty man, our hero, who is kneeling on one knee with his right heel lifted because of the Scorpion's wound. His left foot is ready to crush the head of the dragon called Draco. In his right hand, he carries a great club ready to strike and in his left hand, he holds the triple headed monster called Cerberus.

The brightest star located in the head of this constellation is called Ras al Gethi which means "the head of him who bruises" referencing the already stated Genesis' quote. The next brightest star located in the right arm pit is called Kornephorus which means "the branch kneeling".

Other star names include Marsic located in the right elbow meaning "the wounding". The star Maasyn located in the upper left arm meaning "the sin offering" and Caiam located in the lower right arm meaning "punishing".

Hercules was honored as the greatest hero performing his wondrous feats, which aligns with Jesus' achievements of healing and performing miracles.

In summary, this constellation with its three decans illustrate the conflict between the two opposing forces and who will ultimately be victorious. The next constellation will give the identity of the victor.

<u>SAGITTARIUS</u>

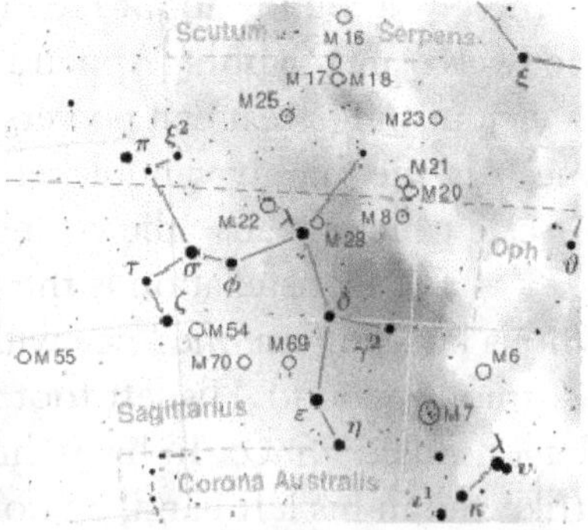

This constellation is the picture of a mighty warrior in the form of a Centaur with his arrow aimed directly at the heart of the scorpion as our hero is ready to conquer the enemy.

Secrets of the Divine

Thine arrows are sharp in the heart of the king's enemies; whereby the people fall under thee
Psalms 45:5

In Latin, Sagittarius means "the archer", the "bowman", or "he who sends forth the arrow". The Greeks call him Toxotes, "the archer" and in Hebrew, he is called Keshith which also means "the archer". In Arabic, this constellation is called Al Kaus meaning "the arrow". In the Dendera Zodiac, this constellation is called Pimaere meaning "the graciousness".

And God was with the lad; and he grew, and dwelt in the wilderness, and became an archer
Genesis 21:20

Many of the star names point to the graciousness of Sagittarius. In Arabic, one of the brightest stars is named Al Naim which means "the gracious one". In Hebrew, this star carries the same meaning. The star Al Warida means "who comes forth" and the star Ruchba er Rami meaning "the riding of the bowman".

Thou art fairer than the children of men: grace is poured into thy lips; therefore God hath blessed thee forever
Psalms 45:2

This sign further expresses the connection to Jesus with the idea of graciousness and his swift triumph over the scorpion. This swiftness is connected to that part of Chiron that is a horse. The coming of Jesus will be swift and with great power and glory.

Behold a white horse: and he that sat on him had a bow; and a crown was given unto him: and he went forth conquering, and to conquer
Revelation 6:2

Looking at some of the numeric values, we have "the Archer", in Hebrew equating to "800" which is the same as "Lord" in Greek. The name Jesus in Greek is always an "8".

In Greek mythology, Sagittarius was Chiron, the chief centaur who was noble and righteous in character. Chiron had greater human intelligence and taught wisdom, medicine, and music. Again we are reminded of the centaur's two natures.

Thou lovest righteousness and hatest wickedness
Psalms 45:7

SAGITTARIUS' FIRST DECAN: LYRA

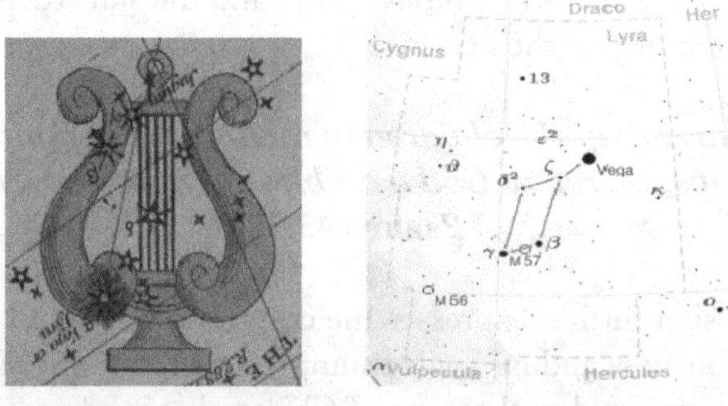

The first Decan of Sagittarius is called Lyra, an ancient harp. In ancient planispheres this decan appears in the shape of an eagle, the enemy of the serpent. The Lyra was strung with human hair and was an instrument used in song and praise. Here it is praising the archer's actions as the warrior is triumphant.

I will sing unto the Lord, for He hath triumphed gloriously
Exodus 15:1

Be thou exalted, Lord, in thine own strength: so will we sing and praise they power
Psalms 21:13

Within this constellation is one of the brightest stars in the northern hemisphere called Vega which means "he shall be exalted" or "the warrior triumphant". Around 12,000 B.C., Vega was the northern pole star. Today, the pole star is named Polaris. Another star called Shelyuk in Hebrew and Al Nesr in Arabic means "an eagle". The star Sulaphat, in Arabic, means "springing up". In the Dendera Zodiac, Lyra is pictured as an eagle named Fent-kar which means "the serpent ruled".

Vega is related to the word "victory" meaning "the overcoming of an enemy" or "success in a struggle or endeavor against odds or difficulties". This is the reason why sometimes this constellation appears as an eagle which is the enemy of the serpent and victorious over his prey. Continuing the theme of Sagittarius and the two natures of the centaur, here we have the two meanings representing praise and victory.

But thanks be to God, which giveth us the victory through our Lord, Jesus Christ
1Corinthians 15:57

Now thanks be unto God, which always causeth us to triumph in Christ, and maketh manifest the savior of his knowledge by us in every place
2Corinthians 2:14

The lyre is the oldest of the stringed musical instruments and was said to be invented by Hermes and given to mankind. The number of strings was seven (7) and equaled the number of the upper "true ribs" on one side of the human rib cage attached to the sternum.

According to Manly P. Hall, "in the mysteries, the lyre was regarded as the secret symbol of the human constitution, the body of the instrument representing the physical form, the strings were the nerves, and the musician the spirit" (Hall 1928, 250).

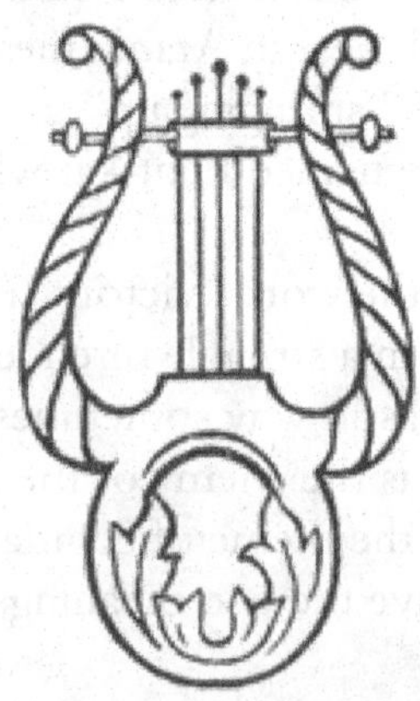

And his brother's name was Jubal: he was the father of all such as handle the harp and organ
Genesis 4:21

King David played the Lyre to praise the Lord and to calm Saul's pain. David was referred to as "the favorite of the songs of Israel".

King David Playing the Lyre
Gustave Dore

My heart is fixed, O God, my heart is fixed: I will sing and give praise. Awake up, my glory; awake, psaltery and harp: I myself will awake early. I will praise thee, O Lord, among the people: I will sing unto thee among the nations
Psalms 57:7–9

The Shekhinah is Coming

And it came to pass, when the evil spirit from God was upon Saul, that David took a harp, and played with his hand: so Saul was refreshed, and was well, and the evil spirit departed from him
1Samuel 16:23

The Lyre was used by the Bards and Troubadours who wrote songs and ballads in a storytelling fashion later in history, particularly in the British Isles. The etymology of the word bard is the same as lyre, "to raise the voice in praise".

According to Greek mythology, Apollo gave the lyre to Orpheus who was considered chief among poets and musicians. He was called "the father of songs" by Pindar (522–433 B.C.) an ancient Greek lyric poet. Pindar places Orpheus as the harpist and companion of Jason and the Argonauts. It was the music of Orpheus' lyre that sank the dragon into a deep sleep so that Jason could capture the Golden Fleece that would rightfully place Jason on the throne.

Apollo with his Lyre
Drinking Cup
5th Century BC

Orpheus Taming Wild Animals
Apollo Gave Lyre to Orpheus
Roman Mosaic–A.D. 204

This constellation truly celebrates the joy and gladness of the universe and the hopes of "what is to come". The ancients claimed that the lyre was the symbol of the "music of the spheres" which was discussed in Chapter 5. This is another indication of the importance of music or more correctly vibrations and future events.

Thy kingdom come. Thy will be done in Earth, as it is in heaven
Matthew 6:10

Thy kingdom come. Thy will be done, as in heaven, so in Earth
Luke 11:2

This thought is truly apparent when you look at the numeric code. The words "harp" and "signs" in Hebrew equate to the word "eagle" in Greek with a value of 576. This constellation is pointing to the coming of the triumphant Jesus as the value of 576 also means "life" in Greek with the etymology stemming from two ancient Greek words: *"etymos"* which means "true" and *"logia"* which means "word". Don't we refer to Jesus as the "logos" or the "word"? This will be discussed in greater detail in Chapter 10.

SAGITTARIUS' SECOND DECAN: ARA

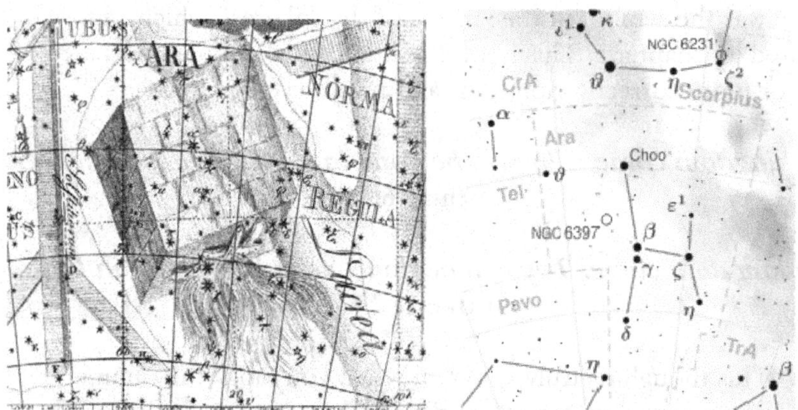

The second Decan of Sagittarius is called Ara. It is the picture of an altar or burning pyre. In Greek mythology, this was the altar on which the Centaur sacrifices the wolf, Lupus, the second Decan of Libra. It signals the victory over the enemy and the enemy's destructive ways.

The altar is upside down so that the fires are in the region of heaven known as Tartarus. Tartarus comes from the Greek word *Τάρταρος* meaning "deep place". It is the abyss of the underworld. Plato wrote in *Gorgias*, that souls were judged after death by Rhadamanthus, Aeacus, and Minos and those who received punishment were sent to Tartarus, the classic Hades (hell), or "the lake of fire".

Then shall He say also unto them on the left hand, depart from me, ye cursed, into everlasting fire, prepared for the devil and his angels

Matthew 25:41

Secrets of the Divine

And the devil that deceived them was cast into the lake of fire and brimstone
Revelation 20:10

The word Tartarus is used once in the New Testament where Peter states:

For if God spared not the angels that sinned, but cast them down into Tartarus, and delivered them into chains of darkness, to be reserved unto judgement
2Peter 2:4

In Arabic, this constellation was called Al Mugamra which means "the completing or finishing" or "the making of an end of what was undertaken". It is the idea of the coming of judgement with victory over the enemy and thrusting him into the darkness of the abyss. Both in Greek and Latin this constellation was called Ara with a connotation of "ruin" or "destruction". The word mara in Hebrew means "curse" or "destruction".

SAGITTARIUS' THIRD DECAN: DRACO

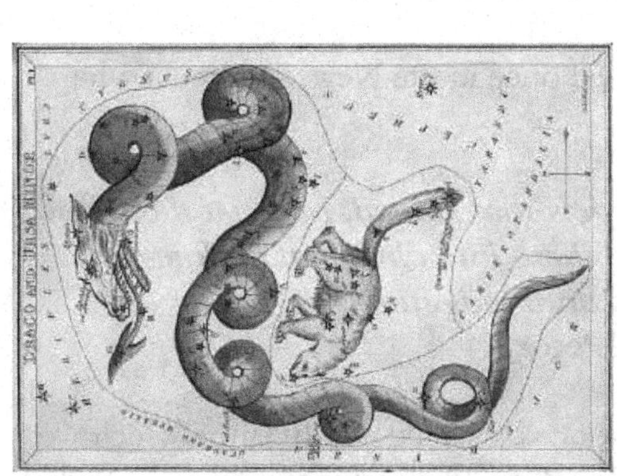

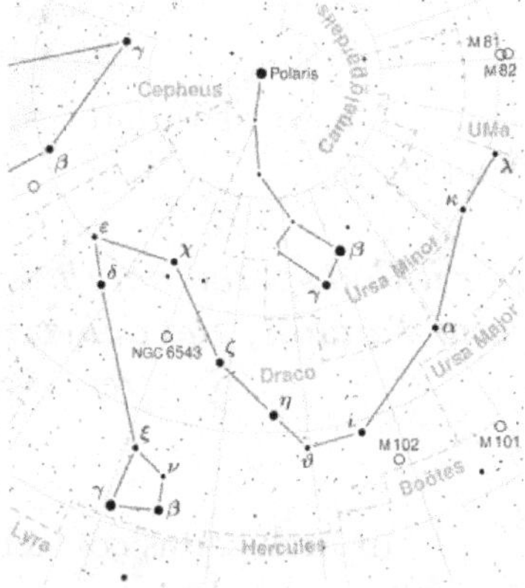

The third Decan of Sagittarius is called Draco. Draco is Latin for "dragon". Draco is evidence that our hero's fight is not yet over. Coiled around the northern celestial pole, Draco is always visible in the northern hemisphere. To the Greeks, Draco meant "trodden on". In Hebrew, this constellation was called Dahrach which means "to tread".

It is the picture of a dragon or serpent coiled and ready to strike. However, Hercules is ready to crush its head. As one of the largest constellations, Draco's body covers one half of the northern sky with its tail extending over one third of the stars. It appears that we are under Draco's influence as it occupies the top of the world. According to Ptolemy, Draco touches into each of the 30 degrees occupied by each of the twelve major constellations.

And there appeared another wonder in heaven; and behold a great red dragon, having seven heads and ten horns, and seven

crowns upon his heads. And his tail drew the third part of the stars of heaven
Revelation 12:3–4

Around 2700 B.C., Draco's famous star called Thuban, located in the tail of the dragon, was the pole star. In Hebrew, Thuban means "the subtle". In Arabic, this same star is called Al Waid which means "who is to be destroyed".

A star located in the head of Draco is called Eltanin which means "the long serpent or dragon". In Hebrew, another star called Rastaban means "the head of the subtle".

Biblically, the dragon was known as the old serpent, the devil and has become the universal symbol of evil. However, it should be noted that dragons in Asian cultures are revered as a representative of the primal forces of nature where they are associated with supernatural powers and wisdom.

And the great dragon was cast out, that old serpent, called the Devil, and Satan which deceiveth the whole world
Revelation 12:9

In Greek mythology, Draco was the offspring of Typhon having one hundred heads and voices. Draco was the guardian of the golden apples that grew in the Garden of Hesperides which Hercules stole for his eleventh labor. Hercules lured the dragon to sleep with music and took the golden apples with ease. The Hesperides were the daughters of Nyx and Erebus.

Dragons can be found in all the ancient cultures in legend, art, pictures on flags and banners as well as on shields. The destruction of the dragon was always done by the hero of the culture. While there is no earthly zoological evidence of dragons, they tend to be interchangeable with slinking serpents and illicit the same fear as they attack with fire. The closest animal to a dragon is the pterosaurs, a huge reptile looking lizard, with wings, that could walk on its hind legs. In Greek mythology, one might consider Typhon.

As the serpent, the image is that of the silent destroyer creeping in to destroy its prey. As the dragon, the image is that of an assailant rushing in to destroy its prey with fire. Either image connotes a great enemy to mankind.

If there is no earthly zoological evidence of dragons, where does this universal image and fear come from? How did this image penetrate the human psyche? However this happened, this universal symbol morphed into the pictures of St. Michael and St. George in slaying the dragon.

St. Michael Killing the Dragon
Painting on a Wayside Shrine
Bildstock in Hof, Denmark

St. George Killing the Dragon
Emmanuel Tzanes
17th Century

Clearly, this constellation with its three decans concerns the destruction of the enemy by our hero who is honored with song and praise.

CAPRICORUS

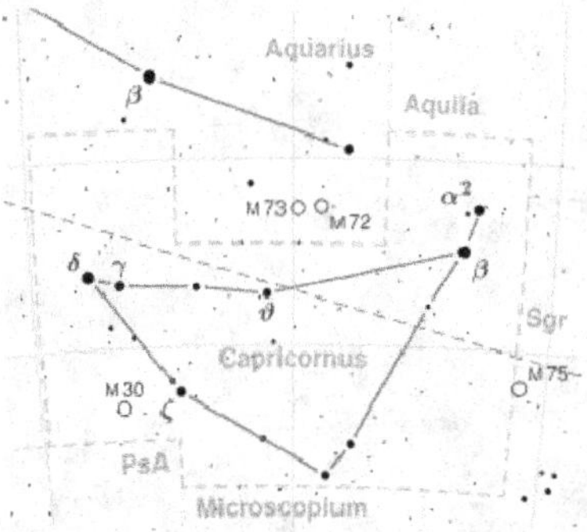

This constellation is the picture of a fallen goat bowing its head. The creature has the tail of a vigorous fish, but is unable to rise. Again, we have the picture of a dual character, half-goat and half-fish, as a transformation is beginning much like the phoenix rises out of its ashes into a new being. We will see the transformed image in the third decan of Capricornus where the animal becomes a full and vivacious fish. In the Dendera Zodiac, it is pictured as a half-goat and half-fish called Hu-penius which means "the place of the sacrifice".

Known as the Sea Goat, in Hebrew, this constellation is named Gedi and in Arabic, it is called Al Gedi. Both names mean "cut off". In Latin, we have the modern term Capricornus which means "goat". It also connotes atonement or bowed in death as the goat was often used in sacrifice.

And Moses diligently sought the goat of the sin offering and behold, it was burnt…to make atonement for them before the Lord

Leviticus 10:16–17

A star located between the horns of the goat is called Geidi meaning "the kid". A star located in the left eye of the goat is called Dabih which means "the sacrifice slain". One star located in the tail of the goat is called Deneb, which means "the sacrifice cometh". Another star located in the tail called Nashira means "the record of the cutting off". And another star is named Ma'asad which means "the slaying".

In this mystical union, the dying goat transforms into a living fish, the symbol of the faithful. As we learned in Chapter 3, the symbol to identify the early Christians was the fish. Again, the Hebrew word for fish is *"Nun"* with a numeric value of "8" the same as Jesus, the one who nourishes us. The horn of the goat becomes the cornucopia, a symbol for food and abundance.

Cornucopia

Oftentimes, the cornucopia is depicted with Ceres the goddess of harvest. In Greek mythology, she was Demeter, the goddess who presided over grains and harvest. Known as the "earth-mother", she was the "bringer of seasons" and gifted mankind with cereal.

Artemis
Glyptothek Museum
Munich, Germany

Ceres, Goddess of Harvest
"Livia Drusilla"
National Archaeological Museum
Madrid, Spain

Oannes was the half-man, half-fish god of the Sumerians/Babylonians that is pictured in ancient temples. He is shown with great dignity carrying a basket filled with treasure. In legend, Oannes rose out of the water to teach the Babylonians wisdom. The same half-man, half-fish god of the Philistines was called Dagon which means "fruitfulness" or "the seed producing". You can see from the image that his head piece is an "open-mouth fish". It is this same symbol that becomes the mitre head piece that the Pope wears.

Dagon

Oannes

Mitre

This image morphed into the "mermaid" and became the original logo for Starbuck's coffee shops. Today, the Starbuck's logo is minus her body and tails as you can only see her head.

Guild of Students
University of Birmingham
England

Twin-tailed Siren
Original Logo
Starbucks

It appears that this "fish symbol" is very ancient and has continued to wind its way throughout history in many different forms.

In Greek mythology, Pan is associated with this constellation. To avoid being attacked by the monster Typhon, Pan dives into the Nile River and transformed his body below water into a fish. Pan was known as a fertility god from Arcadia protecting the fields, shepherds, and goat-herds. Pan is credited with inventing the flute.

CAPRICORNUS' FIRST DECAN: SAGITTA

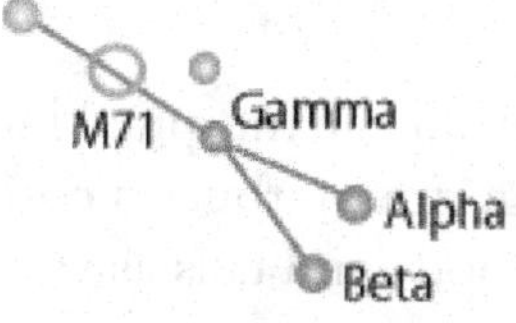

The first Decan of Capricornus is called Sagitta which is Latin for "arrow". The Greeks called this constellation Oistos also meaning "arrow". In Hebrew, this constellation was named Sham which means "destroying". It is the death arrow numerically representing both the numbers "1" and "8" as the word "arrow" in Hebrew is equal to "108" where "1" equals Lord and number "8" equals Jesus.

It is the picture of a lone arrow in flight and known as the arrow that God sent forth as it is shot by an invisible hand. It is the mysterious divine arrow of justice. The brightest star in this constellation is also called Sham. Sham has a numeric value of "8" another reference to Jesus.

For thine arrows (the word) stick fast in me
Psalms 38:2

In Greek mythology, Sagitta was the weapon that Hercules used to kill the eagle Ethon who perpetually tormented Prometheus as punishment for bringing fire to humankind against Zeus' approval.

CAPRICORNUS' SECOND DECAN: AQUILA

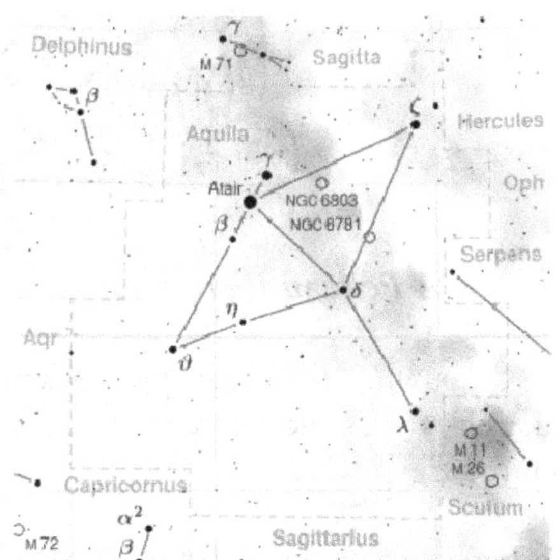

The second Decan of Capricornus is called Aquila. In Latin, the word Aquila means "eagle" and is the picture of a wounded eagle falling having been pierced by the arrow of Sagitta.

The eagle is known as the royal bird that is the natural enemy of the serpent and is very protective of its young. If the eagle cannot find food for its young, it will tear itself to nourish them with its own blood. The same is true for the pelican.

"Pelican in her piety"
A Pelican Piercing its Breast to Feed its Young

So, while the eagle appears wounded, he is still taking care of his family. It was the reference to the eagle that saved the Israelites from the Egyptians.

Ye have seen what I did unto the Egyptians and how I bare you on eagles' wings and brought you unto myself
Exodus 19:4

The brightest star in Aquila, located in the eagle's neck, is named Altair which in Arabic means "the wounded". Another star located in the throat of the eagle is named Alshain which in Arabic means "the bright". In Hebrew, this means the "color or scarlet", hence the color of blood. In the eagle's tail is the star called Dheneb which means "pierced" and on the eagle's back is the star called Tarazed which means "wounded" or "torn".

And one shall say unto Him, what are these wounds in thine hands? Then He shall answer, those with which I was wounded in the house of my friends
Zechariah 13:6

In Greek mythology, Aquila was the eagle that carried the thunderbolts of Zeus. Aquila also abducted the shepherd boy, Ganymede and carried him to Mount Olympus.

CAPRICORNUS' THIRD DECAN: DELPHINUS

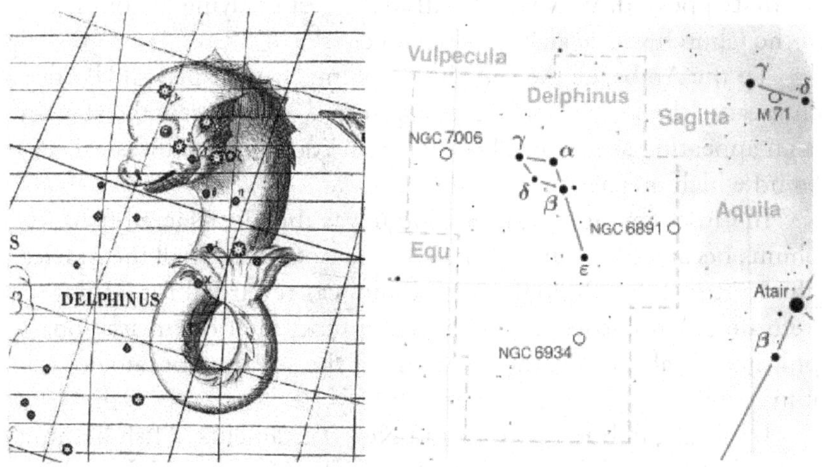

The third Decan of Capricornus is called Delphinus which in Latin means "the dolphin'. In Hebrew, this constellation is called Dalaph which means "the pouring out of water". In Arabic, this constellation is called Al Ka'ud which means "coming quickly". The dolphin was a marine animal considered friendly to man and oftentimes saved drowning sailors.

It is the picture of a fish, full of life, appearing to leap out of the sea. It is the transition of the half-goat Capricornus into the whole fish. So, while there is sacrifice and wounding, the hope remains for the transformation into a full and everlasting life.

The brightest star in this constellation is called Sualocin which is Nicolaus spelled backwards. The second brightest star is called Rotanev which is Venator spelled backwards. The name Nicolaus Venator was an assistant to Giuseppe Piazzi, an Italian astronomer and Catholic priest of the 18th century. Piazzi established an observatory at Palermo and produced the *Palermo Catalogue* in 1803 were these star names first appeared. Why was a Catholic priest studying astronomy when the Church was against this practice?

To the Arabs, all the stars in Delphinus were called Al Ukud which meant "the Pearls" or "Precious stones" as they saw the stars in this sign appearing as a cross. The star in the dolphin's tail was called Al Amud which means "pillar of the cross".

In Greek mythology, the dolphin was the most sacred fish. Delphinus became the name of the most famous seat of all the oracles, Delphi. In Roman mythology, the dolphin was rewarded for finding and returning Amphitrite, a nymph to Neptune, the Roman sea god. Amphitrite was also called the "goddess of the sea" and became Neptune's wife.

Biblically, in both the Old and New Testaments, a fish became the symbol of those that believed in Jesus. The Greek word for fish, *"Ichthus" (ΙΧΘΥΣ)*, became the acronym meaning Jesus Christ, Son of God, Savior as we learned in Chapter 3.

Behold, I will send for many fishers, saith the Lord
Jeremiah 16:16

And he saith unto them, Follow me, and I will make you fishers of men
Matthew 4:19

The constellation Capricornus with its three decans represents the heart of the gospel teachings which is "hope" from Jesus' promise and transformation.

And behold, I send the promise of my Father upon you
Luke 24:49

In summary, this constellation with its three decans is about death and rebirth in all forms. Each time, the new creature is nourished and cared for as it grows. In nature, the tree produces the fruit which dies and falls to the ground. The seeds from the fruit then germinate to produce a new tree that will bring forth new fruit. It is the cycle of life regardless of the species. Again, all the signs are in nature for those who are observant. Is this not the same SEED from the virgin birth of our story?

This constellation signals the key time when the Sun has traveled the farthest in darkness. It is on the Winter Solstice that the Sun will stop and begin its journey into the "light". This "gate of the soul" will be the end of the "Grand Cycle of Time" and the mysterious date of 21 December 2012. The time elapsed will be 25,920 years, the exact number of the Hebrew names for the twelve constellations we learned in Chapter 6. Interestingly, if you add the digits (25,920) of the Grand Cycle of Time you arrive at 18 (2+ 5 + 9 + 2 = 18). This not only contains the "1" and "8" combination we have already studied and will again in Chapter 10, but here again the "18" adds to the magic number "9" (1 + 8 = 9) we studied in Chapter 5.

AQUARIUS

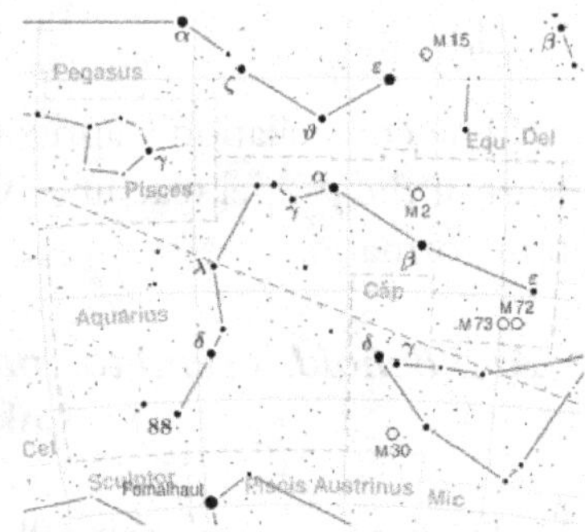

This is the current constellation that the Sun will remain in for the next 2160 years.

The constellation of Aquarius is known as "the water bearer". The word Aquarius means "the pourer forth of water" in both Coptic and Greek. In Latin, it means "the exalted waterman". In Hebrew, this constellation is called Deli which means "the water-urn" or "a bucket". In Hindu, this constellation is called Kumbha which means "water-pitcher".

Along with sunlight, we could not exist without the element water. Biblically, water is used in blessings, atonement, and redemption. And isn't it interesting that so many spiritual healing sites are located adjacent to water like the one in Lourdes, France.

...the glorious Lord will be unto us a place of broad rivers and streams...the Lord, he will save us

Isaiah 33:21–22

This constellation is the picture of a man pouring water from a great urn and seemingly from an inexhaustible heavenly stream of water. As the water flows freely down the stream, it appears to enlarge as its abundance is great.

And it shall be in that day, that living waters shall go out from Jerusalem; half of them toward the former sea, and half of them toward the hinder sea: in summer and in winter shall it be
Zechariah 14:8

In the Dendera zodiac, the man pouring the water is called Hupei Tirion which means "the place of him coming down" or "poured forth". In Babylon, he is named GU.LA which means "the great one".

He shall pour the water out of his buckets, and His seed shall be in many waters...and His kingdom shall be exalted
Numbers 24:7

The brightest star in this constellation is located in the right shoulder and called Saad al Melik which means "record of the out-pouring". In the opposite shoulder is a star called Saad Al Sund which means "who goeth and returneth". This star in Hebrew is called Scheat which carries a connotation of "a wish".

In mythology, Aquarius is sometimes identified with Ganymede, a Phrygian youth known for his beauty. Because of his beauty, he was carried to heaven on eagle's wings (Aquila) to live in glory with the gods and become their cup-bearer.

The story aligns with Jesus who was cut-off from life too early, but who is now immortal and willing to nourishes those in need with water. This water is not only used to germinate the seed, but to quench thirst and provide blessings. The water image connotes abundance and an unending supply.

For I will pour water upon him that is thirsty, and floods upon the dry ground: I will pour my spirit upon thy seed and my blessings upon thine offspring
Isaiah 44:3

AQUARIUS' FIRST DECAN: PISCIS AUSTRALIS THE SOUTHERN FISH

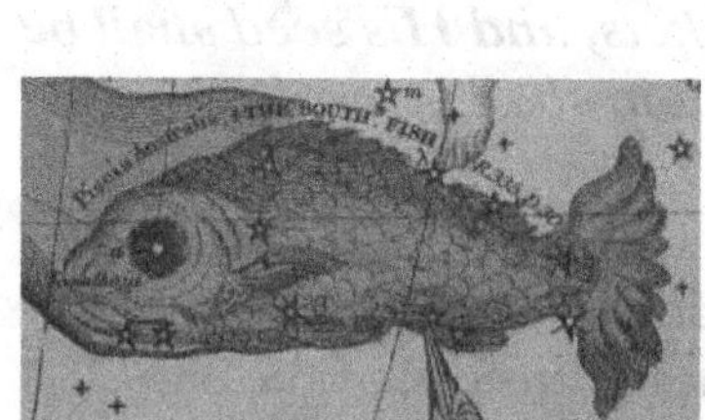

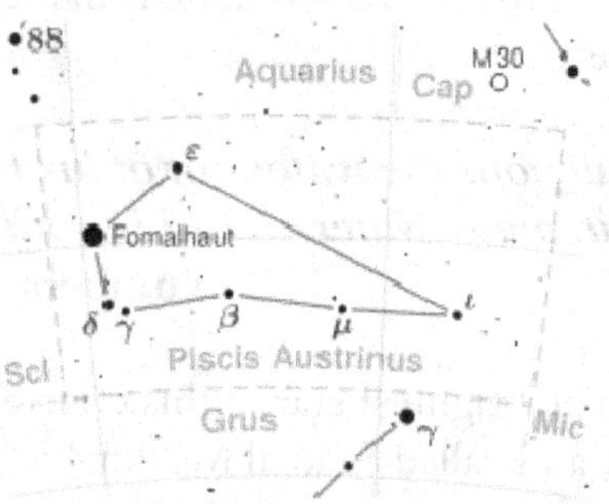

The first Decan of Aquarius is called Piscis Australis which means "the blessings bestowed". It is also known as The Southern Fish. Located at the feet of Aquarius, it appears that the fish, lying on its back, is drinking from the living waters that are being poured from Aquarius' urns. Symbolically, it is a purification of the blessings received.

Every one that thirsteth, come ye to the waters, and he that hath no money; come ye, buy, and eat; yea, come, buy wine and milk without money and without price
Isaiah 55:1

If any man thirst, let him come unto me and drink
John 7:37

The brightest star in this constellation is called Fomalhaut. In Arabic it means "the fish's mouth". This "fish's mouth" image morphs into the mitre worn by the Pope that was shown in the constellation Capricornus.

In mythology, the fish is Astarte, the Semitic goddess of fertility and love. She was pursued and chased by Typhon, the son of Gaia and Tartarus. To escape this deadly monster's advances, she leaped into the river and transformed into a fish.

Amazingly, on 14 November 2008, it was announced that a planet had been discovered orbiting the star Fomalhaut. Extra solar planets (outside our Sun system) have only been discovered since 1988 and that discovery wasn't confirmed until 2003.

AQUARIUS' SECOND DECAN: PEGASUS

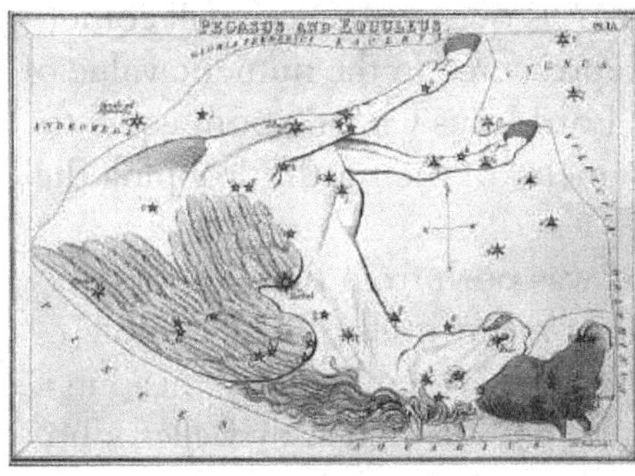

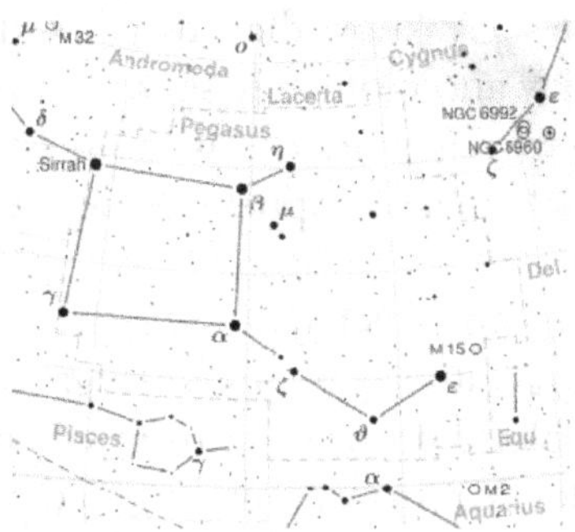

The Shekhinah is Coming

The second Decan of Aquarius is called Pegasus, a beautiful winged horse that means "blessings quickly coming". This is because that everywhere Pegasus struck his hoof to the earth, a holy spring burst forth. Pegasus is known as "the horse of the opening" or "the horse of the gushing fountain". In Hebrew, the word Pegasus means "chief horse".

This constellation is the picture of a great celestial horse pushing forward with heavenly speed and with great wings upon his shoulders. He is the Divine messenger bringing joy with song as God's word spreads with the movement of his wings.

The brightest star in Pegasus is located on the neck between the wings. In Hebrew, the star name is Markab which means "returning from afar". Another star located near the shoulder is named Scheat which means "who goeth and returneth". Another star named Algenib is Arabic for "the side" or "the wing" and the star named Enif means "the branch" in Arabic.

Zechariah saw the horses and heard the Lord say,

These are they whom the Lord hath sent to walk to and fro through the Earth
Zechariah 1:10

We know that the "chief horse" is our hero whom will come quickly and ultimately save us. It is represented in the numeric value of the Hebrew words "salvation" and "Lord Jesus Christ", both equal to 792 which also happens to be the diameter of the Earth (dropping the zeros).

In Greek mythology, Pegasus was born from blood drops mixing with sea foam which gave the horse its brilliant white color. The blood drops were from when Perseus severed Medusa's head in battle. Pegasus was an untamed animal that was ridden by Bellerophon only after he received a golden bridle from Athena. Bellerophon with the help of Pegasus was able to kill the Chimera, a fire breathing monster and another offspring of Typhon.

AQUARIUS' THIRD DECAN: CYGNUS

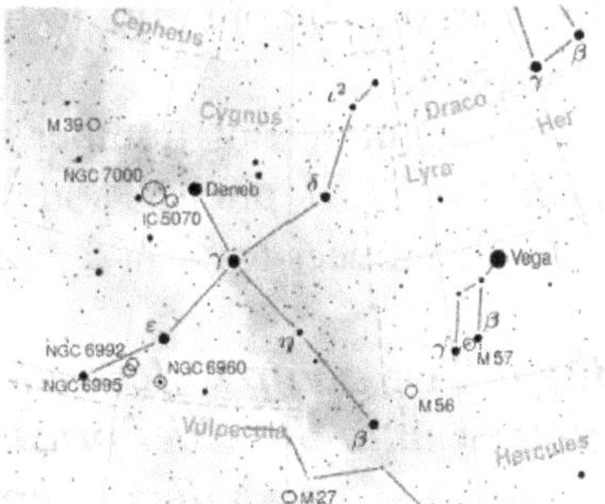

The third Decan of Aquarius is called Cygnus, the swan who is king of the water birds, known as "the blesser circling and returning". The ancient Greeks and Romans considered the swan to be sacred and represent dignity, purity, and grace.

This constellation is the picture of a graceful bird swiftly flying towards Earth in the same direction of the waters flowing forth from the urns of Aquarius. Because of how the stars in this constellation mark the wings and length of the bird's body, it forms a large cross marking the four cardinal directions and sometimes called the Northern Cross.

The brightest star in this constellation located at the bird's tail is called Deneb Adige which means "lord" or "the judge to come". Another bright star is Sadr which in Hebrew means "who returns as in a circle". The double star Albireo located in the swan's beak means "flying quickly" in Arabic. Two stars located in the swan's tail called

Azel means "who goes and returns quickly" the other star is Fafage which means "gloriously shining forth".

This constellation contains the most magnificent binary star in the heavens. Today, it is known as 61 Cygni, but christened in 1804 as Piazzi's Flying Star as it moves faster than any other star. Remember the Catholic priest (Piazzi) from the constellation Delphinus? It was the first star, outside our Sun, to have its distance measured from the Earth in 1838.

Some interesting number codes equate the Greek word for swan and the Greek phrase "son of Man" as the value 2260, which coincidently reduces to "1" (2 + 2 + 6 + 0 = 1), the number for Lord.

Behold, we go up to Jerusalem; and the Son of man shall be betrayed unto the chief priests and unto the scribes, and they shall condemn him to death
Matthew 20:18

In Greek mythology, Zeus disguised himself as a swan to seduce Leda, the Queen of Sparta who gave birth to Helen of Troy. According to a painting by Leonardo da Vinci, Leda is represented with her two sons Castor and Pollux, the twins in Gemini.

Leonardo's painting has been lost, but it was duplicated by Cesare da Sesto. Fortunately, I was able to view this painting when visiting England.

Leda and the Swan
Cesare da Sesto
Wilton House, Salisbury, UK

In summary, Aquarius is about the waters of life and our hero who is bringing this to the world quickly.

He which testifieth these things saith, surely I come quickly Amen. Even so, come, Lord Jesus. The grace of our Lord Jesus Christ be with you all. Amen
Revelation 22:20–21

The Shekhinah is Coming

These are the very last words written in the King James Bible. Isn't it interesting that we are currently in the sign of Aquarius where these last words of the Bible are referenced?

Have all the signs lined up in Aquarius for the second coming? Let's take a look:

- We have the abundant supply of water being poured out by the great one—"atonement"
- We have the fish (faithful) drinking the blessing—water
- We have the chief white house (purity) coming quickly with joy
- We have the King of the water birds (swan) with its prominent stars in a cross formation returning

It appears to align with biblical prophecy as our current sign, the one which the Sun will remain in for over 2000 years.

PISCES

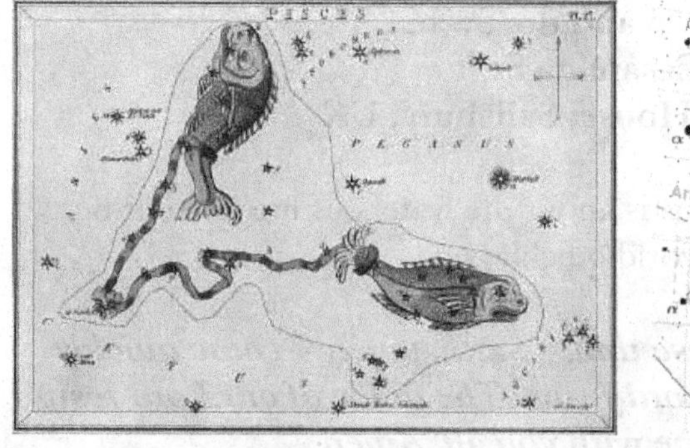

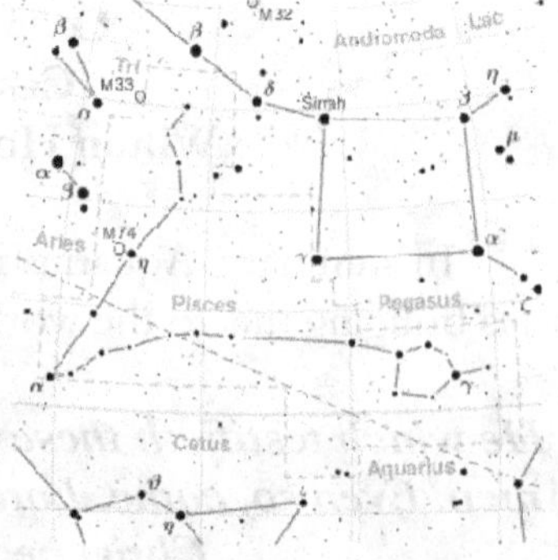

The constellation Pisces is the picture of two fish whose tails are bound separately by the Band, the first Decan of Pisces. The fishes are far apart and swimming at right angles with one pointed upwards towards Polaris, the pole star, and the other fish swimming along the line of the ecliptic (the dotted line in the right picture).

Most ancient languages agree on the meaning of Pisces as being "the fishes". In Syriac, it is called Nuno, "the fish prolonged". In Egypt, this constellation is called Pi-cot Orion, the fish which means "congregation" or "company of the coming prince". In Babylonian accounts, this constellation is called KUN.MES meaning "the tails".

In Hebrew, this constellation is called Dagim meaning "the fishes". Remember the half-man, half-fish god of the Philistines called Dagon from the constellation Capricornus? Notice the similar spelling? In Hebrew, two of the brightest stars are called Okda which means "united" and Al Samaca in Arabic which means "the upheld".

Biblically, the subject of fishes abounds with the connotation being "multitudes". God compared Abraham's seed to the stars in the sky, and the sand upon the sea shore.

Be fruitful, and multiply, and replenish the Earth
Genesis 1:28

Behold, I will make thee fruitful, and multiply thee, and I will make of thee a multitude of people; and will give this land to thy seed after thee for an everlasting possession
Genesis 48:4

Even Ezekiel is shown the great sacred "life-giving" waters and the multitude of fish that will be available to the fisherman. This matches Jesus' teachings to his congregation of believers. The fish represent the multitudes that become "one" in faith, desiring the love of God, and peace from the chaos of this world.

The Shekhinah is Coming

And it shall come to pass, that everything that liveth, which moveth, whitersoever the rivers shall come, shall live; and there shall be a very great multitude of fish, because these waters shall come thither; for they shall be healed; and everything shall live wither the river cometh
Ezekiel 47:9

Some scholars have likened the two fishes to the two churches. One church belonged to the patriarchs and the laws of Moses and the other church was created after Jesus. While they both united the people, the laws changed with Jesus as we will see in Chapter 10.

In Greek mythology, the fishes represent Aphrodite, the goddess of beauty and her son Eros, the god of love. They transformed themselves into fishes and dove into the Euphrates River to escape from the monster Typhon. They had tied their tails together to avoid being separated and lost from each other.

PISCES' FIRST DECAN: BAND

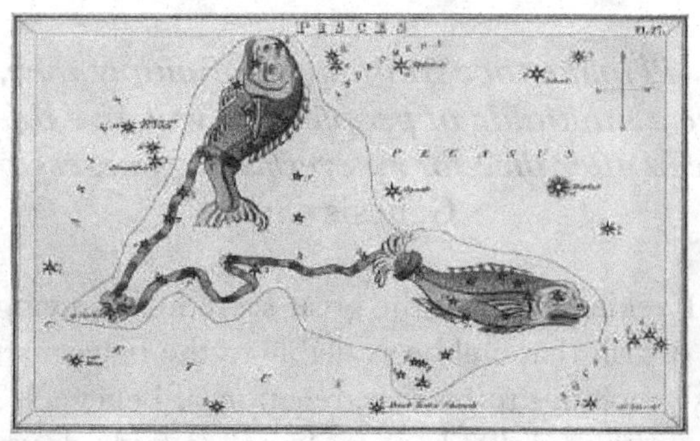

The first Decan of Pisces is called The Band or Ribbon. This is the very long and waving band or the ribbon that binds the two fishes' tails of Pisces. This band demonstrates that the two fishes are forever tied in unity even though they swim in opposite directions. Just as the faithful sometimes lose their footing, they remain connected to Jesus.

The band is so long that it also attaches to the neck of Cetus the monster and the second decan of Aries, who appears to be holding them back from moving forward. It is a challenge for the faithful to overcome living in this world.

In Arabic this constellation is called Al Risha which means "the band" or "bridle". The Egyptians named this constellation U-or, which means "he cometh". Is this the coming redeemer who Hosea speaks of?

I drew them with cords of a man, with bands of love: and I was to them as they that take off the yoke on their jaws, and I laid meat unto them
Hosea 11:4

With this sign we have the binding of the Old and New Testaments' saints. The patriarchal church consistently claimed the hope and promise of the Messiah. The new church fulfills and answers that promise tying them together forever. Again, it is the "two" that become "one" in faith as they are connected to the Messiah.

This decan is no longer considered a constellation by the International Astronomical Union (IAU).

PISCES' SECOND DECAN: ANDROMEDA

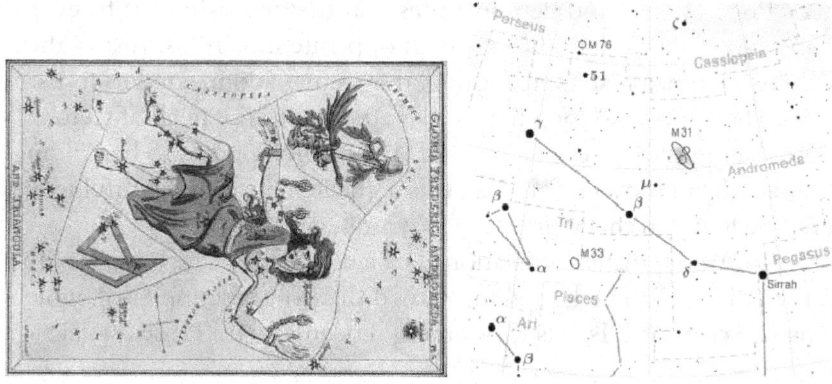

The second Decan of Pisces is called Andromeda or "the chained lady", because she is the picture of a beautiful woman chained to a chair. She is unable to rise as she sits at the top of the world. The chains are attached to both her wrists and ankles. The Hebrews called her Sirrah which means "the chained". The Babylonians referred to her as ANU.NI.TUM.

Andromeda is suffering and weak as one star in her body reflects. The star's name is Mirach in Hebrew and Mizar in Arabic and means "the weak". The brightest star which is located in her head is called Al Phiraiz in Arabic and means "the broken down". The star located in her left foot is called Al Marach which means "struck down".

In ancient planispheres, the Pisces' fishes were pictured with woman's heads. This carried the connotation that churches were referred to as female in the scriptures. In ancient Greek, Andromeda loosely meant "counsel of man", from *Andros* meaning "man" and *medea* meaning "counsel". Doesn't the church give counsel to members?

But, why does this differ from the meaning of the stars as being weak or broken down? I believe it comes from the world-view against the faithful. The world prefers for everyone to think that "there is no hope" for eternity and humanity is forever chained to the world-view.

In Greek mythology, Andromeda is the princess of Ethiopia, a mythical kingdom. She is the daughter of King Cepheus and Queen Cassiopeia. Andromeda had been sacrificed because of her mother's pride. She was chained to a rock near Joppa in Palestine and left to be devoured by Cetus, the sea monster to appease the nymphs. She was rescued by Perseus and became his bride.

PISCES' THIRD DECAN: CEPHEUS

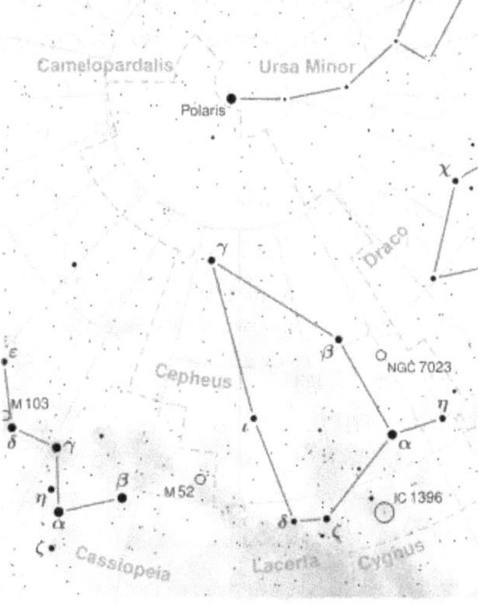

The Shekhinah is Coming

The third Decan of Pisces is called Cepheus. As King of Ethiopia (Joppa), Cepheus represents the crowned king and means "the royal branch" or "the king". In Ethiopia he is called Hyk meaning "the king".

The constellation is the picture of a glorious king wearing his royal robes and carrying his scepter in one hand. He is seated on his throne with a crown on his head and his foot is resting on the pole star. He is reaching out to save his daughter, Andromeda as he is the royal branch who has come to save his family.

This constellation has several stars with interesting meaning. One star, located on the right shoulder is called Al Deramin which means "the quickly returning". One star, located on his stomach is called Al Phirk which means "the redeemer" and the star on his left knee called Al Rai means "the shepherd".

In Egypt, the king is called Pe-ku-hor which means "the ruler that cometh".

He shall bear the glory, and shall sit and rule upon His throne; and He shall be a priest upon His throne; and the counsel of peace shall be between the both
Zechariah 6:13

In Greek mythology, Cepheus was one of the Argonauts who sailed with Jason on his quest to find the Golden Fleece.

Cepheus was the name that Jesus gave to Simon Bar-Jonah. In Semitic, cephas was "a rock" which was translated into Greek as Petros and Latin as Petrus. This is the biblical apostle, Peter. In Hebrew, the word "bar" means "son of" as Peter was the son of Jonah.

Blessed art thou, Simon bar-Jonah...and I say also unto thee, that thou art Peter, and upon this rock I will build my church
Matthew 16:17–18

In some constellation listings, Cepheus is described as the second decan of Pisces and Andromeda the third decan. I prefer the way in which they are ordered in this discussion as it appears to follow the story line.

In summary, Pisces is about the Church, represented as the fishes, bound in the earthly realm waiting for their king, their redeemer, to loosen what binds them. Is it any wonder that King Cepheus, the righteous branch, sits at the top of the world?

ARIES

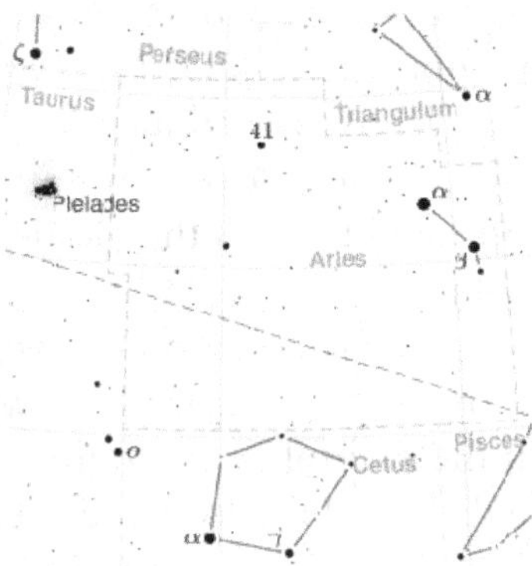

In this constellation we have the picture of a vigorous ram. Aries means “the chief”, “the head”, or “the lordly”. In Arabic, this constellation is called Al Hamal which means “the sheep”, “the gentle”, or “the merciful”. In Hebrew, the ram is called Taleh which means "the lamb". The very ancient Akkadian name for this constellation was Baraziggar which meant "altar" or "sacrifice". The Babylonian name is LU.HUN.GA meaning "the Agrarian worker" which has remained unclear as to its meaning.

A star located in the left horn is called Al Sheratang which means "the bruised" or "wounded". Another star called Mesartim means "the bound" and a bright star named El Nath means "wounded or slain". It was this star that was high in the heaven on the day of the crucifixion. Of course, the ram was another sacrificial animal used in mythology.

Aries, in Greek mythology, represented the golden ram that rescued Phrixos and his sister Helle from their wicked step mother, Ino, who wanted them sacrificed in order to make their crops grow. Their mother Nefele, the divine cloud, sent the golden ram to save them. On the back of the ram, the children headed to the land of Colchis, but Helle became giddy, lost her grip, and fell into the sea. The spot where she fell was name Hellespont or Helle's Sea in honor of her. Phrixos continued onto Colchis, the city of refuge, where he sacrificed the golden ram to the gods. The ram's skin was hung in the temple and became the Golden Fleece that Jason and the Argonauts sought.

While the ram was another sacrificial animal, the Golden Fleece was the highest treasure that was sought by the ancients. It is the lamb that the faithful seek and it was the cloud that provided protection just like the cloud that covered the tabernacle in the desert.

In the right picture, above the constellation and over the head of Aries, there is a small constellation called Triangulum. It was one of the forty-eight constellations listed by Ptolemy and is currently one of the eighty-eight constellations taking the place of "The Band" constellation. This constellation is known as the "triangle" by the Greeks because they believed that the name of God was inscribed on a triangle. The brightest star in this triangle is called Mothallah meaning "the Head" or "the Uplifted". Isn't this the knowledge that Enoch was disseminating to mankind? Is it coincidental that if the star's name is written Moth-Allah, that the last half of the name is the Islamic God?

ARIES' FIRST DECAN: CASSIOPEIA

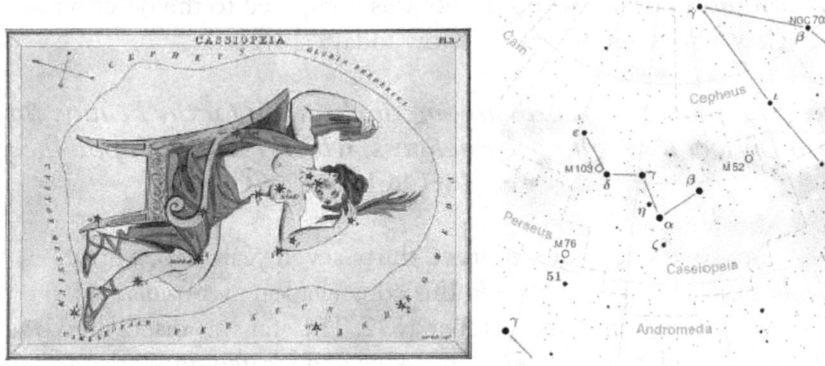

The first Decan of Aries is called Cassiopeia known as the "enthroned woman". She is the royal queen seated on her throne with the branch of victory in her hand. She is the glorified wife of King Cepheus known to be vain and boast about her beauty.

In Arabic, this constellation is called El Shedir which means "the freed". A bright star in this constellation is called Ruchba which means "the enthroned". She is seated at the top of the heavens by the polar star near King Cepheus whose right hand is extending his scepter to her.

Kings' daughters were among thy honorable women: upon thy right hand did stand the queen in gold of O'phir
Psalms 45:9

The Shekhinah is Coming

And the king held out to Esther the golden scepter that was in his hand
Esther 5:2

In ancient times, this constellation was called "the daughter of splendor" or "the glorified woman". It is one of the most beautiful constellations to be seen. Her beauty was compared to the description of Israel, not the church that we know today:

And thy renown went forth among the heathen for thy beauty: for it was perfect through my comeliness, which I had put upon thee
Ezekiel 16:14

Approximately four hundred thirty-seven years ago, a great astronomical mystery occurred in this constellation as a brilliant star suddenly appeared on 10 November 1572. The star was discovered by Tycho Brahe and was brighter than Venus and located under the arm of the chair. The star shined continuous for sixteen months, then disappeared and has never been seen again.

In Greek mythology, Cassiopeia professed to be more beautiful than the daughters of Nereides, the nymphs of the sea. This angered the god Poseidon. To punish Cassiopeia, Poseidon chained her daughter, Andromeda, to a rock as a sacrifice for the sea monster, Cetus. Thankfully, Andromeda was saved by Perseus. Cassiopeia was then banned to the heavens with her head downward to learn humility as she raises a palm branch with her left hand.

ARIES' SECOND DECAN: CETUS

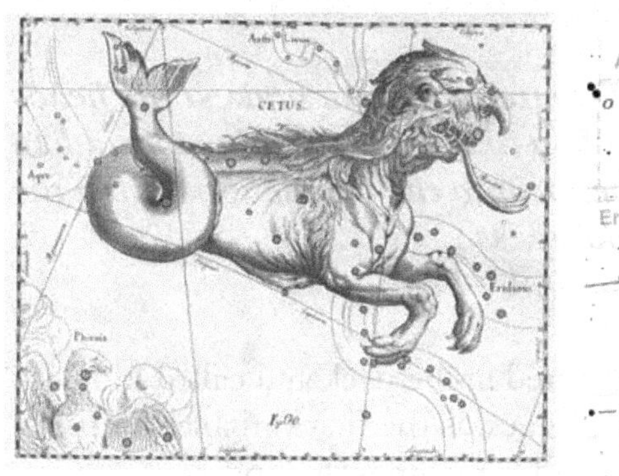

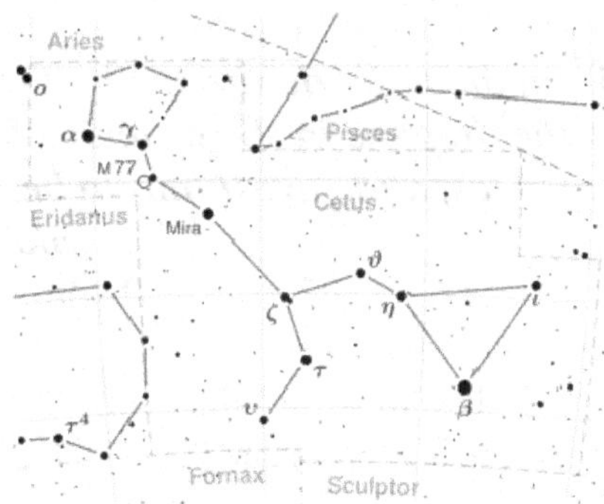

The second Decan of Aries is called Cetus, the sea monster which demonstrates that the conflict is not yet over. With the tail of a whale, Cetus is sometimes referred to as "the whale" since it covers a very large space in the heavens. It is the largest constellation located in the lower regions.

As the whale, it is the natural enemy of other fishes and biblically refers to Leviathan known as "the serpent bound" or Satan. It is the constellation of The Band, the first Decan of Pisces that is around the neck of this monster. Being tied to the fishes, Cetus is unable to escape. This is the same leviathan that Job speaks of:

Canst thou draw out leviathan with a hook? Or his tongue with a cord which thou lettest down?
Job 41:1

The brightest star of this constellation located in the jaw is named Menikar which means "the bound" or "chained enemy".

The Shekhinah is Coming

Another bright star located in the tail is named Diphda which means "overthrown" or "thrust down". Here again is the enemy that must be bound and cast down.

Thou didst divide the sea by thy strength; thou brakest the heads of the dragons in the waters. Thou brakest the heads of leviathan in pieces, and gavest him to be meat to the people inhabiting the wilderness
Psalms 74:13–14

The most notable star is located in the neck and called Mira which means "the rebel". In 1596, Mira was the first variable star to be discovered as its brightness varies and sometimes disappears completely.

In Greek mythology, this is the sea monster sent to devour Andromeda. The sea monster died when it looked upon the head of Medusa held aloft by Perseus.

<u>ARIES' THIRD DECAN: PERSEUS</u>

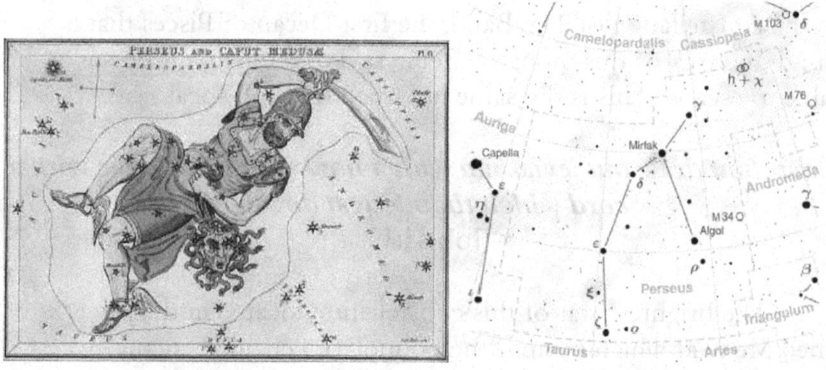

The third Decan of Aries is called Perseus known as "the breaker". In Hebrew, he is called Peretz which translates to the Greek word "Perses" who was the Titan god of destruction. The Babylonians called him SU.GI meaning "the Old One".

The breaker is come up before them: they have broken up and have passed through the gate, and are gone out by it; and their king shall pass before them and the Lord on the head of them
Micah 2:13

This constellation is the picture of the mighty warrior Perseus, the son of Zeus. Loaned to him be Hermes, he wears a helmet on his head and wings on his feet. He holds a great sword in his right hand high above his head and he carries the head of Medusa, the Gorgon, in his left hand. He stands directly above the brightest part of the Milky Way.

Medusa in Hebrew is called Rosh Starn which means "the head of the adversary". In Arabic, Medusa is called Al Oneh which means "the subdued".

A bright star located in the head of Medusa is named Algol which means "head of the demon". This star gives the appearance of "winking" about every three days. Another star located in his left foot is called Athik which means "who breaks". A star located on his waist is called Mirak which means "who helps" and the star located on his right shoulder called Al Genib means "who carries away".

In Greek mythology, Perseus was the son of Zeus and Danae. Danae was the daughter of Acrisius, King of Argos. Danae had been imprisoned by her father, because he had been told by the Oracle of Delphi that his offspring would kill him. Her confinement opened to the sky which allowed Zeus to impregnate her by showering her with gold. She called her son Perseus Eurymedon. Out of fear, Acrisius cast both Danae and her infant son into the sea in a wooden chest. They washed ashore on the island of Seriphos. They were rescued and taken care of by Dictys, a fisherman who's brother Polydectes was king of the island.

In Greek mythology, Medusa so boasted about her beauty that Athena turned her into a hideous monster with her long beautiful hair becoming snakes. She was so ugly that any human looking at her would turn to stone. With the use of Athena's shield, Perseus was able to reflect Medusa's look and cut off her head without looking at her. Upon his adventurous return home, he saw Andromeda about to be killed by the sea monster Cetus and saved her. Perseus married Andromeda and their offspring became the Persians. Perseus continues to guard Andromeda as Cetus remains close by and continues to chase her.

Clearly, Perseus is representative of Jesus, our hero, if you study the numbers revealed. The statement "the breaker has come up" equals 480 and the statement "the coming of the son of man" from Matthew equals 4800. Remembering that you can drop the zeros and not change the meaning they are equivalent.

In addition, Perseus was created with gold dust and we know from prior discussion that gold equated to the Sun and the God image as "One". And, Perseus is rejected and rescued by a fisherman, the symbol of the "faithful". He is victorious and triumphant in killing Medusa and becomes a leader and teacher of wisdom. Need I say more?

In summary, Aries conquers and binds the monsters so that the rightful heirs may be returned to the throne. It is the long awaited outcome of the "faithful".

TAURUS

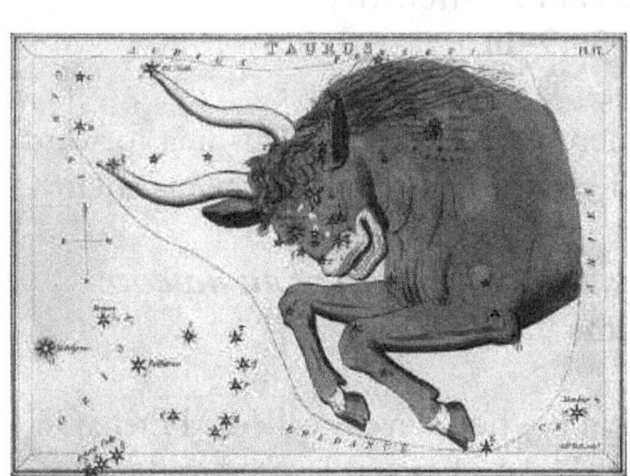

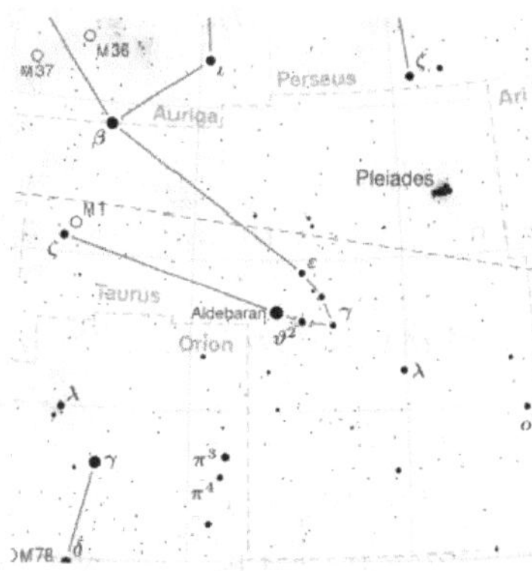

Taurus is Latin for "bull". This was the "heavenly bull" that marked the Bronze Age and the time of the Babylonians. It was listed in the *Mul.Apin Tablets* as GU.AN.AN, which means the "heavenly bull". The Akkadian name for the bull was Shur which means "the ruler coming". The Greeks called him Tauros and the Arabs called him Al Thaur.

The Apis bulls which had special markings were honored and worshiped by the Egyptians who gave them ceremonial burials upon their death. This constellation has the same representation in the Dendera zodiac. To the Egyptians, his name meant "the mighty Chieftain who cometh".

Many ancient translations refer to this ox-like animal as a reem. The reem was a wild, fierce, and untamable animal that is now extinct, but was once common to the biblical area. The reem possessed great strength and speed and had amazing horns. Through the various translations, the term "reem" became "unicorn", a beautiful and mystical creature known to be tamable only by a virgin woman.

The Shekhinah is Coming

Will the unicorn be willing to serve thee, or abide by thy crib? Canst thou bind the unicorn with his band in the furrow? Or will he harrow the valleys after thee?
Job 39:9–10

This constellation is the picture of a fierce bull rushing forward with great strength and force with his horns ready to pierce his enemy.

But my horn shalt thou exalt like the horn of an unicorn
Psalms 92:10

The brightest star located in the bull's eye is called Al Debaran, which means "leader" or "governor". Another star located at the tip of the left horn is called El Nath which means "wounded" or "slain".

Biblically, Taurus represents Jesus coming to claim his own and be the Lord and ruler of the Earth after the "day of judgement". It is Taurus that will carry out that judgement.

And Enoch also, the seventh from Adam, prophesied of these, saying, behold the Lord cometh with ten thousands of his saints. To execute judgment upon all and to convince all that are ungodly among them of their deeds….
Jude 1:14–15

In Greek mythology, Zeus took on the form of a white bull to kidnap Europa, a Phoenician princess and take her to Crete where he made her the first queen of Crete. One of Jupiter's moons is named after Europa and some writers attribute the geographical area of Europe to be named after her.

Within this constellation and located in the neck of this bull is the star cluster known as the Pleiades or the "the seven sisters", the daughters of Atlas and Pleione. Six of the sisters married immortal gods, but the seventh sister, Merope, married a mortal named Sisyphus. Because of this, Merope's star light is dimmer than her sisters.

In Babylon the Pleiades cluster is referred to as MUL.MUL meaning "Star of Stars". The Greeks called them Chima which means "accumulation". The brightest star called Alcyone means "the center".

This star cluster was known to all the ancient cultures and is dominated by hot blue stars, easily seen from Earth. The Pleiades are the rarest as they shine with a power over a million times our Sun's output (stellar classification—Wikipedia).

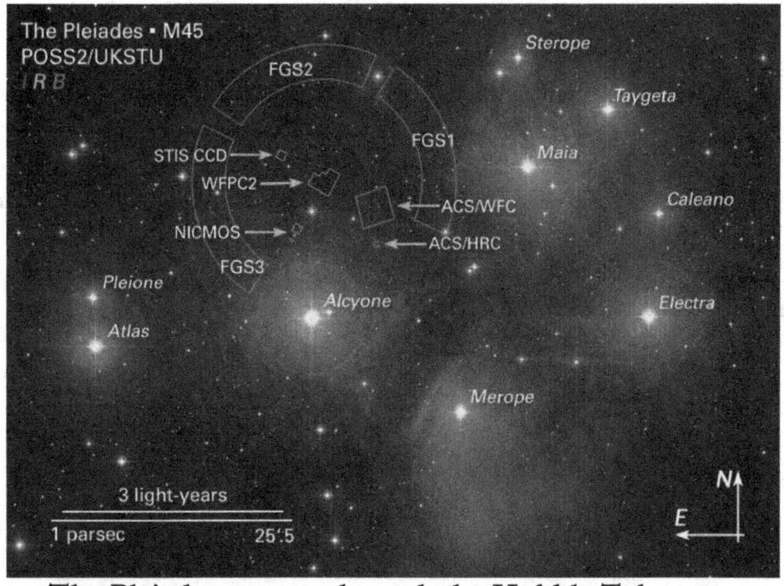

The Pleiades as seen through the Hubble Telescope

The etymology of Pleiades means "flock of doves" from the Greek word *"peleias"* meaning "dove". The reference to doves and blue stars or as some ancients say, "blue apples", makes this a fascinating star cluster along with ancient prophecy and the coming of Jesus. It has also been suggest that the seven stars are the seven churches in John's vision beginning in Revelation 3:7.

Which maketh Arcturus, Orion, and Pleiades, and the chambers of the south
Job 9:9

Canst thou bind the sweet influences of Pleiades, or loose the bands of Orion?
Job 38:31

Also within the constellation Taurus, located in one of the bull's eye, is the star cluster known as the Hyades meaning "the congregated". These bright stars form the "V" shape on the bull's face. The Hyades were the daughters of Atlas and Aethra and the half-sisters of the Pleiades. The sisters were deeply saddened after the death of their brother Hyas, who had been devoured by a lion. Because of their love, they were transformed into stars.

TAURUS' FIRST DECAN: ORION

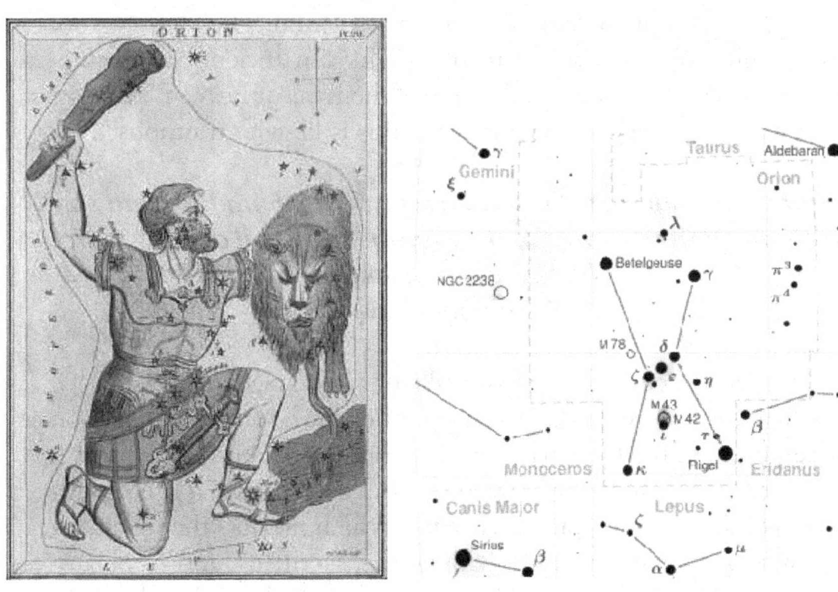

The first Decan of Taurus is called Orion, the great hunter. Orion is known as the "glorious one", "the coming prince", or "light breaking forth". He is the avenger who has come to crush the enemy.

This constellation is the picture of a giant hunter who is in the act of striking with the club in his right hand. A mighty sword hangs from his waist and in his left hand is the skin of a slain lion. His left foot is lifted to crush the head of Lepus, the hare and the first decan of Gemini.

Orion has been called by several names. In Arabic, Al Giauza which means "the branch", Al Mirzan which means "the ruler", Al Nagjed which means "the prince", and Al Gebor which means "the mighty". In Hebrew, Orion was called Nux which means "the strong" or Meissa which means "coming forth". The Babylonians called him SIPA.ZI.AN.AN meaning "the Loyal Shepherd of Heaven".

The ancient spelling of Orion was Oarion. The Hebrew root means "light" or "the coming forth as light". In ancient Akkadian, Orion was called Ur-ana which means "the light of heaven". In Egypt, Orion was called Hagat which means "this is he who triumphs".

And then shall that Wicked be revealed, whom the Lord shall consume with the spirit of his mouth, and shall destroy with the brightness of his coming
2Thessalonians 2:8

Orion is one of the most brilliant and recognizable constellations seen from Earth and can be viewed from any location as it is centered on the Celestial equator. Three of the distinctive and bright stars make up Orion's belt and are known as the Three Kings. In Arabic, the stars are named Al Nitak which means "the wounded one", Mintaka which means "dividing–as a sacrifice", and Al Nilam which means "string of pearls". Many scholars believe that the three pyramids on the Giza plateau align with the three stars of Orion's belt.

This constellation contains many bright stars with the brightest located in the right shoulder named Betelgeuse which means "the branch coming". On Orion's opposite shoulder is the star named Bellatrix which means "swiftly coming" or "suddenly destroying". Another bright star located in the lifted foot is named Rigel or Rigol and means "the foot that crusheth". A star in Orion's right leg is named Saiph which means "bruised". Saiph is the word used for "bruise" in Genesis.

And I will put enmity between thee and the woman, and between thy seed and her seed; it shall bruise thy head, and thou shalt bruise his heel
Genesis 3:15

In Greek mythological, Orion was gifted with strength, beauty, and had the ability to walk on the sea. As the greatest skilled hunter, he often accompanied Diana and Latona, and boasted that he could kill all the animals on Earth. To protect the animals, Gaia, the goddess of Earth, sent a scorpion to sting Orion on the heel. Both were honored by being placed in the heavens, but on opposite sides to avoid further conflict.

Orion is mentioned by name in the Bible in both Job 9:9 and 38:31 as already detailed in the Pleiades discussion along with Amos 5:8.

Seek Him that maketh the seven stars and Orion, and turneth the shadow of death into the morning, and maketh the day dark with night; that calleth for the waters of the sea, and poureth them out upon the face of the Earth: The LORD is his name
Amos 5:8

Orion represents Jesus as the avenger to stamp out the unbelievers and cleanse the Earth. He is shown here as the "branch" and the "light" that comes swiftly to accomplish celestial rule of his kingdom.

An interesting note about the future NASA flights to the moon is that the astronauts will travel in the "Orion Spacecraft". This spacecraft is currently being designed and tested and will most probably travel first to the International Space Station.

TAURUS' SECOND DECAN: ERIDANUS

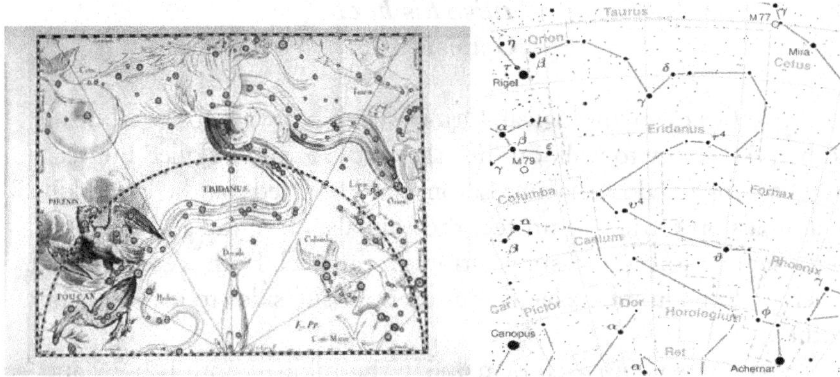

The second Decan of Taurus is called Eridanus and known as the "river of the judge". This refers to the wicked being cast into the lake of fire as seen in Daniel's vision.

A fiery stream issued and came forth from before him; thousands ministered unto him, and ten thousand times ten thousand stood before him; the judgment was set, and the books were opened
Daniel 7:10

This constellation is the picture of a mighty river flowing in a serpentine course from East to West. The river emanates from the foot of Orion and flows to the lower regions of heaven into the underworld as Cetus, the sea monster, and second Decan of Aries, attempts to stop the river's flow. It is the river of judgement and the hope of salvation. However, now it is not salvation by baptism, but salvation by fire. These late believers will be redeemed, but not crowned.

The brightest star of this constellation is located at the end of the river and is named Achernar which means "the after part of the river". The star at the mouth of the river is called Cursa which means "bent down". Another star located in one of the bends of the river is called Zourac which means "flowing".

In Greek mythology, Phaeton had taken the Sun-god, Zeus' chariot drawn by two white horses. Phaeton was not yet skilled in controlling the horses, so his path created the serpentine shape of the river. In anger, Zeus struck Phaeton with a thunderbolt and he fell burning into the river Eridanus, which is now called Po, a river in northern Italy.

A fire goeth before Him, and burneth up His enemies round about
Psalms 97:3

This constellation demonstrates how Jesus' anger and indignation towards the unfaithful will be expressed with fire. It will be the day of judgement. Fire is discussed in greater detail in Chapter 11.

But the day of the Lord will come as a thief in the night; in which the heavens shall pass away with a great noise, and the elements shall melt with fervent heat, the Earth also and the works that are therein shall be burned up
2Peter 3:10

TAURUS' THIRD DECAN: AURIGA

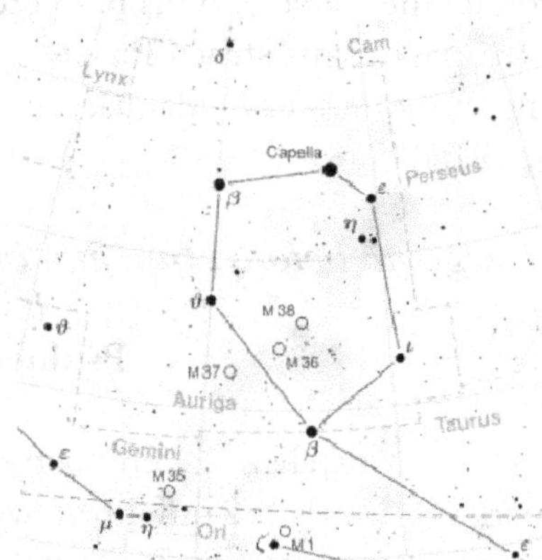

The third Decan of Taurus is called Auriga and known as "a shepherd". In Latin, Auriga means "a coachman" or "a charioteer". His Babylonian name is ZUBI meaning "the scimitar" which is a curved sword used by Arabs in battle.

This constellation is the picture of a kind and gracious man seated on the Milky Way holding bridle reins in his right hand. This is the same band or reins that Cepheus, the king and third decan of Pisces holds and represents the power of this individual. It is because of these reins that the Greeks and Latin refer to him as a charioteer, but he is really a shepherd protecting his young.

In his left hand, he cradles a goat on his shoulder and holds two babies that are frightened by the on-rushing bull located at the feet of Auriga. This is clearly the actions of a shepherd not a charioteer.

He shall feed his flock like a shepherd: He shall gather the lambs with his arm, and carry them in his bosom, and shall gently lead those that are with young
Isaiah 40:11

This constellation represents that even in the midst of judgement; there is still hope for mercy and salvation. Auriga has come to lead the unfaithful who have now made a different choice in their beliefs.

For we which have believed do enter into rest, as He said, as I have sworn in my wrath, if they shall enter into my rest
Hebrews 4:3

The brightest star is called Alioth in Hebrew and located in the body of the goat that the shepherd holds. In Latin this same star is called Capella. Both names refer to a "she-goat". The star located in the shepherd's right arm is called Menkilinon which means "band or chain of the goats". Another star called Prijipati in Sanskrit means "Lord of Creation".

In Greek mythology, this man is called Hephaestus which means "a driver" or "charioteer". Because Hephaestus was born lame with crippled feet, he invented the chariot so it was easier for him to get around. He was a smith or craftsman known to have made Hermes' winged helmet and sandals as well as Athena's Aegis breastplate. In Roman mythology he is called "Vulcan".

In summary, Taurus is the return of Jesus to protect those that believe and judge those that harm others.

But the transgressors shall be destroyed together: the end of the wicked shall be cut off. But the salvation of the righteous is of the Lord; He is their strength in the time of trouble
Psalms 37:38–39

GEMINI

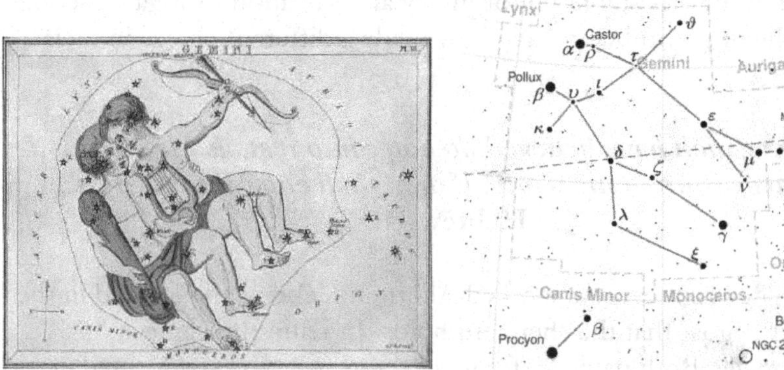

This constellation is the picture of two young heroes sitting peacefully together. They are twins whose heads touch together in a loving way while their feet rest on the Milky Way. In Latin, Gemini means "twins" and names them Castor and Pollux. The Greeks called the twins Apollo and Hercules. As the youths embrace, one youth holds a palm branch in his right hand and the other youth holds both a lyre/harp and a bow and arrow.

In the Dendera zodiac, this constellation is represented by a man and woman walking while holding hands rather than the twins. In

Coptic, this constellation is called Pi Mahi which means "united" as in brotherhood. The man represents the "coming one".

In Hebrew, this constellation is named Thaumin which means "united". It means the same in Arabic and called Al Tauman. The Babylonians called the twins MAS.TAB.BA.GAL.GAL meaning "the great twins".

And they shall be coupled together beneath, and they shall be coupled together above the head
Exodus 26:24

The brightest star in this constellation is located in the head of Apollo and called Castor which means "ruler" or "judge". The bright star located in the head of Hercules is called Pollux and means "who cometh to labor" or "suffer".

The twins represent Jesus in his two roles, one having lived and suffered and the other his second coming. It is the glorious rein of grace. It is the time when the two become "One" as Jesus is joined with the faithful. In each one there is a piece of the other much like the ancient yin/yang symbol.

...the Father is in me (Jesus), and I in him
John 10:38

Believe me that I am in the Father and the Father in me; or else believe me for the very "works" sake
John 14:11

In Greek mythology, one of the twins was the son of Zeus and Leda. He was conceived when Zeus changed into a swan to seduce Leda. Leda was the wife of King Tydareus of Sparta who was the father of the other twin. The twins alternately shared immortality and the young heroes helped Jason and the Argonauts find the Golden Fleece.

GEMINI'S FIRST DECAN: LEPUS

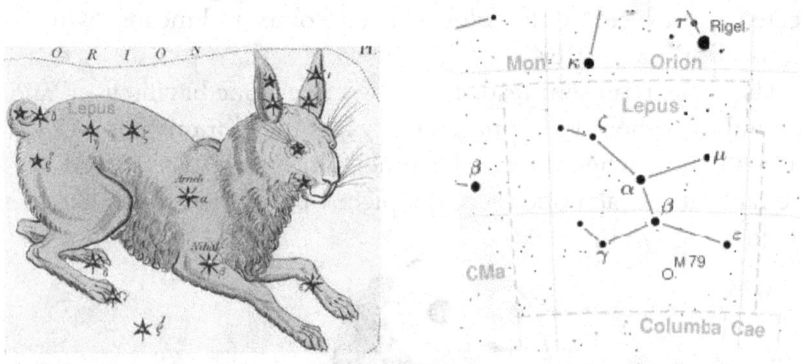

The first Decan of Gemini is called Lepus known as "the hare" or "the enemy". In Arabic, this constellation is called Arnebeth which also means "the hare" or "the enemy of the coming". In the Dendera zodiac, he is a bird called Bashti-beki which means "confounded" and "failing". Orion is poised to crush him as he is the enemy that is being overthrown.

The brightest star in this constellation is located in the body of the hare. In Hebrew, this star is called Arnebo which means "the enemy of him that cometh". Another star is named Rakis which means "the bound" or "the caught". The next star is named Sugia which means "the deceiver". Clearly, all stars are identifying the enemy.

Lepus is the hare that Orion is in the act of crushing as it was his favorite animal to hunt with his hunting dogs Canis Major and Canis Minor. In Greek mythology, Lepus was placed in the heavens for Orion's benefit. The Egyptians viewed Lepus as the boat of Osiris.

GEMINI'S SECOND DECAN: CANIS MAJOR

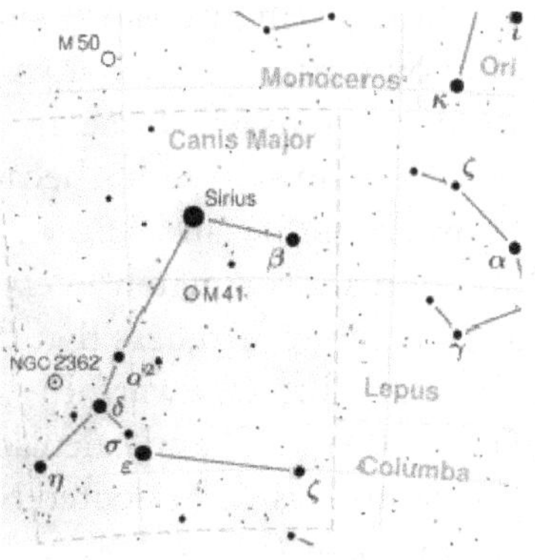

The second Decan of Gemini is called Canis Major and known as "the prince" or "the coming glorious prince". Canis Major is Orion's larger hunting dog that is attempting to devourer the hare, Lepus the first decan of Gemini. Destroying the enemy will lead to victory.

The Akkadian called this constellation Kasista which means "the leader" or "prince of the heavenly host". To the Egyptians, Naz, a hawk, was the picture of this constellation which meant "sent quickly".

The Persians referred to this constellation as the wolf, Zeeb which means "coming quickly". In Latin, Canis Major means "greater dog". It is sometimes referred to as the Dog Star Sirius.

Located in the dog's head, Sirius is the brightest star in this constellation. It is also the brightest star in the night sky and sometimes appears as bright as the planet Venus.

In Persia, Sirius was called Tistrya or Tistar which means "the chieftain of the East". In Greek, Sirius means "the sparkling". The brightness associated with Sirius also implied great heat from the Greek word Seirios which means "scorcher". This has morphed into the phrase "the dog days of summer" related to the summer months being the hottest.

Sirius is an interesting star and can be seen from almost every location on Earth. In 1862, it was discovered that Sirius was actually a binary star system which means there is a smaller star revolving around Sirius. The main star, Sirius became known as Sirius A and the smaller white dwarf star became known as Sirius B. The two stars complete a full rotation approximately every fifty years. In 1995, it was suggested by two French researchers that there could be a third star called Sirius C known as a brown dwarf. In 2005, the Hubble Space Telescope was able to view Sirius B and calculate its diameter.

Sirius was documented by all ancient cultures. Within the Sumerian poem *Epic of Gilgamesh*, Gilgamesh dreams of a heavy star that descends from heaven and described as a "potent essence". This would be Sirius B.

In Egyptian mythology, Sirius, known as Sopdet, was the foundation of the Osiris and Isis religion where Orion represented Osiris after his death. This star was also very significant, because it alerted the Egyptians to the annual flooding of the Nile prior to them planting their harvest for the year. During the middle kingdom, Egyptians based their calendar on Sirius' heliacal rising. Sirius is also aligned with one of the shafts in the Great Pyramid coming out of the Queen's chamber.

We even find Sirius mentioned in the Qur'an by three different translators:

Yusufali: "That He is the Lord of Sirius (the Mighty Star)"
Pickthal: "And that He it is who is the Lord of Sirius"
Shakir: "And that He is the Lord of the Sirius"
53:49

It is evident that many ancient cultures attached great significance to the star Sirius. Some scholars say that Sirius comes from the word Seir which means "victorious prince". This is then combined with the Egyptian constellation name to yield Naz-Seir, "the prince sent quickly". If you add the letters "ene" to the end, it yields Naz-seir-ene. This is none other than the branch that came from Nazareth.

And He came and dwelt in a city called Nazareth: that it might be fulfilled which was spoken by the prophets, He shall be called a Nazarene.
Matthew 2:23

Another star located in the left forefoot is called Mirzan which means "the prince" or "the ruler". A star located in the animal's body is called Wesen which means "the bright", "the shining", "illustrious", or "scarlet". Another star located in the right hind leg is called Adhara which means "the glorious".

The identity of the prince is clear as this relates to the second part of our hero's story. Isn't it interesting that Sirius is the brightest star in the sky?

For unto us a child is born... and the government shall be upon his shoulder and his name shall be called Wonderful, Counselor... The Prince of Peace
Isaiah 9:6

GEMINI'S THIRD DECAN: CANIS MINOR

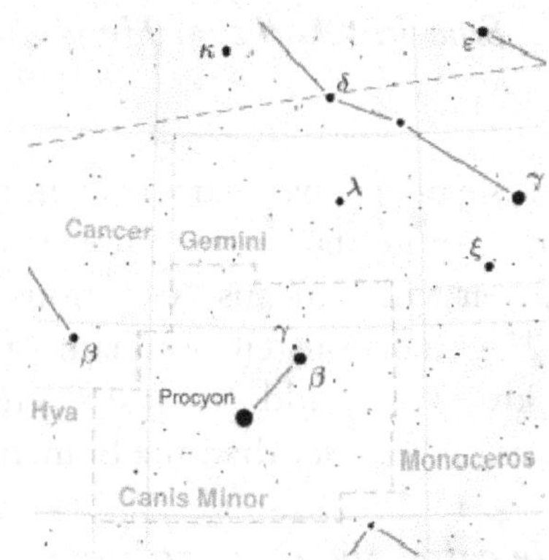

The third Decan of Gemini is called Canis Minor. In Latin, Canis Minor means "smaller dog" and known as "the exalted redeemer". In Arabic, this constellation is called Al Kalf al Asghar which means "the lesser dog". It is Orion's second and smaller hunting dog. In the Dendera Zodiac, this constellation is called Sebak which means "conquering victorious".

The brightest star in this constellation located in the dog's body is called Procyon which in Greek, means "before the dog". The star name is derived because this star rises one hour prior to Sirius rising in Canis Major.

Another star located in the neck of the dog is called Al Gomeisa which means "redemption". The star Al Shira or Al

Shemeliya means "the prince of the left hand". These are the saints following Jesus in his judgement, power, and authority over the enemy.

In summary, clearly Gemini and the three decans alert us to the completed task and the return of the Prince of Peace.

CANCER

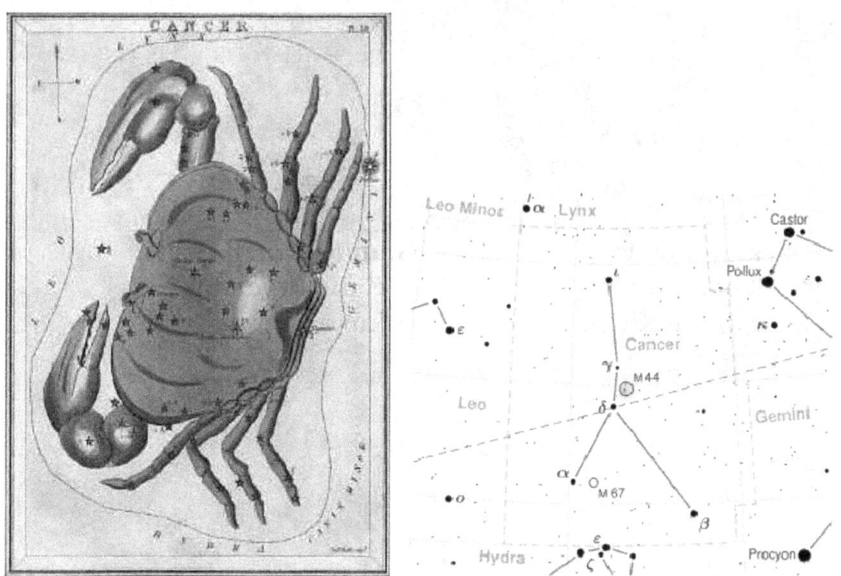

The constellation Cancer comes from the Latin name meaning Crab. Hence, this constellation is the picture of a gigantic crab. The Babylonians called this constellation AL.LUL meaning "the crayfish". All ancient zodiacs reflect the same picture except for the Egyptians. The Egyptians picture this constellation as a Scarabaeus, the sacred beetle and the Egyptian symbol for immortality. The Scarabaeus was called Klaria which means "the folds" or "the resting place". The

Scarabaeus is found throughout Egypt on temple walls, cartouches, and monument carvings.

Scarab Beetle
Wall of a Tomb
Valley of the Kings
Luxor, Egypt

Granite Scarab Beetle
Karnak Temple
Luxor, Egypt

Cartouche–Tuthmosis III
Karnak Temple

Winged Scarab Beetle
Edfu Temple

The crab is a creature of transformation and undergoes many changes during its development as it periodically discards its old shell and develops a new one. It has a tail as well as two powerful claws for grasping. The Scarabaeus also undergoes changes during its development from a worm of the Earth to a winged denizen.

In Arabic, this constellation is called Al Sartan which means "who hold or binds". In Greek, it is called Karkino which means "holding or encircling". In Akkadian, it is called Su-kul-na which means "the seizer" or "possessor of seed". In Hebrew, it means "to bind together".

The brightest star is located in the tail of the crab and called Tegmine which means "holding". Another star located in one of the claws is called Acubene which means "the sheltering" or "hiding place". An additional star called Ma'alaph means "assembled thousands".

The Shekhinah is Coming

The faithful are sheltered as the crab, with its powerful grasp, does not allow anything to escape. As the crab is born in water so are the faithful born again by baptism in water. The faithful have transformed and obtained their long awaited rest and promised inheritance having been steadfast in their beliefs. Their journey is almost over.

Cancer contains the closest open cluster to our solar system with approximately one hundred stars brighter than our Sun. There are over three hundred stars in this open cluster and was one of the first objects studied by Galileo in 1609. Identified as M44, it is known as the Beehive Cluster or Praesepe which in Latin means "hive", "crib" or "manger". Remember our discussion of beehives and the number six in Chapter 3?

The Greeks and Romans viewed this as two donkeys eating from this manger. One donkey is called Aselius Borealis and the other is called Asellus Australis. It was the tribe of Issachar that was assigned the two donkeys to their tribal standard when Jacob gave his blessing to his twelve sons.

Issachar is a strong ass couching down between two burdens
Genesis 49:14

Cancer is the beginning of bringing all the faithful together in one place. The final day of rest is almost here.

CANCER'S FIRST DECAN: URSA MINOR

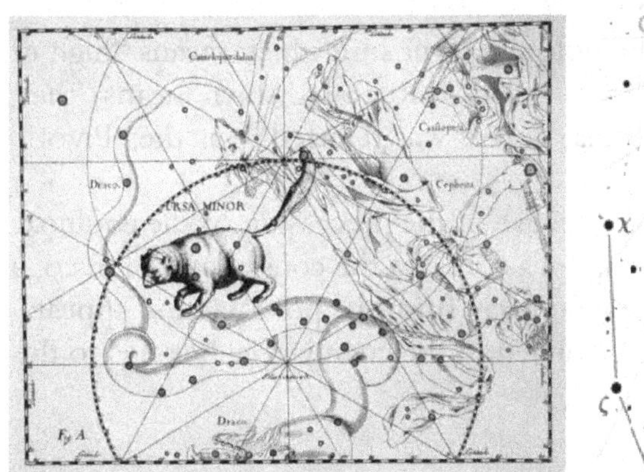

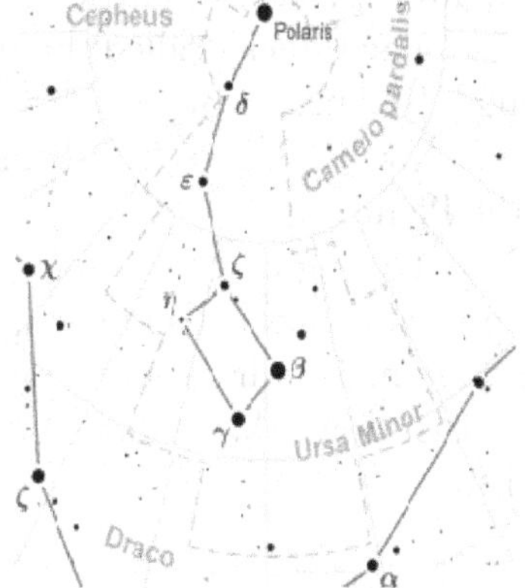

The first Decan of Cancer is called Ursa Minor from the Latin name meaning "little bear". It is also known as "the lesser bear" or "the lesser sheepfold", but most commonly referred to as the "Little Dipper" from the seven brightest stars that form the shape of a dipper or ladle. These stars are also called Septentriones which means "the seven which turn".

The bear reference is interesting as they do not have tails, but this figure has a long uplifted tail unlike those known on Earth. In addition, no bear reference is found in any of the ancient zodiacs and probably was a reference to sheep.

This constellation is most notable for its northerly position and the fact that it contains the Pole Star called Stella Polaris. The pole star is the central star of the heavens and located far out on the tail of the bear and almost directly overhead of the Earth's North Pole.

The Pole Star is extremely important to sailors who navigate the seas and often referred to as Stella Maris, the "Star of the Sea".

The Shekhinah is Coming

Appearing to be motionless as the central point of heaven, Polaris is continually circled by all the other stars. This is why the constellation is sometimes called Septentriones.

The Greeks called the pole star Cynosure which means "high in rising". In Arabic, the pole star is called Al Ruccaba which means "the turned" or "ridden on". In India, Polaris was referred to as the "Pivot of the Planets".

Throughout time and because of the precession of the equinox, the pole star shifts. The pole star was once in the constellation Draco, the dragon. The dragon is now far away from the pole star and appears to be cast down. What once belonged to the enemy now belongs to the faithful.

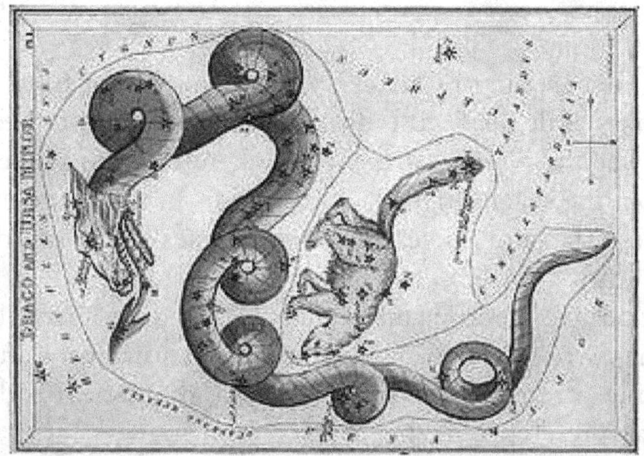

Ursa Minor, with Draco looping around it

And the great dragon was cast out, that old serpent, called the Devil, and Satan, which deceiveth the whole world
Revelation 12:9

The Greeks referred to Ursa Minor as Arcas or Arktos *(αρκτος)* which means ""bear". It is derived from the word Arx which means "the stronghold of the saved". The term Arctic region comes from this definition. The legendary King Arthur's name is derived from the word Arktos as well.

The definition of Arktos is how you can differentiate which Arctic region contains polar bears and which one contains penguins. Arctic region (North Pole) means with bears and Antarctica (South Pole) region means without bears. This is where the penguins live.

Polaris is the brightest star in this constellation followed by Al Pherkadain which means "the calves" or "the young". Other stars include Al Gedi which means "the kid" or "the chosen of the flock" and Al Kaid which means "the assembled" or "the gathered together".

In Greek mythology, Arcas was the son of Zeus and Callisto, a nymph whom he seduced in betrayal of his jealous wife Hera. In her rage, Hera turned Callisto into a bear while Zeus hid Arcas to protect him. Arcas remained safe until King Lycaon attempted to sacrifice him to the gods when Zeus intervened and turned King Lycaon into the first werewolf. As the new king, Arcas went hunting and came upon a bear, his mother. When he raised his bow and arrow to kill the bear, Zeus transformed both of them to the heavens as the big and little bears. The mother is reunited with her son.

The area in which Arcas was hidden as a child became known as Arcadia a secluded area of Greece where the inhabitants tend to led a more simple and spiritual life. Mount Lycaeum in Arcadia has been listed as the birthplace of Zeus. Interestingly it is the same term used by Aristotle for the name of his academy as we learned in Chapter 3.

Some writers like Virgil referred to Arcadia as an imaginary paradise in his work *Eclogues*. More recently the famous painting by Nicolas Poussin known as "The Arcadian Shepherds" has been linked to grail stories related to Mary Magdalene. On the tomb is written the words, "*Et in Arcadia ego*", which has been interpreted as "Even in Arcadia I am found". I was fortunate to see this painting as well as its location first hand while visiting France.

Les Bergers d'Arcadie
Et in Arcadia Ego
Nicolas Poussin
Louvre Museum
Paris, France

In Greek mythology, the seven stars of the little dipper were called Hesperides, the nymphs and daughters of Zeus (Atlas). Hera's orchard was known as the "Garden of the Hesperides", where a tree grew the immortality-giving, golden apples. The tree was tended to by the Hesperides and protected by the hundred-headed dragon named Ladon. The tree was a gift from Gaia when Hera agreed to marry Zeus.

Known as the "Sunset Goddesses" or "the Daughters of Evening", the three nymphs are named Aegle meaning "dazzling light", Erytheia meaning "the red one", and Hesperia meaning "the evening". The maidens not only tended the garden but sang beautifully.

The Garden of Hesperides
Frederic Leighton
1892
Lady Lever Art Gallery
Liverpool, UK

CANCER'S SECOND DECAN: URSA MAJOR

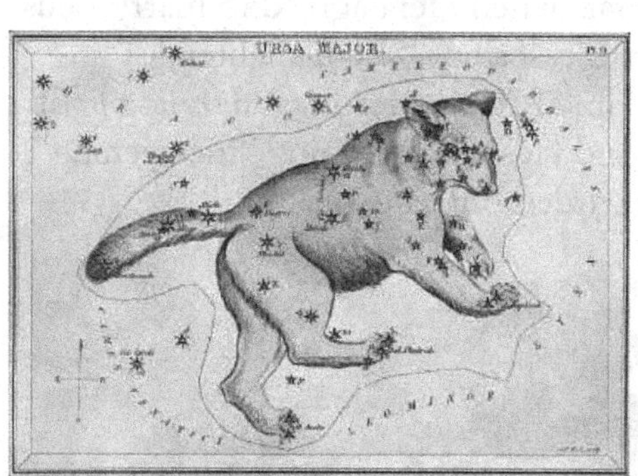

The second Decan of Cancer is called Ursa Major from the Latin name meaning "The Great Bear". It is most commonly referred to as the Big Dipper or Plough. As in Ursa Minor the seven brightest stars of Ursa Major form the shape of a dipper or ladle.

In Arabic, this constellation is called Al Naish which means "the ordered" or "assembled together" as a herd of sheep. It is the picture of a great bear. Anciently, this constellation was seen as a great sheep resting with its flock.

Hear the word of the Lord, O ye nations, and declare it in the isles afar off, and say, He that scattered Israel will gather him, and keep him, as a shepherd doth his flock
Jeremiah 31:10

Here the faithful are assembled in an orderly fashion. God's faithful have taken dominion over the enemy and are now resting after their many trials.

The brightest star in this constellation is located on the back of the bear and called Dubhe which means "a herd of animals" or "a flock". Dubhe is also known as one of the "pointer stars" used in locating Polaris, the pole star identifying true North.

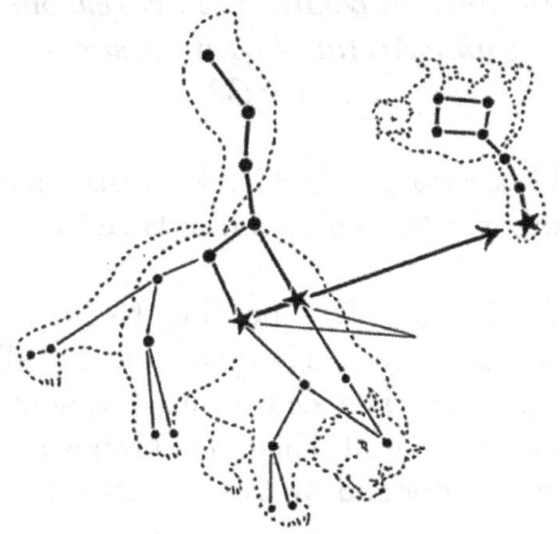

Pointer Stars identifying Polaris

The second brightest star is called Merak or Merach in Hebrew which means "the flock". In Arabic, it means "purchased". Merak is the other "pointer star" in locating Polaris. A star located to the left of Merak is called Phaeda which means "visited", "guarded", or "numbered" as a flock. In the middle of the ladle's handle are two stars Alcor and Mizar that appear as double stars.

When the King James Version of the Bible was translated from the Latin Vulgate, the phrase "the bear" was termed "Arcturus". It is this word, Arcturus, which is found in scripture.

The Shekhinah is Coming

Which maketh Arcturus, Orion, and Pleiades, and the chambers of the south
Job 9:9

Canst thou bring forth Mazzaroth in his season? Or canst thou guide Arcturus with his sons?
Job 38:32

The word Mazzaroth is the Greek translation of the Hebrew word Mazarot. Both words have been translated to mean zodiac or constellations.

In Greek mythology, Hera the wife of Zeus was jealous of him lusting after Callisto so she turned her into a bear. Callisto's son Arcas was about to slay the bear when Zeus realized what was happening and turned Arcas into a bear as well. They were both placed in the heavens. Callisto became Ursa Major and Arcas became Ursa Minor.

CANCER'S THIRD DECAN: ARGO

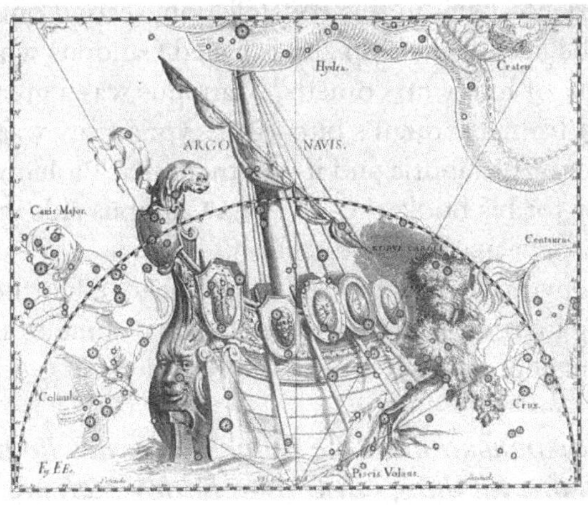

The third Decan of Cancer is called Argo, "the swift one". This is the famous ship that Jason and the Argonauts used to bring back the Golden Fleece. The Argonauts were a group of heroes assembled to help Jason on his quest. Some of the heroes were Hercules, Orpheus, Castor, and Pollux. The fleece belonged to the winged ram Chrysomallos and was considered magic. When the ram was sacrificed, it became the constellation Aries.

The name Jason is the Greek translation of the Hebrew Joshua (*Yĕhōšuă'*), which means "Yahweh delivers or rescues". The same feat that Jason and the Argonauts perform in delivering the Golden Fleece. Our hero is returning victorious as the faithful have obtained eternal life.

In the Dendera Zodiac, this constellation appears as an ox with an ankh around his neck, the Egyptian symbol for life. This ox was called Shes-en-Fent which means "rejoicing over the serpent".

The Shekhinah is Coming

Rejoicing is exactly what the Argonauts did upon returning home with their ultimate treasure.

The brightest star in this constellation, second only to Sirius, is located near the keel of the ship and is called Canopus which means "the possession of him who cometh". Canopus was a great Egyptian hero who died from a serpent's bite. An Egyptian city was named after him very close to Alexandria and it was there that Ptolemy charted the stars in the sky for his book, the *Almagest.* Canopus aids in navigation and is an important marker for direction.

In summary, Cancer appears to gather together those in Christ after their long journey in the Earth realm. It is a time of rest which will be peaceful and joyful. It will be the Kingdom of God.

That in the dispensation of the fullness of times he might gather together in one all things in Christ, both which are in heaven, and which are on Earth; even in him
Ephesians 1:10

LEO

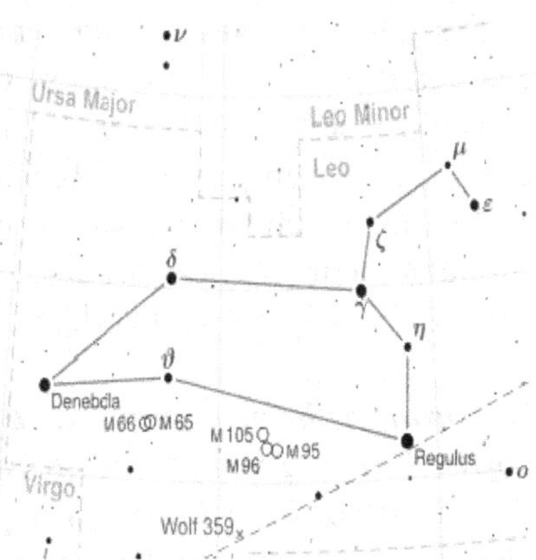

The constellation Leo is Latin for lion, the majestic king of the jungle that is revered by all. The lion has forever been associated with royalty and dominion. The Babylonians called Leo UR.GU.LA meaning "the lion". In the Dendera Zodiac, this constellation is also a lion that stands on and crushes the serpent.

The lion is a very fierce and powerful animal and in Hebrew there are five words for lion which include: Aryeh which means "he who rends" or "hunting down his prey". Ger which means "a lion's whelp", Ciphir which means "a young lion when first hunting for himself", Sachal which means "a mature lion in full strength", Laish which means "a fierce lion", and Labia which means "a lioness".

The Shekhinah is Coming

The lion is pictured in all the ancient zodiacs from all cultures. To the Persians, the lion was called Ser and to the Syrians, the lion was called Aryo which means "the pourer out of rage". It was the lion's tail that later became the constellation Coma Berenices, the first decan of Virgo.

This is the lion of the Tribe of Judah that has come to destroy his enemies. Throughout the long genealogy of Judah, the tribe has been characterized as one that has warred against its enemies and been victorious in those fights. This will conclude in the second coming of our hero Jesus, no longer the lamb, who will prevail in the final fight with the enemy which will be torn to pieces. The pronouncement of the final judgement will be swift and align with the characteristics of this majestic animal, the final zodiac constellation.

God brought him forth out of Egypt; he hath as it were the strength of an unicorn; he shall eat up the nations his enemies, and shall break their bones, and pierce them through with his arrows. He couched, he lay down as a lion, and as a great lion; who shall stir him up? Blessed is he that blesseth thee, and cursed is he that curseth thee
Numbers 24:8–9

The brightest star in Leo is located in the heart of the lion and called Regel or Regulus which means "treading under foot" or "the feet which crush".

Thou shalt tread upon the lion and adder: the young lion and the dragon shalt thou trample under foot
Psalms 91:13

The second brightest star in Leo is located in the tail's tip and called Denebola which means "the judge" or "lord who cometh with haste".

In Greek mythology, it was Hercules' first of his twelve labors to kill the lion Nemean. The lion had come to Earth from the Moon in the form of a meteor and caused havoc to the Greeks in Corinth. The Lion's hide was so strong that Hercules killed the lion by strangling it. Hercules then used the lion's thick hide as a shield in battle.

LEO'S FIRST DECAN: HYDRA

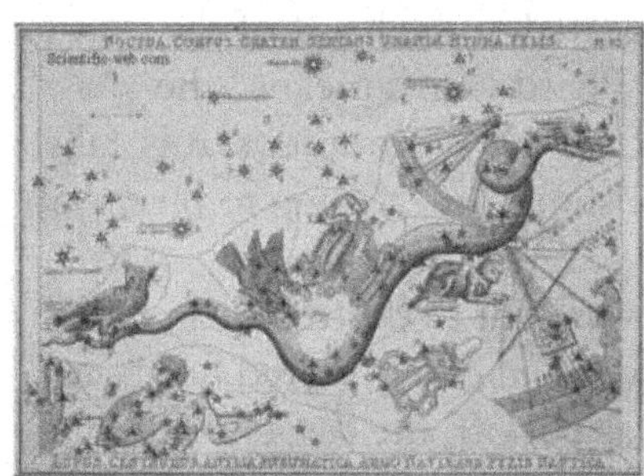

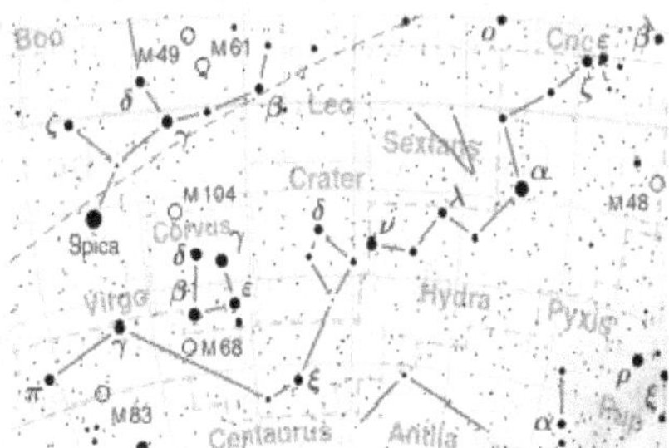

The first Decan of Leo is called Hydra, the serpent and means "he is abhorred". It is fitting that the final battle with the enemy that has influenced the whole of humanity is represented in this first decan. Especially, since this constellation is the largest modern one and is so immense that it covers one-third of the heavens as it lies beneath the constellations of Virgo, Leo, and Cancer.

The constellation is the picture of a twisting serpent attempting to flee from the Lion who is about to seize the serpent's neck. He knows that the punishment will tear him apart as this will be the final battle. This is the enemy that has come in different forms, but the same deceiver who has been cast out for the last time. Regardless of his form, the enemy's dominion has ended.

> ***In that day the Lord with His sore and great and strong sword shall punish leviathan the piercing serpent, even leviathan that crooked serpent; and He shall slay the dragon that is in the sea***
> **Isaiah 27:1**

In Babylon, this constellation was known as MUL.DINGIR.MUSH, the serpent and was sacred to the god Ningishzida, the Lord of the Underworld.

The brightest star in Hydra is located in the heart of the serpent. In Arabic, this star is called Al Phard which means "the separated, the excluded" or "put out of the way". Another star is called Minchir al Sugic which means "the punishing" or "tearing to pieces of the deceiver".

In Greek mythology, Hercules was sent to destroy this great serpent as one of his twelve labors. Hydra had one hundred heads and could only be killed by fire. If a head was cut off, the serpent would grow two new heads. Hercules with the help of his companion, Iolaus was successful by applying a red hot iron to each of the heads as they were cut off until they were all gone.

LEO'S SECOND DECAN: CRATER

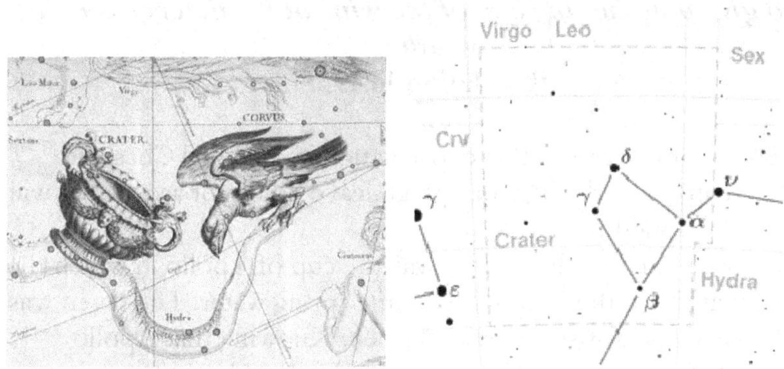

The second Decan of Leo is called the Crater which is Latin for "cup". This constellation is the picture of a wide and deep cup that is full. The base of the cup is attached to Hydra as they share some of the same stars. Clearly, the enemy cannot escape the coming wrath and his ultimate destruction.

For in the hand of the Lord there is a cup, and the wine is red; it is full of mixture; and he poureth out of the same
Psalms 75:8

It is the cup of divine wrath poured out upon the Earth to destroy any remaining enemies.

The same shall drink of the wine of the wrath of God, which is poured out without mixture into the cup of his indignation; and he shall be tormented with fire and brimstone in the presence of the holy angels, and in the presence of the Lamb
Revelation 14:10

The Shekhinah is Coming

And the great city was divided into three parts, and the cities of the nations fell; and great Babylon came in remembrance before God, to give unto her the cup of the wine of the fierceness of his wrath
Revelation 16:19

The brightest star in this constellation is called Al Ches and means "the cup". The descriptions given leave no doubt as to what will be done to the unfaithful.

In Greek mythology, Crater was the cup of Apollo in which the raven was sent to Earth to fetch him some spring water. The raven was delayed as he waited for some fruit to ripen. Knowing that Apollo would be unhappy with his delay, the raven brought back the serpent. The raven claimed that the serpent had attacked him and caused the delay. Of course, Apollo knew that this was not true and flung all of them out of their heavenly abode.

LEO'S THIRD DECAN: CORVUS

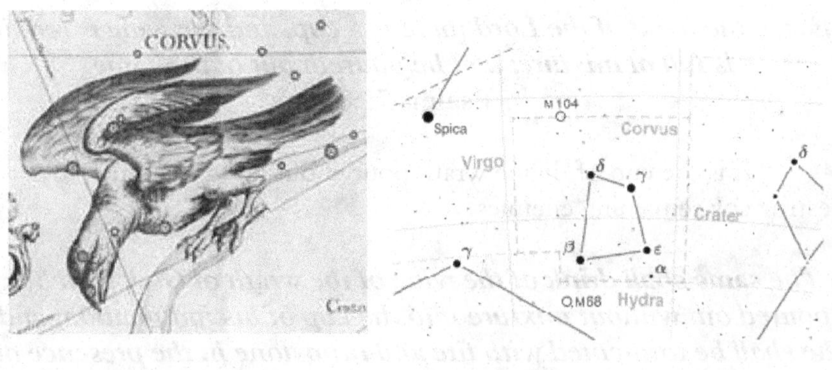

The third Decan of Leo is called the Corvus which is Latin for "raven". In myth, a raven is known as a bird of prey and considered a bad omen. In the Dendera Zodiac, he was called Her-Na meaning Her—"the enemy" and Na—"breaking up".

This constellation is the picture of the raven grasping the body of Hydra, the serpent. As a bird of punishment, the raven joins the lion in tearing the serpent apart. This is the same raven as referenced in the Greek mythology of Crater.

The brightest star in this constellation is located in the eye of the raven and called Al Chibar which in Arabic means "joining together". In Hebrew, this star is called Chiba and means "accursed" or "the curse inflicted". Another star named Minchir al Gorab means "the raven tearing to pieces".

And one of the elders saith unto me, Weep not: behold, the Lion of the tribe of Judah, the Root of David, hath prevailed to open the book, and to loose the even seals thereof
Revelation 5:5

The inheritance of the faithful has been returned as this completes the circle and the final chapter of *THE STARS: HIS LIFE IN LIGHTS*. The stars were studied and revered by the ancients as far back as Zep Tepi or the First Time. As we learned early on, information was passed by word of mouth and the ancients created stories that would help them to remember this information. That is exactly what the Bible does. As the written word, it documents the story written in the stars as the ancient patriarchs learned through their travels and saw in the monuments that where built to align with them. There is no doubt that the message remains for all to see now as it was in the beginning untainted by humanity.

We begin and end the story with the same Bible verse:

The Shekhinah is Coming

The heavens declare the glory of God; and the firmament sheweth his handiwork. Day unto day uttereth speech and night unto night sheweth knowledge. There is no speech nor language, where their voice is not heard
Psalms 19:1–3

Metaphorically, I refer to this study of the stars as our nightly bedtime story as I see them as a blanket to cover us and keep us warm until we see the "morning star". They will remain our constant reminder until that time giving everyone the choice to embrace.

We have spent a considerable amount of time discussing stars. So, let's take one last look at the gematria of the word "star". In Hebrew, the gematria value of the word "star" equals 48. This is the same value of the Greek phrase "the coming of the Son of Man" (dropping the zeros). Is there any doubt what this connection is or who is being referred to?

NOTE:
ALL STAR IMAGES ARE FROM URANIA'S MIRROR OR URANOGRAPHIA. URANIA'S MIRROR WAS A BOOK AND SET OF CONSTELLATION CARDS PUBLISHED IN LONDON IN 1832. URANOGRAPHIA WAS COMPLETED BY JOHANNES HEVELIUS.

URANOGRAPHY WAS A GREEK WORD FOR "SKY" OR "HEAVEN". DURING THE RENAISSANCE, THIS TERM WAS USED IN CELESTIAL ATLASES AS A DESCRIPTION OF THE HEAVENS.

ALL IMAGES CAN BE FOUND ON WIKI COMMONS.

THE CITY OF GOD

Jerusalem is the one place on Earth considered sacred and holy by the three major religions of the world as it stands in the middle of the nation of Israel. It is one of the oldest cities in the world dating back to the fourth millennium B.C.

For Islam, the Dome of the Rock mosque is especially sacred for two reasons. First, it covers the rock that Abraham used when he was prepared to sacrifice his son, Isaac to God. Secondly, it is the site where the great prophet Muhammad ascended to paradise.

Omar Mosque—Dome of the Rock

The Shekhinah is Coming

For Christianity, the Church of the Holy Sepulcher is sacred because it covers the tomb of Jesus Christ where he rose from the dead.

Church of the Holy Sepulcher

For Judaism, Jerusalem was the capital of Judea about 1000 B.C. during the reign of King David. It was also the site of Solomon's temple which was built to house the Ark of the Covenant. Today, only the Western Wall—"wailing wall" remains from the Roman destruction of the Second Temple in A.D. 70. In Hebrew, the Western Wall is known as the *"kotel"*. It is the site that the Jews pilgrimage to for the mourning of the lost temple oftentimes writing prayers on small pieces of paper and shoving the paper into the cracks created where the large blocks, forming the wall, come together.

Western Wall (Dome of Rock in Background)

Western Wall up Close

Jewish tradition holds that the city was founded by Shem and Eber in the line of Enoch. Eber was the great-grandson of Shem. The city's name was originally called Salem, the capital of King Melchizedek. This is confirmed by both Josephus (*Antiquities I:10:1*) and the cuneiform tables known as the *Amarna Letters* found in 1888 at Tell Amarna, Egypt.

According to the Columbia Encyclopedia, Sixth Edition, "Salem is the Hebrew word for peace in the Bible and the royal city of Melchizedek traditionally identified with Jerusalem".

In Salem also is His tabernacle and His dwelling place in Zion
Psalms 76:2

Shalom, the greeting word used by the Jewish people means "peace" and stems from the word Salem. In Arabic, the word for peace is "Salaam" and the standard Arabic greeting *Assalamu Alaikum* is "peace be upon you." Do you see a similarity in both spelling and sound?

The Shekhinah is Coming

The etymology of the city name "Jerusalem" according to Wikipedia is a compound of two Semitic roots:

"s–l–m" meaning wholeness, peace, harmony, or completeness

"y–r–h" meaning to show, instruct, or teach

The Zohar states that Melchizedek is King of Salem who rules with complete sovereignty. In the Book of Jasher, an Apocrypha writing, Melchizedek is referred to as Adonizedek meaning Righteous Lord, the same name used by Joshua (Joshua 10:1). In the book of Hebrews 7:2, he is referred to as King of Righteousness, King of Salem, and King of Peace.

According to Strong's, the name Melchizedek (קדצ-יכלמ, *Malkiy-tsedeq)* comes from the Hebrew root words "melek" meaning "kings" and "tzedek" meaning "righteousness" rendering Melchizedek as King of Righteousness.

Within the Dead Sea Scroll (11Q13), called *Genesis Apocryphon* 22:14–17, Melchizedek is referred to as Elohim which means a "divine being". Interestingly, in the Book of Enoch it states that Melchizedek was born of a virgin named Sofonim who became the wife of Nir, the brother of Noah. At birth, Melchizedek was fully developed and began speaking by blessing the Lord. It is said that he was taken to the Garden of Eden by Archangel Gabriel and survived the flood without being on Noah's ark. Melchizedek's divine birth is actually confirmed in the book of Hebrews:

Without father, without mother, without descent, having neither beginning of days, nor end of life; but made like unto the Son of God; abideth a priest continually

Hebrews 7:3

Biblically, Abram (not yet Abraham) was blessed by the King of Salem, Melchizedek, the priest of the God Most High as he received bread and wine.

And Melchizedek king of Salem brought forth bread and wine; and he was the priest of the Most High God. And he blessed him, and said, blessed be Abram of the Most High God, possessor of heaven and Earth
Genesis 14:18–19

Melchizedek
Offering Bread & Wine
Dieric Bouts
The Church of St. Peter
Leuven, Belgium

Melchizedek
Blessing Abram
Charles Foster
1897

This blessing is repeated in Hebrews 7:1 after which Abram gives tithes to Melchizedek:

Now consider how great this man was, unto whom even the patriarch Abraham gave the tenth of the spoils
Hebrews 7:4

After Abram had been blessed by Melchizedek, Abram prayed to God for a son. It is through this prayer that Abram was promised that his seed would be greater than the stars in heaven and his first son, Ishmael would be a wild, fighting man. Remember, Ishmael was conceived with his wife's Egyptian handmaiden, Hagar.

Located at the equator, Jerusalem's sunrise is due East while the sunset is due West, a perfect alignment as the ancients believed that the location channeled the Earth's energies along with the heavenly energies making it a divine spot for communicating with the gods. In Greek, the gematria values for the words "God" and "Jerusalem" are 864 matching the Sun's diameter, confirming the ancient's beliefs.

But I have chosen Jerusalem, that my name might be there; and have chosen David to be over my people Israel
2Chronicles 6:6

According to Christopher Knight, "The name 'Jerusalem' in the Canaanite language means 'foundation for observing Venus rising'" (Knight 2007, 13). In addition, he states "that the latitude of Jerusalem is 31 degrees 47 minutes north, which means that the angle of the shadows cast by the winter and summer solstices is precisely 60 degrees" (Knight 2007, 12).

This is the same 60 degrees that relates to the "Delta of Enoch". However, Knight also states that on the winter solstice using sticks to cast shadows both easterly and westerly the resulting 30 degree shadows would "form a perfect six-pointed star that is known as either the Seal of Solomon or the Star of David" (Knight 2007, 13—Appendix I).

Salem was also the name used for the planet Venus and was the site of a temple dedicated to Venus and built by Roman Emperor Hadrian around A.D. 100. It was one of the pagan temples built in the city that once stood where the Church of the Holy Sepulcher currently stands.

Tradition holds that in A.D. 326, Constantine's mother, Helena accompanied by Eusebius made a pilgrimage to Jerusalem. Along the way she had a vision that the tomb of Jesus lay beneath the temple to Venus. Helena ordered that the temple be demolished to uncover the tomb after which a church was built on the site in A.D. 335.

As the only planet named after a goddess (Astarte or Aphrodite), Venus is the third brightest object in the sky after the Sun and the Moon. It is brightest shortly before sunrise when it is called "the morning star." It is also brightest shortly after sunset when it is called "the evening star." In representing the goddess, the symbol for Venus is the same as the biological symbol for the female—♀.

Venus was known as the "goddess of love" who was born from the sea and symbolized maidenhood as she was depicted in art with long abundant red hair. Many ancients associated Venus with the life principle as it proceeds the dawn of the Sun considered a rebirth of that life-giving force.

The Birth of Venus
Sandro Botticelli
Galleria degli Uffizi
Florence, Italy

Venus' orbit around the Sun is almost a circle causing it to pass between the Earth and the Sun every 584 days. It is at these times when it switches between being a "morning star" or an "evening star." Pythagoras, in the sixth century B.C., was the first to recognize this phenomenon as the ancient Egyptians and Babylonians believed that Venus was two separate bodies.

Even more interesting, as Venus revolves around the Sun, the path creates a five pointed star (pentagram) every eight years which takes us back to our discussion on sacred geometry and the golden mean in Chapter 3. Venus is also the name given to Friday that is sacred to Islam representing their holy day.

The purpose of discussing Venus is that we are told that the glory of God is in the face of Jesus, who is often referred to as the "morning star."

Secrets of the Divine

For God, who commanded the light to shine out of darkness, hath shined in our hearts, to give the light of the knowledge of the glory of God in the face of Jesus Christ
2Corinthians 4:6

I, Jesus have sent mine angel to testify unto you these things in the churches. I am the root and the offspring of David, and the bright and morning star
Revelation 22:16

In the book of Hebrews, Jesus is likened unto Melchizedek as a priest forever in the order of Melchizedek (Hebrews 5:6 and 7:17) which quoted Psalms 110:4 where David refers to the future Messiah. Yet, from Moses' time, the priesthood was always within the tribe of Levi. Some Jewish tradition teaches that Melchizedek gave Adam's robes to Abram which then established the future priesthood with Aaron, the First High Priest.

We know that the genealogy of Jesus is within the tribe of Judah which was never connected to the priesthood. So, how did the priesthood change tribes? Let's first look at the parallels between Jesus and Melchizedek?

1. Melchizedek and Jesus experience virgin births
2. Melchizedek shares bread and wine with Abram as Jesus shares bread and wine with his disciples at the Last Supper documented in all four gospels
3. Melchizedek and Jesus are both priest of the Most High God
4. Unbeknownst to most people, Melchizedek was killed and hung on a tree as he was one of the five kings left who fought against Joshua. After winning all the battles, Joshua ordered their death. ***"And afterwards Joshua smote them, and***

slew them, and hanged them on five trees; and they were hanging upon the trees until the evening" **(Joshua 10:26)** Jesus also died hanging on a tree (the cross)

5. Both are said to be the "sons of God"
6. Melchizedek is from a place called "peace" and called the King of Peace. Jesus is said to be the "Prince of Peace" in Isaiah 9:6

   Note: In Chapter 3, we found Jesus, in art, on the royal portal of Chartres Cathedral. Melchizedek, along with Abraham and Moses, is also displayed at Chartres Cathedral on the porch of the northern transept (12th century). Melchizedek is shown with his symbols of the chalice and loaf of bread while Jesus is shown in the recurring symbol of the Vesica Pisces.

When Abram paid tithes to Melchizedek, it established Melchizedek's superior status and greatness over all. The tribes of Israel had yet to be born, because Abram had not yet birthed Isaac whose son Jacob produced Levi and the future priesthood of Aaron.

Once Moses was established, all the tribes that came out of Egypt paid tithes to Aaron, the first High Priest and continued with successive priest in the line of Levi. Aaron, being gifted in speech had represented his brother Moses well, but he had rebelled against God at the water of Meribah (Exodus 17:1–6). Because of this, Aaron was stripped of his priestly garments which were given to his son, Eleazar and Aaron died on Mount Hor (Numbers 20:22–28).

We know from the Torah, the first five books of the Bible, that none of the men that came out of Egypt with Moses were allowed to cross the Jordan River into Canaan except for Joshua and Caleb. This was due to the Israelites' rebellious nature. This included both Aaron and Moses as the spiritual mantel and leadership was past to Joshua which means "savior" upon the death of Moses. Joshua was the son of Nun, of the tribe of Ephraim. Joshua had also accompanied Moses part way up the mountain where he received the Ten Commandments.

When the children of Israel finally cross the Jordan River and enter the Promised Land, Joshua informs us that Jerusalem was the territory given to the tribe of Benjamin.

And Zelah, Eleph, and Jebusi, which is Jerusalem, Gibeath, and Kirjath; fourteen cities with their villages. This is the inheritance of the children of Benjamin according to their families
Joshua 18:28

Benjamin was the twelfth and last son of Jacob and the only son born in Canaan. His mother Rachel died while giving birth to him as they traveled from Bethel to Bethlehem. Rachel wanted to name her son Benoni which means "child of my sorrow", but Jacob named him Benjamin which means "son of my right hand."

It is then upon Joshua's death that the children of Israel inquired as to who would lead them. And the Lord said:

Judah shall go up; behold, I have delivered the land into his hands
Judges 1:2

So, the spiritual direction of the children of Israel switches to the tribe of Judah, the fourth son born of Jacob, son of Isaac.

In the line of Judah is David, a tenth generation descendant according to Ruth 4:18–22. The complete genealogy of David is:

Judah—Pharez—Hezron—Ram—Amminadab—Nahshon—
Salmon—Boaz—Obed—Jesse—David.

The Shekhinah is Coming

David was born in Bethlehem and enjoyed a special relationship with God due to his faithfulness. Because of his faithfulness, God made a covenant with David that it would be his seed that would establish the royal line of the Hebrews.

I have made a covenant with my chosen, I have sworn unto David my servant, thy seed will I establish forever, and build up thy throne to all generations. Selah
Psalms 89:3–4

The word "Selah", at the end of this quote, is an interesting word. While it is used frequently in Psalms it can be confusing to understand. The simplest explanation would be to "ponder"—to pause and reflect or as the Bible frequently states: "Let those with eyes see and with ears hear."

The book of Hebrews reaffirms that because God is unhappy with the Levi priests, he will make a new covenant with the tribe of Judah from which the lineage of David comes.

For finding fault with them, he saith, behold, the days come, saith the Lord, when I will make a new covenant with the house of Israel and with the house of Judah
Hebrews 8:8

God goes on to say that this is a different covenant than what He had with the people of Israel when He brought them out of the land of Egypt, because they had not kept His covenant.

So, upon one death (Joshua) not only did the priesthood change tribes, but the law changed and the new law revolved around the coming Messiah, the anointed one, and the hope of everlasting life.

It is in the line of Judah that the priesthood will remain until the Messiah returns.

The Sceptre shall not depart from Judah, nor a lawgiver from between his feet, until Shiloh come; and unto Him shall the gathering of the people be
Genesis 49:10

Shiloh was a city north of Bethlehem where the whole congregation of the children of Israel assembled and set up the tabernacle to house the Ark of the Covenant as Joshua directed (Joshua 18:1–2). But, from the above reference, Shiloh refers to a person. If you look at the gematria of the Hebrew phrase "until Shiloh=358", it is the same as the word "Messiah=358", the one bringing peace. The word Shiloh actually means "the one who brings rest". The word Shiloh is also a palindrome with "I AM" as discussed in Chapter 5:

Shiloh = 345 / 543 = I AM

According to Christianity, this Messiah is Jesus and his genealogy according to the Bible is stated in Luke 3:23–38 and Matthew 1:1–17. According to Luke, Jesus is the seventy-seventh in the line from God and hails from the tribe of Judah.

The initial building of the tabernacle while the children of Israel were in the desert was done by Bezalel. Bezalel which means "in the shadow of El" was the son of Uri from the tribe of Judah (Exodus 31:1–6 and Exodus 35:30–31). Bezalel not only built the tabernacle, but the Ark of the Covenant and all the sacred furniture and utensils. He was also in charge of the holy oils, the incense, and the high priest vestments.

The Shekhinah is Coming

Bezalel was filled with wisdom and understanding and combined Hebrew letters and sound to complete his task. Even though God told Moses how to construct the specific spiritual items, he did not understand, but when Moses relayed the information to Bezalel, he understood immediately and made the items as God commanded.

And Moses said unto the children of Israel, see, the Lord hath called by name Bezalel the son of Uri, the son of Hur, of the tribe of Judah; and he hath filled him with the spirit of God, in wisdom, in understanding, and in knowledge, and in all manner of workmanship
Exodus 35:30–31

Obviously, the future was being set up as it appears that the tribe of Judah was honored from the beginning when it related to the true spiritual information and communication with God.

The Qur'an upholds the virgin birth of Jesus who is called Isa in Arabic. Islam believes that Jesus is an "honored servant" (Qur'an 21:26), but denies His "divinity". However, Jesus is compared to Adam who was created without father or mother (Qur'an 3:59).

The Qur'an further states that Isa was the Messiah and was supported by the Holy Spirit. As a messenger of God, Isa spoke as a baby in the cradle, performed various miracles including healing and raising the dead.

Islam does not believe that Jesus was crucified, but they do believe that he ascended to Allah (Qur'an 4:157). According to Islam, Allah sent Muhammad to correct this misunderstanding of the crucifixion.

According to Islamic tradition, they also believe in Jesus' second coming:

And Jesus shall be a sign the hour therefore have no doubt about the hour, but follow ye me this is a straight way
Qur'an 43:61

This verse in the Qur'an parallels the verse in John 14:6 where Jesus says, "***I am the way, the truth, and the life; no man cometh unto the Father, but by me.***"

The Psalter Map (ca. 1250)
British Library
London, UK

The Psalter Map was part of a thirteenth century copy of the Book of Psalms. It depicts Jerusalem in the center with Christ as the world overseer. Around the inner circumference of the world are pictures of many Biblical events. This is the earliest surviving map symbolizing Christ's future role.

And the Lord shall inherit Judah his portion in the holy land, and shall choose Jerusalem again
Zechariah 3:12

Throughout time, various map makers have displayed Jerusalem at the center of Earth. I think this is significant when you consider what we are discussing and what the ancients' prophesized.

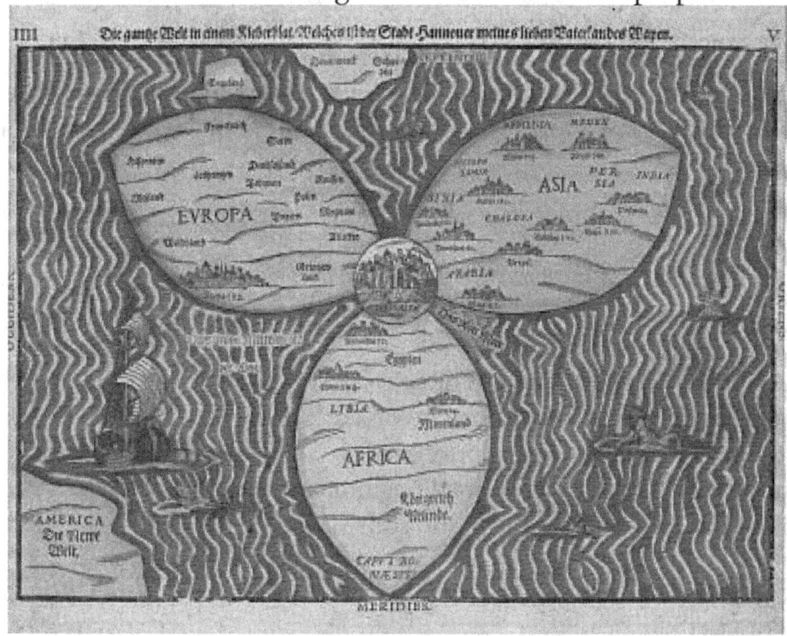

Ancient Map of Jerusalem
Surrounded by three continents: Europe, Africa, and Asia
Magdeburg, Germany–1581

The Shekhinah is Coming

Interestingly, the gematria value for both the "world" and "Jerusalem" in Hebrew equals 432. In Greek, the number value of Bethlehem is also 432 when the numbers are multiplied which was the birth place of both David and Jesus. The number 432 is also the value of the Hebrew word for "savior". We know that both Jesus and Joshua means "savior" and that Joshua was the first Israelite leader in Canaan, the future state of Israel.

Bethlehem was originally known as Ephrath (Micah 5:2) and literally means "house of bread" and what is bread, but nourishment for our bodies. During the desert encampment, this bread or "manna" came down from heaven as was discussed in Chapter 8.

And Jesus said unto them, I am the bread of life: he that cometh to me shall never hunger; and he that believeth on me shall never thirst
John 6:35

Jesus said, I am that bread of life
John 6:48

But the references continue related to the City of God and the New Jerusalem and who will be involved. Throughout scripture, the twelve tribes of Israel play a prominent role. These are the sons of Jacob whose births are described beginning in Exodus 37.

In order of their birth, the sons of Jacob are:

SON'S NAME	MEANING	MOTHER	GEMATRIA VALUE
Reuben	Behold a son	Leah	630
Simeon	God hears me	Leah	1495
Levi	Joined to me	Leah	445

Judah	One who praises	Leah	485
Dan	Making me to forget	Bilhah	700
Naphtali	My wrestling	Bilhah	650
Gad	Granted good fortune	Zilpah	8
Asher	Happy am I	Zilpah	309
Issachar	Purchased me	Leah	1112
Zebulon	Dwelling	Leah	1360
Joseph	God will add to me	Rachel	1518
Benjamin	Son of his right hand	Rachel	168
		TOTAL	**8880**

Leah was Jacob's first wife, and Zilpah was her handmaiden. Rachel was Jacob's second wife and Bilhah was her handmaiden. Leah and Rachel were sisters and the daughters of Laban.

By now, you can recognize the number and its meaning. It represents Jesus, the coming Messiah whose number "8" is magnified in the triple "888", the ultimate level of attainment. The phrase "Lord of the Sabbath" also carries the value of "888" when multiplied by two.

888 = *I am the life* (John 14:6)
888 = *The light dwells in him* (Daniel 2:22)

The names of the twelve tribes of Jacob, who God called "Israel" meaning "struggles with God", were so important that they were part of the High Priest Breastplate. The High Priest, known as the "*Kohen Gadol*", is shown wearing his entire spiritual vestments.

HIGH PRIEST IN ROBES AND BREASTPLATE.
—*Lev.* viii. 8.

Kohen Gadol
The High Priest

The detail for the spiritual vestments begins in Exodus where Moses is commanded by the Lord to make the holy garments for Aaron, the first High Priest and his sons. Great detail is given not only to the various pieces, but also the size and color. The garments included a robe, an ephod, coats, a girdle, a mitre, and the breastplate and were referred to as "for glory and for beauty."

On the shoulders of the ephod were attached two onyx stones that were engraved with the names of the twelve tribes. There were six names on the left shoulder and six names on the right shoulder (Exodus 28:9–10) both encased in gold settings. Onyx stones were first mentioned as part of the Garden of Eden (Genesis 2:12) and when set upon the High Priest shoulders, they represent a "memorial" unto the children of Israel for Aaron to bear their names before the Lord (Exodus 28:12).

The breastplate held twelve stones to represent the twelve tribes of Israel with the tribe name engraved on the stone like a signet or seal also encased in gold. The exact order and arrangement of the twelve stones are given twice in Exodus 28:17–21 and Exodus 39:9–13. "The breastplate was to be foursquare with four rows of three stones each and attached tightly to the ephod:

> The First Row of stones were Sardius, Topaz, and Carbuncle
> The Second Row of stones were Emerald, Sapphire, and Diamond
> The Third Row of stones were Liguere, Agate, and Amethyst
> The Fourth Row of stones were Beryl, Onyx, and Jasper"
> (Remember that Hebrew is read right to left)

Because of lost knowledge and translations, these twelve stones may differ from what is known today and is an area that is frequently debated among the scholars. What is clear is that the stones came out of Egypt so they had to be only those stones known during that time. It should be mentioned that Josephus documents the breastplate with its twelve stones in *Antiquities 3:7:1* describing the stones' extraordinary beauty and immense value.

The tribe ascribed to each stone was not given in the Bible and that knowledge has also been lost. This has created much discussion by many learned biblical scholars each with their own opinion. According to John P. Pratt, the order is: row one: Zebulon, Issachar, Judah, row two: Gad, Naphtali, Dan, row three: Levi, Simeon, Reuben, and row four: Benjamin, Joseph, Asher.

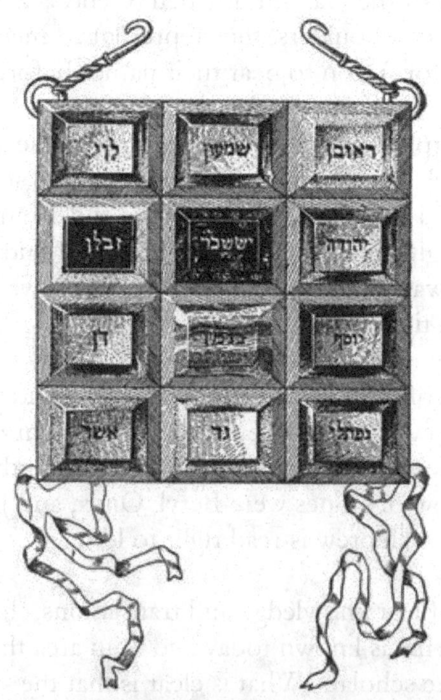

High Priest Breastplate
Jewish Encyclopedia

Just as Aaron was to bear the names of the twelve tribes on his shoulders, the breastplate bore their names upon his heart as it was known as the "breastplate of judgment". Nine of these twelve stones were referenced by Ezekiel when discussing the Garden of Eden, but relate more likely to the constellations (*covering*–remember the blanket discussion at the end of Chapter 8?) as it speaks of a time prior to man's creation and the sons of Jacob being born.

Thou hast been in Eden the garden of God; every precious stone was thy covering, the sardius, topaz, and the diamond, the beryl, the onyx, and the jasper, the sapphire, the emerald, and the carbuncle, and gold: the workmanship of thy tabrets (tambourine) and of thy pipes was prepared in thee in the day that thou wast created
Ezekiel 28:13

Interestingly, after Ezekiel talks about the precious stones of the Garden of Eden, he refers to them as ***"stones of fire"*** (Ezekiel 28:14). These same stones are the ones used to garnish the twelve level foundation of the New Jerusalem. However, here the names of the twelve apostles are used with the foundation of the New Jerusalem as opposed to the twelve tribes.

And the foundations of the wall of the city were garnished with all manner of precious stones. The first foundation was jasper; the second, sapphire; the third, a chalcedony; the fourth, an emerald; the fifth, sardonyx, the sixth, sardius; the seventh, chrysolyte, the eighth, a jacinth; the twelfth, an amethyst
Revelation 21:19–20

The twelve apostles of Jesus listed in order of Acts 1:13 were:

APOSTLES' NAME	MEANING	GREEK SPELLING
Peter	Faith	Πέτρος
James (John's brother)	Wisdom and Good Judgement	Ἰάκωβος
John	Love	Ἰωάννης
Andrew	Strength	Ἀνδρέας
Philip	Power	Φίλιππος
Thomas	Understanding	Θωμᾶς
Bartholomew	Imagination	Βαρθολομαῖος
Matthew (Levi)	Will Power	Μαθθαῖος or Λευί
James (son of Alphaeus)	Order	Ἰάκωβος
Simon (the zealot)	Zeal	Σίμων
Judas (brother of James)	Life–generative function of the body	Ἰούδας
Thaddeus (Jude or Lebbaeus)	Renunciation	Λεββαῖος

According to Bonnie Gaunt, the apostle's Greek names, when converted to numbers, adds to 10,656 and is the same number that identifies the New Jerusalem in this verse written by John while on the Island of Patmos (Gaunt 1995, 184).

And I will write on him the name of my God, and the name of the city of my God, the New Jerusalem
Revelation 3:12

The gates of the New Jerusalem will be made of pearl and named after the twelve tribes of Israel (Revelation 21:21). Pearls are a gift from nature as the only gem made by a living animal, the mollusk, and symbolic of purity and humility. As the oldest known gem, the word pearl in Latin means "unique" as no two are alike. Certainly an appropriate reference to Jesus as Saint Augustine had declared.

In the Hindu Vedic tradition, the pearl is associated with their deities, especially Vishnu. The sacred "nine pearls" are described in the Garuda Purana text. Purana means "of ancient times" in Sanskrit. The Qur'an states that those who believe and work righteous deeds will be adorned with pearls (Qur'an 22:23, 35:33, 52:24).

In the New Testament, Jesus compares the Kingdom of Heaven to ***"a pearl of great price"*** (Matthew 13:45–46). In addition, holy things are compared to pearls (Matthew 7:6). It appears that pearls are held to be more sacred than other stones and venerated by all the ancients. Pearls are mentioned nine times in the Bible mostly related to wisdom or as a symbol of Divine Spirit. As we learned in Chapter 5, the color "white" contains all the other colors and means "made whole". The color of the pearl is white, but also iridescent and reflects light. It is a "white stone" that Jesus will give to those that hear Spirit.

...To him that overcometh will I give to eat of the hidden manna, and will give him a white stone, and in the stone a new name written, which no man knoweth saving he that receiveth it
Revelation 2:17

John does not identify the tribes with the sides of the New Jerusalem as was done when they encamped during their desert sojourn in which the camp was also set to the four cardinal directions. According to Numbers 2:3–29, while in the desert encampment, the tribes on the East side were Judah, Issachar, and Zebulon. On the

South side were the tribes of Reuben, Simeon, and Gad. On the West side were the tribes of Ephraim, Manasseh, and Benjamin. Ephraim and Manasseh represented the tribe of Joseph. On the North side were the tribes of Dan, Asher, and Naphtali. As the priesthood, the tribe of Levi was within the center of the camp.

However, it is in Ezekiel's vision that we are given the cardinal directions related to the twelve tribes and the gates of the New Jerusalem. The three gates on the East side are Joseph, Benjamin, and Dan. The three gates on the South side are Simeon, Issachar, and Zebulon. The three gates on the West side are Gad, Asher, and Naphtali. And the three gates on the North are Reuben, Judah, and Levi (Ezekiel 48:31–34).

...And the name of the city from that day shall be, The Lord is there
Ezekiel 48:35

The High Priest breastplate was said to glow with the "Glory of God" when the Urim and Thummin were inserted behind the breastplate as the High Priest mediated between God and the children of Israel. Moses did not require this type of communication device as he spoke directly with God.

King Belshazzar of Babylon
Rembrandt
National Gallery–London, UK

The breastplate was described as being doubled which I believe allowed the Urim and Thummin to be put between the two pieces that were specifically made of a certain material and color with threads of pure gold weaving through the design.

No real descriptions exist as to what the Urim and Thummin were, but clearly they activated the breastplate and it became a "Divine Oracle" giving guidance to the children of Israel as great "rays of light" were upon the stones. There is much speculation with many scholars believing that YHVH, the unspoken Divine name of God, was used as part of this activation. Could it be that the "Delta of Enoch" was used to activate the breastplate? Or, is the Urim and Thummin a reference to Ezekiel's "stones of fire"?

The root meaning of Urim is traditionally upheld to be "lights", "revelation", or "truth" with Thummin meaning "perfection", "completeness", or "integrity". Some scholars believe that the Urim and Thummin were black and white stones used in casting lots.

Many have compared the breastplate with the Assyrian/Babylonian "Tablet of Destiny" which also rested upon the breast of their deity. These magical tablets of power used the words *"urtu"* meaning "oracle" and *"tamitu"* meaning "command". The writing on the tablets was said to contain "all that was", "all that is", and "all that would be." I find it interesting that these "words of power" begin with the same letters as the Urim and Thummin.

As time progressed, the children of Israel used three methods to communicate with the Divine. The methods included the Urim and Thummin, dreams, and prophets. As the number of prophets grew, the use of the Urim and Thummin diminished and by the time of the Babylonian captivity, that form of divination was lost. Eleazar was the last priest who communicated with God in this fashion.

Cyrus, the King of Persia released the children of Israel to return to Jerusalem to rebuild the house of the Lord God of Israel. Some of the Israelites had mated with non-Israelites and it was difficult to prove their genealogy upon their return. As discussed in the books of Ezra and Nehemiah, this would be determined by ***"the priest with Urim and Thummin"***. This phrase has a gematria value of 888, an obvious reference to Jesus.

Secrets of the Divine

And the Tirshatha said unto thee, that they should not eat of the most holy things, till there stood up a priest with Urim and Thummin
Nehemiah 7:65

Since the terms "Urim and Thummin" are mentioned only seven times in the Old Testament (Exodus 28:30; Leviticus 8:8; Ezra 2:63; Nehemiah 7:65; Deuteronomy 33:8; Numbers 27:21; 1Samuel 28:6), the stones appear to fall from the human consciousness until 1823 when Joseph Smith is told of the Golden Plates and the Urim and Thummin as "two stones in silver bows" by the angel Moroni.

These two stones which Smith referred to as the "interpreters" were to be used to help translate the Golden Plates into the Book of Mormon. Smith describes the stones as a pair of large spectacles and his mother describes them as "two smooth three-cornered diamonds". To me the term three-cornered gives the image of a triangle and aligns with prior divine shapes. After translating the plates, the Urim and Thummin along with the golden plates were returned to the angel Moroni.

Golden Plates

Joseph Smith Accepting Interpreters

Throughout history and especially within the Bible, stones have been used symbolically to represent God's unchanging manifest nature. Unhewn stones were always distinguished as Divine because they were formed by God and not man. Oftentimes they were referred to as "the ladder" as they led to the upper levels. Stones were used for altars and pillars to identify a site or an experience. These stones would remain throughout time as even today many megalith sacred stone sites are found around the world and referenced in many cultures.

The Egyptians built their pyramids with rock on what is believed to be the center of the world's land mass. The Greeks had their sacred site on the rocks of Delphi. Jacob slept on a rock pillow that he anointed with oil near Lux, meaning "white", "light", or "bright". He renamed the place Bethel meaning "house of God" (Genesis 28:10–22). Moses wrote his ten commandments on stone and Joshua set up stone pillars where the children of Israel crossed the

Jordan River. Solomon built his temple with unhewn stones on the rock of Mt. Moriah. Even King Arthur was declared the Righteous King when he pulled his sword, Excalibur from a large stone. Finally, Jesus built his church upon the rock and the alchemist is in constant search for the "philosopher's stone" which is known to change lead into gold.

Through the three major religions, through the location of the city, through the numbers presented, and through the various scriptural references, the signs confirm that Jerusalem is the sacred connection between heaven and Earth. According to John Michell, the phrase "Jerusalem, the City of God" has a gematria value of 1746 in Greek. This same value is equal to the Greek phrases "the Universal Spirit", "the Glory of the God of Israel", "the Hidden Spirit", "the Treasure of Jesus", and "the Divinity of Spirit" (Michell 2001, 194).

As we will see in Chapter 11, there is no doubt that the New Jerusalem is the "light" of the future as it shines like a most precious stone. Known as the "Golden City", it shares the same gematria value of 56, in Hebrew, with the words "forever" and "everlasting". Truly, the Shekhinah is coming.

And the building of the wall of it was of jasper; and the city was pure gold, like unto clear glass
Revelation 21:18

The New Jerusalem is believed to be in the shape of a "cube" from the dimensions given in Revelation. The shape of the cube takes us back to the number six and what the Greeks called "The Perfection of Parts" as discussed in Chapter 2.

Many believe that Jerusalem represents two cities. One is the physical city that we can visit and the other is the spiritual city that is "to come". "Early in the third century, a beautiful walled city became apparent in the skies over Judea. According to Tertullian, it was seen every morning for forty days, fading away as the dawn lightened. Some eight hundred years later, bands of poor pilgrims, struggling across Europe towards Jerusalem during the People's Crusade, were sustained by visions of a glorious city in the air above them to which ghostly crowds were flocking" (Michell 2001, 11).

The New Jerusalem
Viewed by John on the Island of Patmos
Tapestry of the Apocalypse
14th Century

For, behold, I create new heavens and a new Earth; and the former shall not be remembered, nor come into mind…I create Jerusalem a rejoicing and her people a joy
Isaiah 65:17–18

Secrets of the Divine

In John Michell's book *The Dimensions of Paradise*, he describes the New Jerusalem as the dodecahedron. This is the fifth platonic solid the Greeks called "ether" as it related to Spirit. It is this platonic form that was a closely guarded secret by the Greek Pythagoreans. If you look closely, you will see many of the items we have discussed in Chapter 3.

The New Jerusalem
Dodecahedron

WHERE DOES THAT LEAVE US?

"Sapere aude"
Dare to Know

This phrase was originally used by Horace (65 B.C.–8 B.C.), the great Latin poet, in his book, *Epistles*. The whole statement reads:

Dimidium facti qui coepit habet: sapere aude
He who has begun is half done: dare to know!

If you truly desire to know the attributes of the "One", you can begin by studying the stars along with nature. This is something that can be done outside the dogma of religion or any other belief structure as the "laws of nature" are always operating. In nature, you will find the true blueprint of creation and the signs to guide your understanding as you follow the same path and order as the "One" during creation. First, there is wisdom in the design which leads to understanding and finally knowledge.

The Lord by wisdom hath founded the Earth; by understanding hath he established the heavens. By his knowledge the depths are broken up and the clouds drop down the dew
Proverbs 4:19–20

No one understood this more than King Solomon. When God asked Solomon to tell him what he wanted, Solomon did not hesitate in asking for "wisdom" instead of wealth, honor, or riches (2Chronicles 1:7–10).

The Shekhinah is Coming

Don't let the dogma of religion and the schism between science and religion interfere with your understanding the Divine plan of creation and how you fit into that plan. As I have delineated in previous chapters, the various translations of sacred documents, along with the destruction of libraries, and cultures have all contributed to confining people within the box instead of viewing the bigger picture.

This is evident by certain words that are used and the connotation in the meaning of those words. For example, it can be disturbing how religion is preoccupied with the words "sin" and "fear". The word "fear" wasn't intended for one to be afraid, but to "be in awe" or have "reverence" for the Divine.

In Biblical Hebrew, the word for sin is *"het"* which means "to err" or "to miss the mark". The Greek word for "sin" is *"hamarto"* which means "to miss the mark". This would be similar to an arrow being shot at the bull's eye target, but misses the center mark. Sin is the same concept. The great Socrates believed that "ignorance" was a sin.

"Hamarto" is the Greek word that Paul used when he wrote:

For all have sinned (Hamarto), and come short of the glory of God
Romans 3:23

Of course we fall short of the glory of God. The Divine essence that created the Universe in which we live is considered perfect. I have shown you pictures of our Universe and where the solar system fits into the overall grand design. How could any human claim to be in the same league as this Divine essence? Of course we will always "MISS THE MARK" as we are not capable of such perfection.

The ancients knew that they were not perfect, but combined the study of geometry, astronomy, and music to obtain an understanding of the Divine, nature, and man defining how all could exist in harmony. Isn't it interesting that the Gnostics believed that sin was in creating the world and trapping the Divine "sparks of spirit" in the darkness, in the material prison of the human body? One of the reasons that Saint Irenaeus considered the Gnostics dangerous to the Christian movement was because they shared their personal experiences of interacting with the Divine. The Gnostics did this by following the ancient teachings of "walking the path."

Instead of the word "sin", another word to use is "iniquity". The meaning of "iniquity" is "unequal" and appears approximately three hundred times in the Bible. Isn't it far more meaningful to understand that we are "unequal" to the "One" rather than the connotation that we are morally evil? I think the real "sin" is when we believe that we are separate from the "One".

But your iniquities have separated between you and your God
Isaiah 59:2

We can't even comprehend nor do we have the vocabulary to understand the "One" or the "ineffable". Our scientists are only beginning to understand quantum physics and string theory. While technology and science are advancing exponentially, we are still falling short of the mark in creating a Universe which our scientists are forever exploring to understand how it all began.

In recent years, it has been proven that we are all united in energy and that our thoughts have an impact on the behavior of energy which encompasses celestial bodies as well. This body of work is known as the Unified Field Theory and ties in nicely with the latest mantra of "Change your Thoughts and you Change your Life." This is none other than the Law of Cause and Effect which Newton adopted from Galileo. Basically, the law states that nothing changes until there is a force applied to something. Or, for every action there is an equal and opposite reaction.

It is man's frontal lobe that uniquely separates him from other animals and God gave us dominion over our thoughts. Advanced research is being done not only on the brain, but how our thoughts can change energy outside of us. I believe Dr. Valerie Hunt from UCLA was the first to conduct studies on this phenomenon and documented in her book *Infinite Mind.* Additional work related to the brain is being conducted by Joe Dispenza, D.C. and documented in his book *Evolve Your Brain* as well as Daniel Amen, M.D. and his book *Change Your Brain Change Your Life*. There is also the fascinating work from the Institute of HeartMath in Boulder Creek, CA and the ongoing Global Consciousness Project.

Currently, outside of Geneva, Switzerland, twenty-member states representing the European Organization for Nuclear Research are in the process of conducting an experiment using the Large Hadron Collider (LHC), a particle accelerator. More commonly known as CERN, this world-wide effort is supported by the most highly skilled and gifted scientist of our time. They are looking for the sub-atomic particle better known as the "God Particle"—that substance that is found in all things. Remember the "Azoth" that the ancients called the universal medicine in Chapter 4? We saw how the symbol for this universal medicine was the caduceus in Chapter 8.

It is out of the CERN project that the World Wide Web (www) was born and initially called ENQUIRE. It was designed so that all the researchers on the project could share their information in real-time with the first web site going on-line in 1991.

Outside the CERN building is the statue of the Hindu Shiva dancing in a circle of flames. A gift from India, Shiva represents the cosmic symbol for life, death, and rebirth.

Nataraj
The Dancing Form of Lord Shiva
Unveiled on June 18, 2004

The first line in the gospel of John states, ***"In the beginning was the Word"*** (John 1:1). The Greek translation of "word" is "logos" a philosophical term for wisdom, reason, and discourse. It dealt with the principles governing the cosmos or the creative power of God. From Genesis, we know that this was the first source of God's activity in creation.

According to the Jewish philosopher, Judaeus Philo of Alexandria (15 B.C.–A.D. 45) in his book *De Profugis*, "the logos of the living God is the bond of everything, holding all things together and binding all the parts, and prevents them from being dissolved and separated" (Friedlander 1912, 114–115). Philo also taught that the "logos" was the intermediary between God and the cosmos.

Doesn't this sound like the "God particle" that CERN is searching for? Is it that illusive substance that binds everything together?

As John continues, he states, ***"And the Word was made flesh…full of grace and truth"*** (John 1:14). He goes on to say, ***"For the law was given by Moses, but grace and truth came by Jesus Christ"*** (John 1:17).

Even the Qur'an refers to Jesus as the "word" in three separate passages:

God gives you good news of John to confirm a word from God
Qur'an 3:39

…Behold, God gives you good news of a word from Him, who shall become known as the Messiah, Jesus, son of Mary…
Qur'an 3:45

…The Messiah, Jesus son of Mary, was only a messenger of God, and His word which He conveyed unto Mary…
Qur'an 4:171

Conclusively, Jesus is the Word, Grace, and Truth. And the words "truth and word" are linked to Jesus:

Jesus says … I am the truth
John 14:6

Jesus says …thy word is truth
John 17:17

Secrets of the Divine

...as the truth is in Jesus
Ephesians 4:21

...his name is called The Word of God
Revelation 19:13

The students of Pythagoras wore the "*Littera Pythagorae*" a symbol which represented the Greek letter "Upsilon" or "Y". It was said that the symbol represented the image of human life which was a central stem divided into two horns. The symbol signified the "power of choice" as the right branch led to "Divine wisdom" while the left branch led to "Earthly wisdom" reminding the student that Earth is a "free will" environment.

From the *Anthologia Latina*, it states:

> *Littera Pythagorae, discrimine secta bicorni, Humanae vitae speciem praeferre videtur. Nam via virtutis dextrum petit ardua callem. Difficilemque aditum primo spectantibus offert, Sed requiem praebet fessis in vertice summo. Molle ostentat iter via laeva, sed ultima meta. Praecipitat captos volvitque per aspera saxa. Quisquis enim duros casus virtutis amore. Vicerit, ille sibi laudemque decusque parabit. At qui desidiam luxumque sequetur inertem, Dum fugit oppositos incauta mente labores Turpis inopsque simul miserabile transiget aevum.*

Translation:

The Pythagorean letter, divided into two horns, seems to present an image of human life. For the steep way of virtue, to the right, offers the viewer a difficult approach up a mountainside, but at the top it provides the weary with rest. The left way shows s pleasant journey, but at the end it hurls down the trapped traveler among rough rocks. For whoever

> has conquered hardship from his love of virtue will be rewarded with praise and honor. But he, who follows a life of idle decadence, thoughtlessly skiving, will spend eternity or a lifetime poor, ugly, and miserable.

Both Saint Jerome and Saint Augustine wrote about the Pythagorean letter "Y" and the *Golden Verses* of Pythagoras. The concept expressed in the Pythagorean "Y" is what Jesus is referring to in John 14:6 when he says, ***"I am the way"***. Everything Jesus says is pointing us back to nature and numbers and how evolution proceeded from the "One". He is reminding us that ***"I and my Father are One"***, the yin-yang concept we discussed in Chapter 8. He is also emphasizing that making choices is an active process that involves opposing forces and we must take action to complete. Doesn't this sound like Galileo and Newton's Law of Cause and Effect? Is it the Gnostic ancient teachings of "walking the path"?

From a gematria point of view, the Hebrew words, "the way", "scales", and "victory" all have the same gematria value of 148. In Greek, you have the words "truth", "signs", "wonders", "miracles", and "the light" all having a gematria value of 264. All of these words are "the keys" to our discussion.

The right path (Pythagorean "Y") is referenced in both the Bible and the Qur'an:

Enter ye in at the strait gate: for wide is the gate, and broad is the way, that leadeth to destruction, and many there be which go in threat, because strait is the gate, and narrow is the way, which leadeth unto life, and few there be that find it

Matthew 7:13–14

Secrets of the Divine

The worldly life is made to seem attractive to the disbelievers who scoff at the faithful, but the pious, in the life hereafter, will have a position far above them. God grants sustenance to anyone He wants
Qur'an 2:212

Would that you knew what the uphill path is! It is the setting free of a slave or, in a day of famine, the feeding of an orphaned relative and a downtrodden destitute person, the believers who cooperate with others in patience, and kindness
Qur'an 90:12–17

I believe that one of our major purposes in life is to fully understand that we are a "spark" of the Divine essence and that we can learn to balance and harmonize our dual natures to reach union with the Divine (Hieros Gammos) by following "the way" left by the last great avatar, Jesus. Wasn't that really what our hero story in Chapter 8 was all about?

The Zohar discusses the polarity of the spiritual and the mundane when it states, "The difference, by means of which light, is distinguishable from darkness is by degree only; both are one in kind, and there is no light without darkness and no darkness without light" (Hoffman 1998, 25). This is another yin-yang concept.

When Jesus was baptized, the dove anointed him with the Divine wisdom. The dove carries the connotation of "pure" and usually shown as the symbol of the Holy Spirit or the Divine messenger. In Hebrew, the word for dove is "Yonah" with a gematria value of 801. Here again is the combination of the "1" and "8". Remembering that "1" is equal to Lord and "8"is equal to Jesus, he becomes the messiah or the anointed one. Notice that we normally see the "1" coming before the "8" when they are combined as we learned in Chapter 3, but here it is the reflection.

At the beginning of this book the question, "*What if this is truth?*" was asked. The Hebrew word for "truth" is written "emet" (תמא) and represents the letters Aleph, Mem, and Tav or the first, middle, and last letters of the Hebrew alphabet. Some scholars state that the word "emet" actually comes from the verb "aman" meaning support, firmness, stability, or security. This clearly supports the word "truth" when you consider the gematria for the word reduces it to "nine" meaning wholeness. It is also a palindrome with the word eternity as was discussed in Chapter 5.

The word "emet" also begins and ends with the first and last letters of the Hebrew alphabet, the Greek concept of "alpha and omega" we have discussed throughout this book where alpha is equal to "1" and omega is equal to "800" or "8" dropping the zeros. The references to the concepts "First and Last" or "Alpha and Omega" are clearly revealed throughout the Bible, but especially in the books of Isaiah and Revelation. Here are a few examples:

Who hath wrought and done it, calling the generations from the beginning? I the Lord, the first, and with the last; I am he
Isaiah 41:4

Thus saith the Lord the King of Israel, and his redeemer the Lord of hosts; I am the first, and I am the last, and beside me there is no God
Isaiah 44:6

Hearken unto me, O Jacob and Israel, my called; I am he; I am the first, I also am the last
Isaiah 48:12

Secrets of the Divine

And he said unto me, it is done. I am Alpha and Omega, the beginning and the end
Revelation 21:6

I am Alpha and Omega, the beginning and the end, the first and the last
Revelation 22:13

Throughout his ministry Jesus conveyed two essential keys by which to live by and they both related to "love": Love the Divine and Love thy neighbor. He didn't leave a list of commandments; he just wanted us to simply "see God in all things." And through understanding sacred geometry and numbers, it is possible to see God in all things.

Jesus said unto him, Thou shalt love the Lord thy God with all thy heart, and with all thy soul, and with all thy mind. This is the first and great commandment and the second is like unto it, Thou shalt love thy neighbour as thyself. On these two commandments hang all the laws and the prophets
Matthew 22:37–40

To "see as God sees" and feel Divine love was brilliantly shown in the movie *Avatar.* The film is set in the year 2154 on the fictional planet Pandora that is inhabited by the Na'vi, a blue-skinned humanoid that is ten foot tall. The Na'vi lives in harmony with both plants and animals along with great reverence for their planet. Their spiritualism revolves around a large tree that provides guidance and healing. The Na'vi has tails with sensitive ends and can connect to other Na'vi or animals so that they can "feel" another and be "one" with it. If you can disregard the other parts of the movie and concentrate on this aspect of the movie, you will walk away with a profound feeling of spirit and connection to the "One". Interestingly, the word "Navi" in Hebrew means "prophet". I also find the use of the word Pandora, the name of the planet, interesting as there was only one thing left in Pandora's jar and that was "hope", a nice subliminal message from the movie.

Jesus continually taught that the kingdom and spirit of God is within you and meditating on Him will lead your soul on its amazing journey. It is represented by that still small voice that was heard by many of the ancients including Elijah, Job, and Zechariah.

...and after the fire a still small voice
1Kings 19:12

...there was silence, and I heard a voice
Job 4:16

Be still, and know that I am God
Psalms 46:10

This still small voice is your soul and within the silence, a secret meeting takes place as the mortal communes with the immortal. It is a place well beyond the five senses of this world. Jesus tells us that this is where you will find the true kingdom. According to Hartmann, this is what the I.N.R.J.—"In Nobis Regnat Jesus" really meant: "Within ourselves reigns Jesus" (Hartmann 1919, 326).

...The kingdom of God cometh not with observation...the kingdom of God is within you
Luke 17:20–21

This is where the "light" can shine upon your "seed thoughts" and allow the silence to germinate them to be ignited by that same "charge" we discussed in Chapter 4 and become manifest in the physical world. Your soul is your "battery pack"—the electric force that sustains your life. Isn't that what Luke Skywalker of *Star Wars* was referring to when he said, "May the **Force** be with you"? I also find his last name very telling as well with what we are discussing in this work.

It is this "kingdom within" that relates to the Mer-Ka-Ba we discussed in Chapter 3. Practicing this form of meditation ignites your body's energy field and brings your body, spirit, and soul into alignment, balance, and harmony. It then becomes the "chariot" of ascension, the vehicle for Hieros Gammos.

Abstractly, this "kingdom within" was how Solomon constructed the First Temple. Solomon used his wisdom and knowledge of the "chariot" in designing the outer court, the inner court, and the holy of holies. Could this be why the Shekhinah was always present in Solomon's temple as the "Ever-present Light"?

While this still small voice might be invisible to us, it is certainly measurable. In 1907, Duncan MacDougall, M.D. of Haverhill, Massachusetts, demonstrated that the soul had mass and therefore could be measured in weight. Through his experiments with six patients, he was able to measure ¾ of an ounce (21 grams) decrease in a person's weight upon death. His work was published in the *New York Times* and *American Medicine*, a medical journal.

Behold my hands and my feet, that it is I myself; handle me and see; for a spirit has not flesh and bones, as ye see me have
Luke 24:39

Anyone that has been present with a loved one, when they die, witness an open mouth as the person exhales their last breath and the soul exits the body. Just as God breathe life into man and he became a living soul (Genesis 2:7), it stands to reason that upon death the soul exits the body in the same fashion. Remember, we are always in a cycle of life as everything in the Universe is always moving in some circular motion.

Then shall the dust return to the Earth as it was; and the spirit shall return unto God who gave it
Ecclesiastes 12:7

If someone gives you something, it is considered a gift, an expression of love. It is meant to be free without expectation of something in return. Considering this along with the discussion of breath, let's look at some gematria. The phrase "his mouth", referenced in Psalms 33:6, has a value of 96. The word "gift", referenced in John 4:10, has a value of 960. Equaling the same value, God gave us life as the "gift" from His mouth.

In Alexander Hislop's book, *The Two Babylons*, he quotes Major Moor on the Vedas, "Speaking of Brahma, it is expressly stated that 'all beings' are created from his mouth". The Vedas are the oldest sacred books that have been dated to 1500–1000 B.C. The word "Veda" comes from the Sanskrit word "Veda" meaning "knowledge" or "wisdom". The word "Brahma" is derived from the Sanskrit word "Brh" meaning "to grow" as in "expand" (Hislop 1999, 16). It appears that this identical concept has come down through the ages in various cultures and religions.

This life-giving breath was well known to the Egyptians and appeared in their art. Remember the discussion of the "ankh" in Chapter 8–Crux, the first decan of Libra? It symbolized their connection between "life" and "breath". Here's the picture again.

Ankh Giving Life

The Hebrew word for "breath" is "pneuma" with a numeric value of 576. The English word "spirit" comes from the Latin word "spiritus" which means "breath". It is this vital essence that animates our bodies. Interesting, the Greek word for eagle also has the numeric value of 576 and birds were used biblically to represent the Holy Spirit.

The Shekhinah is Coming

Even the Egyptian hieroglyph for soul was the Bau bird as shown in Chapter 8. The English word "pneumonia" comes from the Greeks meaning "to flow". If one has pneumonia, they have difficulty with air flowing in their lungs and without air (breath), there is no life. It appears that "spirit" and "breath" are related.

God is a Spirit: and they that worship Him must worship Him in spirit and in truth
John 4:24

The ancient Egyptians practiced a funeral ritual known as "The Opening of the Mouth Ceremony". Using a special tool called the adze; they would cut a slit over the mummy's mouth so the soul could be reanimated and continue to communicate with the family. It was the Egyptian belief in resurrection and the afterlife. This ritual is documented in the *Pyramid Texts*, on tombs, and the *Book of the Dead.* Many believe that this is parallel to Psalms 51:

Book of the Dead: ***"My mouth is opened by Ptah"***—(Ptah—Egyptian Supreme Being)

Psalms 51:15: ***"O Lord, open thou my lips; and my mouth shall shew forth thy praise"***

During the ceremony, the priest would recite various hymns. One hymn to Pa-nefer is:

"*Awake!...May you be alert as a living one, rejuvenated every day, healthy in millions of occasions of good sleep, while the gods protect you, protection being around you every day*" (McDowell 1999, 160).

Opening of the Mouth Ritual
Valley of the Kings
Thebes, Egypt

By the word of the Lord were the heavens made; and all the host of them by the breath of His mouth
Psalms 33:6

For this they willingly are ignorant of, that by the word of God the heavens were of old, and the Earth standing out of the water and in the water
2Peter 3:5

In more recent times, we have had numerous accounts of near-death experiences (NDE) that document the presence of a "being of light" or "a tunnel of light" during this transition and reported after an individual has been pronounced dead. The "light" is reported to be of an unusual, indescribable brilliance that emanates love. Today's scientific study on NDE began with Raymond Moody's book *Life After Life* in 1975 and has continued with Dannion Brinkley and his own personal NDE documented in *Saved by the Light*.

The ancients were also well aware of NDE. At the end of the *Republic*, Plato includes a NDE in "the myth of Er". Er returns from heaven after being dead for twelve days to be a witness to others regarding life after death and how that relates to choices one makes on their living path. Er speaks of the rewards for the just man and how nothing known on Earth can compare to the magnitude of heaven. Clearly, Plato and the Greeks believed in an afterlife.

There are many foundations that have been set up to study the NDE phenomenon with thousands of detailed individual reports. A simple internet search will provide a vast amount of information along with various books that have been written on this subject. Some of these stories are truly amazing. I personally like the work done by Brian Weiss, M.D. and Michael Newton, PhD.

Interestingly, the most reported experience that people share after a NDE is the overwhelming feeling of "love". Other experiences include how they view things differently and how they make different choices upon their return to the body. Additionally, they are no longer afraid to die as they know that another, more beautiful world exists for them.

Was it a NDE that Hieronymus Bosch experienced when he rendered this painting?

The Ascent of the Blessed
Hieronymus Bosch
Palazzo Ducale
Venice, Italy
ca. 1490

I see this picture as the "tunnel of light" that many have experienced during a NDE. To me this picture appears as a "reverse birth canal" with the circle emphasizing a return to the "One" as we are born into the afterlife. Maybe this is the original meaning behind the Christian's statement "they are reborn" or "born again".

Judaism believes in resurrection of the dead during the messianic age. In Hebrew, this time is referred to as *"Olam Ha-Ba"* (הַבָּא עוֹלָם) or "the World to Come". This principle is derived from Rabbi Moshe ben Maimon's (Rambam) *13 Principles of Faith*, which is a widely accepted list of Jewish beliefs. Maimon is better known to the secular world as Maimonides. The term "the world to come" first appeared in Enoch 71:15.

To the Muslim, death is an unavoidable part of life and so is judgement.

Every soul has to experience the taste of death. We test you with both hardships and blessings. In the end you will all return to Us
Qur'an 21:35

Based upon all the evidence presented, there is only one conclusion to be reached: "Jesus is the way" and his life has been documented in the original Divine writing of God: *THE STARS: HIS LIFE IN LIGHTS*. Regardless of where you live, the stars are free to gaze upon as no one can hide them or destroy them and they are exempt from the divisions of race, religion, culture, or creed. Maybe we should re-read Chapter 8 with new eyes.

Heaven is already here for those with eyes to see it. Search the living law not the written word
Gospel of Thomas

While the information presented in this work can be debated between subjective and objective, a vast amount of detail was presented to aim toward a quality of fact and reality. Can you step outside your box and take a new look? If you did nothing more than to consider sacred geometry, nature, the stars, and the gematria comparisons, it should give you pause to ponder "*what if?*" Will you make different choices now? What really is truth?

Magna est veritas et praevalet
The truth is great and shall prevail
Book of Edras
Vulgate Bible

TRUTH
Olin Warner–1896
Library of Congress

Symbolically, this image of "Truth" resembles the Pythagorean "Y". She is in the process of taking action by deciding what path to take as she looks between the mirror and the snake. Will she choose ego (mirror) or wisdom (snake)? Remember the picture of the Egyptians weighing the person's heart against Maat in Chapter 8? It was all about a person's choices during life on Earth that created the weight of the heart.

Much like the sphinx, the snake has been regarded as both negative and positive. On a positive note, the symbol of the snake meant wisdom or potent guardians. Even the Buddha was guarded by Naga, a snake, as he sat in meditation.

Buddha Meditating with Naga
Wall Painting in Laos Monastery

The Shekhinah is Coming

As you ponder *"what if"* and make your decisions, remember how often you daydream about the simplicity of your childhood when you could *"Wish Upon a Star"*. The second line of that famous Walt Disney song (Appendix P) says, "Makes no difference who you are" and ended with "your dreams come true."

Is there more to the stars? Are you not humbled when you view the stars? Could the stars be His Divine signature of "light" shinning the truth? What is your truth and what choice will you make? Some say that "time will reveal the truth", but can you afford to wait?

I call heaven and Earth to record this day against you, that I have set before you life and death, blessing and cursing; therefore <u>choose life</u>, that both thou and thy seed may live
Deuteronomy 30:19

This chapter began with the phrase "Dare to Know" and we have all heard the phrase that "knowledge is power". Along the road of life, don't we often wonder "why we are here" and "what's it all about"? Our choices are made based upon our personal beliefs and hopefully, if you have made it this far, you are pondering those beliefs. Regardless, there is no denying the enormous impact made by one individual that has lasted over two millennia.

Secrets of the Divine

WHAT IF AND THE FUTURE

Engraving–Mechanics Magazine–London, UK–1824
"Give me a place to stand on, and I will move the Earth"
δῶς μοι πᾶ στῶ καὶ τὰν γᾶν κινάσω
Archimedes
200 BC

We have come full circle as Pascal said, "That God is a circle, of which the center is everywhere and the circumference nowhere."

My goal in presenting this information was to give you the "leverage" to move your world and embark upon your soul's journey of true potential, leading to enlightenment. Can you use this information to begin to unlock the "keys of knowledge" and "the mysteries" for yourself just as Jesus showed his personification of the Divine knowledge?

Canst thou by searching find out God? Canst thou find out the Almighty unto perfection?
Job 11:7

Each one of us is a sort of Hercules, here to experience the human life in all its forms. This includes life's tests, trials, and challenges including pain and suffering which all contribute to our soul's growth. But, Hercules was also a hero which entitled him and us to blessings and rewards. Our soul's journey is not in vain as each of us has the opportunity to find the truth without anyone's approval. This journey can take us to new levels of understanding to enhance our lives.

That is what the Buddha did sitting under the shade of the Bodhi tree (pippala tree) and working on his spiritual awakening. It was during that time that he discovered his four noble truths:

1. The Noble Truth of Suffering
2. The Noble Truth of The Arising of Suffering
3. The Noble Truth of the Cessation of Suffering
4. The Noble Truth of The Path leading to the Cessation of Suffering

In the Gospel of Thomas, Jesus says, ***"I have cast fire upon the world, and see; I am guarding it until it blazes".*** **(Saying # 10)** He also informs us that, ***"I shall give you what no eye has seen and what no ear has heard and what no hand has touched and what has never occurred to the human mind".*** **(Saying # 17)**

That fire must be some spiritual awakening that is due to take place much like the Holy Spirit that came onto the apostles in Acts. Will that come in the form of some cosmic event during the 2012 alignment? No one really knows, but could that be why there is so much space exploration taking place that is happening without much fan fare? Are our scientist trying to obtain an "advance warning" of a cosmic event as it would allow a small window of opportunity for the citizens of Earth to react?

This book has detailed many stars, but did you know that when a star dies, it burst into radioactive light that is a million, trillion times brighter than our Sun? This burst of gamma rays is the most powerful force in the Universe that only last a few milliseconds but travels at the speed of light. First detected in 1967, these bursts of light beamed massive amounts of energy in two narrow, oppositely-directed jets. On a recent *20/20* television broadcast, this phenomenon was listed as the seventh deadliest threat to humanity and the Earth. If this happened near Earth, it would appear as if there were two Suns in the sky and the protective ozone layer would be destroyed and the gamma rays would penetrate the Earth killing the very molecules of all life.

The Hubble Space Telescope recently discovered the largest known star which has been named Pistol. And isn't it fire that ignites a pistol? Scientist believes the Pistol star to be one hundred times as massive as our Sun and ten million times as bright. Considering our Sun is three hundred times more massive than Earth, I find these numbers hard to comprehend don't you? According to the NASA website, "They are unsure how this massive star was formed or how it will act in the future." Pistol is located at the center of our galaxy and would be visible to the naked eye if it weren't for all the cosmic dust.

Is this an announcement like the Star of Bethlehem? Or is this the Wormwood Star from the book of Revelation 8:10–11? Does this star have anything to do with the 2012 alignment?

The Shekhinah is Coming

Isaiah also speaks of a bright light in the end times, when he says:

Moreover the light of the Moon shall be as the light of the Sun, and the light of the Sun shall be sevenfold, as the light of seven days, in the day that the Lord bindeth up the breach of his people, and healeth the stroke of their wound
Isaiah 30:26

Can you imagine the Moon being as bright as the Sun or the Sun being sevenfold times seven days brighter? Does this sound like the Pistol star found by NASA? Remembering what we learned in Chapter 5 related to order and harmony as well as where we live in the Universe, Isaiah's statement of "what is to come" would certainly disrupt that balance and drastically change life as we know it.

Pistol Star and Nebula
Hubble Space Telescope • NICMOS

Maybe the Pistol star is the Shekhinah reappearing, the Divine glory of God that dwelled in the Tabernacle and Solomon's Temple. Some interesting gematria related to this discussion is the Hebrew phrases "to give light" and "Shekhinah" are both equal to 256.

Even the Qur'an makes reference to the Shekhinah as a sign:

And their messenger said to them: Verily! The sign of his kingdom is that there shall come to you At-Tabut (the lost Ark), wherein is Sakhinah from your Lord and a remnant of that which Moses and Aaron left behind, carried by the angels. Verily, in this is a sign for you if you are indeed believers

Qur'an 2:248

The Shekhinah is Coming

Documentation from all ancient cultures holds a belief that as each cycle changes, one ending and one beginning, that the cycles alternate between water and fire. In addition, this same documentation states that the water cycle has already transpired.

And I will remember My covenant, which is between Me and you and every living creature of all flesh; and the waters shall no more become a flood to destroy all flesh
Genesis 9:15

So, is it time for the fire cycle? Could that be what Jesus is referring to in the Gospel of Thomas referenced earlier?

We have seen how the cycles appear to "go in a circle" so doesn't it make sense that if we began with "Light", in essence a fire, that we will end with "Light" or fire? Biblically, references to "light" alone abound in both the Old and New Testaments as I have found over one hundred. Even the one that sits upon the white horse called Faithful and True has eyes that are ***"flames of fire"*** (Revelation 19:11–12).

In Chapter 5, we discussed the palindrome and how comparisons can be made in a reflective way. The Hebrew word "*Shabbos*" (Sabbath) has a gematria value of 702 which is the reflection of the Hebrew word "*ohr*" (light), a value of 207. So, you have the Sabbath, meaning "Divine rest" meditating on the "light". Isn't this what was discussed in Chapter 10? Is this "light" or "fire" the God particle that CERN is searching for?

Let's review some of the greatest mysteries that took place in ancient history and how many times it involved "fire" or "light".

Chaos–State 2
Wenzel Hollar
17th Century

The "breaking forth of light" was the first act of creation. This Hebrew phrase has a gematria value of 528 which is the same as the Hebrew word "key". This clearly identifies "light" or "fire" in a very lofty place. Remember we are looking for "the keys of knowledge" and "the mysteries".

According to Manly P. Hall, the word pyramid is "derived from the ancient Greek word πῦρ (pŷr) meaning 'fire', thus signifying that it is the symbolic representation of the One Divine Flame, the life of every creature" (Hall 1928, 116). Let's look at some comparisons.

Pyramid–Egypt

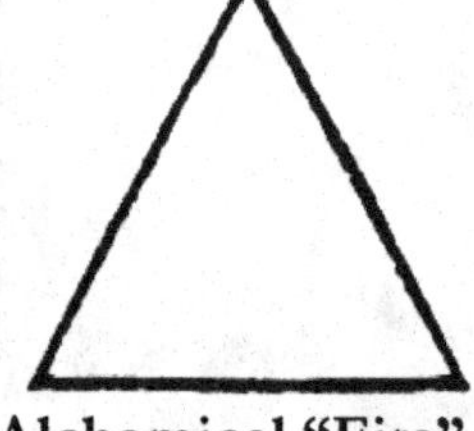

Alchemical "Fire"

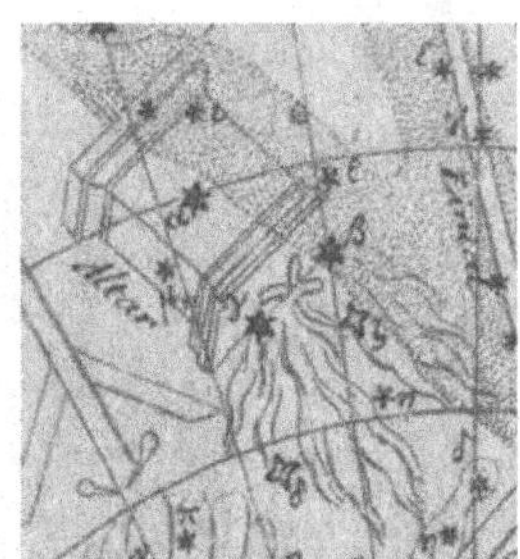

Constellation Ara

The sides of the pyramid are shaped like equilateral triangles which we have already learned is the alchemical symbol for "fire" and the constellation Ara is the altar of "fire" used in sacrifices to the gods. At the height of the Egyptian civilization, the pyramids were covered in highly polished white limestone that shone like gold in the Sun and seen from far distances. It was said to be "blinding". Interestingly, in the *Book of the Dead*, the pyramids are called "The Light".

I find this fascinating when you consider that the pyramids are the only surviving wonder of the ancient world. In addition, the ancients left information that clearly directs our attention to Egypt. We are also guided by Jeremiah that there are "signs" in Egypt as was discussed in Chapter 7. I don't think this is a coincidence.

Reference to the shape of the fire symbol brings up the discussion of the "Delta of Enoch" as it was shaped like the equilateral triangle with the name of the Divine written upon it. There was also the hand position of the Priestly Blessing that forms the equilateral triangle and sent "rays of light" upon the children of Israel during times of blessings. In Chapter 4, we learned that this hand position resembled the Hebrew letter "shin" which looks like a flame of fire. We will discuss "shin" a little later in this Chapter.

We are told, in both the Bible and the Qur'an, that one of the first uses of fire by God to make a point was the destruction of

Sodom. Lot was warned to leave with his family during the night as the city was destroyed at dawn along with its unrepentant inhabitants. Lot was Abraham's nephew and survived the city's destruction along with his two daughters.

Then the Lord rained upon Sodom and upon Gomorrah brimstone and fire from the Lord out of heaven
Genesis 19:24

Lot, we are the Messengers of your Lord. They (the unbelievers) will never harm you. Leave the town with your family in the darkness of night and do not let any of you turn back. As for your wife, she will suffer what they (unbelievers) will suffer. Their appointed time will come at dawn. Surely dawn is not far away!
Qur'an 11:81

The Shekhinah is Coming

Destruction of Sodom and Gomorrah
John Martin–1852
Laing Art Gallery
Newcastle, England

As Moses is tending to the sheep, a burning bush catches his attention as it is not consumed by the flames. As he approaches, he is instructed by a voice to take off his sandals as this is "holy ground". Moses then receives instruction from the voice on the bringing of the Israelites out of Egypt.

Moses and the Burning Bush
Holman Bible
1890

And the angel of the Lord appeared unto him in a flame of fire out of the midst of a bush: and he looked, and beholds, the bush burned with fire, and the bush was not consumed
Exodus 3:2

Looking at the gematria related to this passage, we have YHVH and the phrase "appeared unto him" both equal to 26. The gematria value for "holy ground" is also 26.

After the children of Israel are freed from their Egyptian oppression, they journey into the desert. Moses again visits the "burning bush" and receives the Torah. After spending time on the mountain, Moses' countenance begins to shine. When he rejoins the rest of his people, they are afraid to look upon him, because he is brightly shinning like the Sun.

Moses Face Shone Like the Sun
Gemalde von Jose Ribera
1638

When Aaron and all the children of Israel saw Moses, behold, the skin of his face shone; and they were afraid to come nigh him
Exodus 34:29

In art, Moses' shining face is depicted with rays of light coming off his head or with horns. References to Moses abound in the Qur'an as he is mentioned more often than any other individual, especially in his dealings with the Pharaoh.

They were wicked people. When the Truth from Us came, they called it simply magic
Qur'an 10:75–76

Isn't this an interesting comment from the Qur'an? Especially, since the Church accused people of doing "magic" as a way to condemn and punish them. This goes along with our discussion in Chapter 1 and how the Church wanted to control the people.

While in the desert, the children of Israel constructed a tabernacle unto their God. The tabernacle is protected by a cloud during the day and a column of fire by night. This cloud also guides their journey in the desert.

The Shekhinah is Coming

The Tabernacle in the Wilderness
Holman Bible
1890

Then a cloud covered the tent of the congregation, and the glory of the Lord filled the tabernacle
Exodus 40:34

...it were the appearance of Fire, until the morning
Numbers 9:15

Moreover thou leddest them in the day by a cloudy pillar; and in the night by a pillar of fire, to give them light in the way wherein they should go
Nehemiah 9:12

Moses referred to the Israelites as stiff-necked as they were always complaining. When they continued to complain, they angered the Lord. In anger, He sends fire to consume the disgruntled ones. It was only when Moses prayed unto the Lord that the fire was quenched.

The fire of the Lord burnt among them and consumed them that were in the uttermost parts of the camp
Numbers 11:1

Aaron, Moses' brother, is also reference in the Qur'an. In Arabic, Aaron is called Harun and usually appears alongside his brother. As Levites representing the priesthood, Aaron's sons Nadah and Abihu suffer and die when disobedient to the Lord. They are consumed by fire for offering unauthorized fire upon the altar instead of incense.

Aaron's sons Nadah and Abihu offer unholy fire and die
Matthaus Merian

And there went out fire from the Lord and devoured them and they died before the Lord
Leviticus 10:1–2

As we learned in Chapter 9, when the Israelites crossed the Jordan River into Canaan, Joshua was their leader and Eleazar was the High Priest. In a continual choice to be in alignment with God, Joshua would consult and receive guidance and direction from the High Priest. The breastplate would light up and reflect the Hebrew letters that were appropriate for his inquiry.

And he (Joshua) shall stand before Eleazar the priest, who shall ask counsel for him after the judgement of Urim before the Lord: at his word shall they go out, and at his word they shall come in, both he, and all the children of Israel with him, even all the congregation
Numbers 27:21

In reference to the breastplate, Josephus writes, "For so great a splendor shone forth from them before the army began to march, that all the people were sensible of God being present for their assistance. Whence it came to pass that those Greeks, who had veneration for our laws, because they could not possibly contradict this, called the breastplate 'the Oracle'" (*Antiquities 8:59:9*).

The High Priest
Breastplate Glowing

The Shekhinah is Coming

Did you know that all the sacred items used in the Temple were made with gold or covered in gold? Even the High Priest Breastplate had threads of pure gold weaving through the material. Was the gold the conduit that created the "light" of the breastplate?

The symbol for gold was a circle with a dot in the center ⊙ which was the same as the astrological sign for the Sun that provides both light and life. It looks like the bull's eye target we discussed in Chapter 10. In Hebrew, the gematria value for the word "gold" is 15 while the word "golden" in Greek is 1500 aligning with the value of the Greek words "light" and "life".

In Hebrew, the word "life" is "chai" with a gematria value of 18. The Hebrew word for "maker" has a gematria value of 180. Here again is the combined "One" and "8 = Jesus" clearing identifying our origin. Remember in Chapter 3, Jesus was often depicted in ancient art sitting within the vesica piscis and the title of the art would include the word "majesty"? We learned that "majesty" also has a gematria value of 18, another combination. Here are some more keys of the "One" and "8" combinations in Greek: "The Holy Spirit" when added and the "Kingdom of God", "truth", and "great" when multiplied.

Chai–Life

For approximately eighty years, the children of Israel oscillated between their God and Baal, the god of the Canaanites. Elijah summons all the people to Mt. Carmel where he challenged both sides to call upon their God. Whichever God answered with fire would end the dispute and identify the supreme One. Elijah was then challenged by the tribe of Moab. Elijah answered the challenge by stating he was a man of God and proved it by calling down fire from heaven and consumed all who challenged him.

Elijah Calling Fire Down from Heaven
Destroys the Messengers of Ahaziah
Dore's English Bible
1866

The Shekhinah is Coming

Elijah answered and said to the captain of fifty, if I be a man of God, then let fire come down from heaven, and consume thee and they fifty. And there came down fire from heaven and consumed him and his fifty.
2Kings 1:10

Elijah is also one of Islam's prophets and listed in the Qur'an. In Arabic, he is called Ilyas or Elyas. Throughout his life, Elijah served God faithfully. He was awarded for his faith and taken into heaven by a whirlwind of fire. This is the Mer-ka-ba or chariot we discussed in Chapter 3. When Elijah ascends to heaven, he drops his powerful cloak for Elisha to use. In Arabic, Elisha is called Al-Yasa' and is mentioned as one of the Islamic prophets in the Qur'an.

Prophet Elijah and his Fiery Ascent
Joaquim Goncalves da Rocha
1812

And it came to pass, as they still went on, and talked, that behold, there appeared a chariot of fire, and horses of fire, and parted them both asunder; and Elijah went up by a whirlwind into heaven
2Kings 2:11

The Shekhinah is Coming

King David ruled in Judea for some time, but it was his son Solomon who built the great temple for the Lord. Solomon's temple was blessed and forever filled with Divine light.

The Zohar states, "I will place My mishkan in your midst…My mishkan is Shekhinah" (Matt 1983, 153). Mishkan means "to dwell" and was the word used when referring to both the desert Tabernacle and Solomon's Temple.

The Ever Present
Temple of Solomon
William Brassey Hole
Bible Picture Gallery

Secrets of the Divine

...for the glory of the Lord had filled the house of God
2Chronicles 5:13

We know that the first act of creation was "light" and the closest light to Earth is the Sun. We learned in Chapter 1 that the ancients worshiped the Sun as representative of God and we learned in Chapter 5 that the Sun's diameter is 864,000 miles. Here are some interesting gematria words and phrases that equal 864.

In Hebrew, the phrases "the Sun shines" and "Holy of Holies" equal 864. In Greek, the phrase "God is fire" and the words "Jerusalem" and "topstone" equal 864. We are also told in Revelation that the New Jerusalem will be 864,000,000 furlongs in a cube shape.

According to Manly P. Hall, "the name Solomon may be divided into three syllables, SOL–OM–ON, symbolizing light, glory, and truth collectively and respectively. The Temple of Solomon is, therefore, first of all 'the House of Everlasting Light', its earthly symbol being the temple of stone on the brow of Mount Moriah" (Hall 1928, 574).

Hall's statement contains both the "Sol for Sun" and the "OM of the Hindu original creation symbol" we discussed in Chapter 5. All something to consider the next time you watch a beautiful sunset.

Within Solomon's Temple, the Ark of the Covenant was the dwelling place of the Shekhinah. It is the same as the pillar of fire that protected the Israelites in the desert. The Talmud teaches that the Shekhinah is present during prayer, "Whenever ten are gathered for prayer, there the Shekhinah rests" (Talmud Sanhedrin 39a). This is similar to the Christian belief stated in Matthew:

For where two or three are gathered together in My name, there am I in the midst of them
Matthew 18:20

The Ark and the Mercy Seat
Treasures of the Bible
Henry Davenport Northrop–1894

In the book of Daniel 3:1–30, we are informed that Nebuchadnezzar had made an image of gold. Upon presenting the image to his people, he commanded that upon hearing the sound of music that all should fall down and worship the image or be cast into a burning fiery furnace. There were three Jews, namely Shadrach, Meshach, and Abednego that refuse to worship this golden image. Nebuchadnezzar was furious and demanded that the furnace be heated seven times hotter. The three men were then bound and cast into the burning fiery furnace.

When Nebuchadnezzar gazed into the furnace, he saw four men walking in the fire unharmed. The fourth man had the form of the Son of Man. Nebuchadnezzar was so astounded that he called the men out of the fiery furnace and made a decree that no one could speak against their God again and promoted the three men.

Shadrach, Meshach, and Abednego
Nebuchadnezzar's Fiery Furnace
Simeon Solomon–1863

The Shekhinah is Coming

In His last attempt to show that "life" and "light" were related, Jesus is transformed into His "light body" during the transfiguration. This is "enlightenment", the transformation of the body into light. Could this process of transformation been the markings left on the Shroud of Turin? In Buddhism and Hinduism, enlightenment is a blessed state in which the individual transcends desire and suffering to attain Nirvana—a state of bliss. We saw these images in Chapter 5.

Through this process, Jesus' face had shown like Moses after he descended the mountain with the Torah. And look who is standing on each side of Jesus. It is the two prophets, Elijah and Moses, who most knew about the true meaning of the element "fire".

His face shone like the Sun and his clothes brilliant white
Matthew 17:2–3 and Luke 9:28–31

The Transfiguration
James Joseph Jacques Tissot
Brooklyn Museum
New York City

Jesus—Flanked by Elijah and Moses
On the Ground: Peter, John, and James

The Shekhinah is Coming

Before Jesus leaves Earth and ascends, he instructs His apostles to meet him in the upper room. He has promised to leave each one with a comforter. This comforter is "fire".

In Acts 2:1–4, it states: ***And when the day of Pentecost was fully come, they were all with one accord in one place. And suddenly there came a sound from heaven as of a rusting mighty wind, and it filled all the house where they were sitting. And there appeared unto them cloven tongues like as of fire, and it sat upon each of them. And they were all filled with the Holy Ghost, and began to speak with other tongues, as the Spirit gave them utterance.***

Pentecost
Manuel Perez Paredes
Nuestro Senor del Veneno Temple
Mexico City, Mexico

It appears that "Fire" is the ultimate "sign" of God's presences as stated in Deuteronomy 4:24 ***"For the Lord thy God is a consuming fire"*** and Hebrews 12:29 ***"For our God is a consuming fire".*** In describing the relationship between the physical and the spiritual, the Zohar states: "If one wishes to know the wisdom of the holy unification, let him look at the flame rising from a burning coal or from a kindled lamp. The flame cannot rise unless it is unified with something physical" (Kaplan 1997, 63).

"Light" is synonymous with "fire" as fire is defined as a chemical change that releases heat and light. It is a feeling of intensity that is synonymous with passion. It is an active process of change that can be a severe ordeal or an inspiration. Clearly, this process has dominated some key junctures or decision points described throughout scripture. There are so many references to "light" in art, in scripture, and in symbols. So, we have been left with numerous "signs". I doubt anyone can deny that "light" is one of the "keys of knowledge". Is it any wonder that the ancients worshipped the Sun?

Dating to the late eighth century B.C. and included in Hesiod's *Theogony*, myth tells us that "fire" was given to the human race by Prometheus, who stole it from Zeus. Fire is considered the most powerful of the four elements as it is both a life-giver and a death-bringer. We know from the Bible that "fire" was also the first element of creation in the form of "light". It was also "fire" that shaped this Earth during the primitive volcanic times. The heat from that process is now part of the lower mantle where it circulates. As our planet cooled and life was produced, "fire" kept people warm and cooked their food. "Fire" also produced pots from fired clay, tools, and weapons. "Fire" is definitely responsible for the advancement of civilization. In an age of prolific nuclear weapons and world leaders' quest for power, will "fire" be the death-bringer?

The Shekhinah is Coming

From all the "light" and "fire" examples presented, you can see how the outcome was either positive or negative based upon "choice". Is this why the "Dancing Shiva" is dancing in a circle of fire outside the CERN building?

As we leave this discussion, let's take a final look at the Tetragrammaton and how "fire" is related to it.

יהוה

YHVH—THE TETRAGRAMMATON
"HaShem—The Name"

Some scholars take the Tetragrammaton and add the letter "shin" in the middle rendering it YHShVH, for Jesus, as the "shin" image is symbolic of a "flame". When this is done, it is called the Pentagrammaton, a Greek word meaning five-lettered name. It is the Greek concept of "ether" and "spirit's" descent into matter. Remembering our discussion in Chapter 1, the Tetragrammaton is symbolic of the four elements where Yod is Fire, Heh is Water, Vav is Air, and Heh is Earth. In his book, *De Verbo Mirifico (Concerning the Miraculous Word)*, Johannes Reuchlin (1455–1522) explores the Pentagrammaton in detail as he called it "the wonder-working word".

Shin—The Eternal Flame
The Changeless Divine Essence of God

Secrets of the Divine

The Hebrew work known as *Sefer Ha-Temunah (Book of the Image)* discusses the theory of "Shemittot" or "cosmic cycles" which deals with the Hebrew alphabet as an expression of God's manifestations. According to Edward Hoffman, this book "teaches that one letter is currently missing from the Hebrew alphabet. Every seeming defect that we see in the cosmos is mysteriously linked to this missing consonant, which will become manifest in the future. Some Jewish mystics have suggested that this unknown letter is a 'Shin' with four prongs" (Hoffman 1998, 82).

In Judaism, Shin begins the word "Shaddai", meaning "almighty" and is the name of God that was known to Abraham, Isaac, and Jacob.

And I appeared unto Abraham, unto Isaac, and unto Jacob, by the name of God almighty, but by my name Jehovah was I not known to them
Exodus 6:3

Shin is also the "sign" formed during the Priestly Blessing as shown in Chapter 4. Shin is also the beginning of the words shalom and Shabbat. Shalom, meaning peace, reminds us of the city of peace, Jerusalem and Shabbat means Sabbath, the sacred time of rest and Divine thought.

In John 14:13–14, Jesus instructs us to ***"ask in my name"*** when we pray. In Aramaic, it is the word "shema", another word beginning with "shin", which is used in this phrase. The word "shema" carries the connotation of listen, hear, or do. It's about obedience and our relationship with God and the ultimate blessings that follow. This is clearly shown in Daniel.

And the kingdom and dominion, and the greatness of the kingdom under the whole heaven, shall be given to the people of the saints of the most High, whose kingdom is an everlasting kingdom, and all dominions shall serve and obey him
Daniel 7:27

We need to peal the film from our eyes and transform our thoughts into the "light" by seeking the truth through meditation and understanding the mysteries to unfold our enlightened soul. It is a cycle that is much like the metamorphosis of the caterpillar into the butterfly. What once was an egg turns into a beautiful creature that feeds primarily on the nectar of flowers. Hopefully, I have provided you with some nectar to feed your mind and soul.

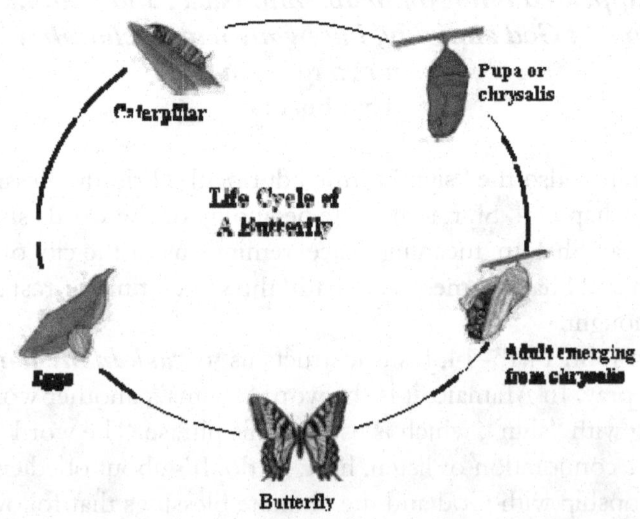

http://www.kwiz.com/

Secrets of the Divine

Along with the analogy of the butterfly, there is a concept known as the "Butterfly Effect" or "sensitive dependence on initial conditions". This concept is related to chaos theory and the work done by Edward Lorenz. Basically, it states that a small difference or change (the movement of the butterfly's wings) in a dynamic system can produce a larger change impacting many, like the domino effect.

Take a moment to think about this. How small that movement of the butterfly's wings would be and how great the resulting changes? How would this open our minds to the bigger picture and change our soul's journey? Have you embarked upon a new path? In a time of great world division and strife, can you see that humanity's beliefs are really more alike than different? I have given numerous references from all the major religions (Islam, Judaic, Christianity, Buddhist, and Hinduism) to demonstrate that very point. Just remember that the circle equaled "One", "unity", and "love" and everything began with it.

So, where does all of this leave us? My first hope would be that you would never look at the numbers "1" and "8" again without thinking that they are "signs" for something greater. A second hope would be that what you see in nature will be with new eyes. My final hope would be that your thoughts and choices would be considered with great care.

In Hosea 2:15, the phrase ***"Door of Hope"*** is used. In Hebrew, the letter "D" (ד) is spelled "daled" and means "doorway" and "knowledge". In the dictionary, the synonyms listed include "portal" and "gateway".

A door is nothing more than an access or transition from one place to another. It is our opportunity to reconcile with the "One" and embrace what we have learned. As some would say, that means "atonement" or "at–*one*–ment", recognizing that we are not separate from the Divine and remembering where and how everything originated from the "One". It is keeping spiritual awareness in our mind and thoughts as well as "to see as God sees" which will lead to a heart filled with "love". Remember, Jesus left us with only two commandments and both were about "love". We feel "love" in our hearts, that amazing organ with no limits on the amount of love one can give or take in. Does that make "love" the greatest "light" of all?

Siehe! ich stehe vor der Thüre und klopfe an.
Offenb. 3,20.

Behold, I stand at the door, and knock: if any man hear my voice, and open the door, I will come in to him, and will sup with him, and he with me
Revelation 3:20

Just as the breastplate was the mediator between God and the children of Israel, so Jesus is now the mediator, our doorway. In Greek, the phrase "mediator between God and Man" has a gematria value of 3168 matching the Greek words "Lord Jesus Christ".

For there is one God and one mediator between God and men, the man Christ Jesus
1Timothy 2:5

Look at the view of Earth, the beautiful "blue marble" first photographed by the Apollo 17 crew, the last manned lunar mission, in 1972. It is a circle representing the "One". Does this not change your view about the interconnectedness of life on Earth as we float in space? What could be a bigger "sign" than this?

God shall bless us and all the ends of the Earth shall fear (revere) him
Psalms 67:7

The Blue Marble–2000

There is only one final question: "So *what if* this is Truth"?

And ye shall know the truth, and the truth shall make you free

John 8:32

352 = "The Way"

352 = "The Light"

OR

352 = 3 + 5 + 2 = 10 = 1 = "The One"

Secrets of the Divine

We have returned to the "ONE" and our "sign" is the everlasting stars in the night sky. We have come "full circle" on our path to apotheosis.

ABOUT THE AUTHOR

One's life journey is usually dynamic with many twist and turns and mine is no exception. As we all believe that we plan our lives with various goals, we are often surprised at how things turn out when we take the time to reflect. For me, where I am today in my life is nowhere near what I was preparing for when I left the parental nest to begin directing my own life and making my own independent choices.

It was over 30 years ago when I completed my formal education with a BS and MBA in Business Administration while concurrently embarking on my professional career in the financial arena of healthcare and beginning my own family. For me, it was a dream come true and time past as life became a routine that was both fulfilling and enjoyable.

Through my experiences, I had developed a core belief that success was based upon material possessions and what one had accomplished in life was measured by education, career, and the people that you knew. I seemed to be living this dream as my husband and I had been extremely fortunate in all areas of our life. I believed that through continued hard work that things would maintain and the ultimate reward would be one of coasting into retirement while enjoying my grandchildren.

In 1996 that all changed and my dream died. I was jolted out of my comfort zone of life and confronted with some major life changing events that I was unprepared to deal with. My husband and I separated after a 25+ year marriage and headed down the slippery slope to the divorce courts. It was purely agonizing as everything crashed around me. No longer was I in reach of that retirement dream.

The Shekhinah is Coming

I was totally lost, stripped of my identity of who I thought I was. I was in the agony of the "valley of despair" as I struggled to find the answers to the life changing events that were occurring. I felt hopeless and had no idea what to expect as it felt like someone else was in control of my life, making all the choices, and I could not get off the train. At one point, I was suicidal as I didn't have the tools to cope with what was being expressed in my life.

I needed to find some strength to continue with life. I kept thinking of the prophet Job and his struggles as I read:

With the ancient is wisdom, and in length of days understanding. With Him is wisdom and strength, He hath counsel and understanding
Job 12:12–13

Somehow, I garnered my strength and stumbled onto a spiritual path and a study of ancient wisdom. It became an inward search and a journey of evaluating my core beliefs with what I was learning from this ancient knowledge and what was happening in my life. My studies became a catalyst to see things differently. It was like I stepped out of my old life and was awakened into something fresh and new as I remembered the words of Emerson who said, "What lies before us and what lies behind us is but a small matter compared to that, which lies within us". He also said "What we know is a point to what we do not know" (Emerson 2007, 55).

This inward search opened doors to subjects and disciplines that were totally foreign to me and not part of my accepted truths or what I had learned growing up. I had always known that we had two guarantees in life, dying and paying taxes, but I discovered that there was a new guarantee and that was CHANGE.

Secrets of the Divine

As I stopped reacting and resisting change, I found the courage to face my fears and embrace my faith in the supreme being of creation. As I was able to do this, Spirit provided the synchronicity of events that have enriched and enlightened my life and brought me into my soul awareness.

I had learned from Rev. Fred Price, Faith Dome (Los Angeles) that FEAR stood for "False Evidence Appearing Real." As I changed my beliefs, my reality shifted as I was no longer limiting myself to the black and white box I had been living in. My new spiritual insight became a vehicle for change by expanding my knowledge and my world view. I was now walking in the world of "faith" as opposed to the "material".

I was learning to balance my outward life with my internal thoughts and began to move forward in life. I was learning to trust in the flow of life and how to co-exist in harmony with it rather than to make choices out of fear and judgement. My new way of looking at life was helping me to heal both my physical and emotional pain.

I became an ordained minister after completing a two-year certification program in spiritual studies with an emphasis in healing. I have continued with extensive training in this arena which has encompassed several different healing modalities. Spirit has blessed me with being a conduit in helping others as well as healing my own self from three painful conditions, one being cancer.

I continued my in-depth study to expand my own self awareness, understanding, and the searching out of deeper truths. This culminated with a pursuit of a Ph.D. in Philosophy with a concentration in ancient wisdom which I completed in 2003. I have gained tremendously from my studies and at the same time I have been humbled by them. What I thought where major differences in the major religions was wrong. When you begin with ancient wisdom, you see how they are more alike than different. It's like the old saying "Many roads lead to Rome".

My journey has been quite amazing and while it may appear that I have reached a level to eliminate challenges in my life, this is not true. As long as we live in the third dimension, we all struggle with the challenges of life be they relationships, finances, politics, or just the pressure of watching the daily world events on TV.

If you can change how you view challenges and learn to embrace them, you begin to see them as opportunities to grow and expand. I continue to remind myself what EGO really means: "Edging God Out". Ego will keep you in the illusion and hinders your growth. My friends will tell you that I continually say, "Everything is in Divine right order" and that there are no accidents or coincidences.

I now know that one must learn to balance their worlds, the material (mundane) with the spiritual. It goes back to the saying "Living in the World, but not being of the World" as similarly stated in Romans 12:2. We must constantly remember that we are "Spirit" here to have an earthly and human experience. When all is said and done, we will return to Spirit.

Daily, one must make the commitment to honor who we are– "Spirit". One of my spiritual teachers is Jimmy Twyman and while on retreat in Joshua Tree, CA, Jimmy was constantly reminding us, "To See as God Sees". We chanted this phrase throughout the retreat. This powerful little phrase echoes in my ears daily, especially when I get upset about something that is really meaningless in the grand scheme of things. Let this phrase be a mantra for you as well to help transverse difficult challenges.

There are many avenues to maintaining balance. For myself, I am constantly reading and searching out new pieces of the puzzle, attending seminars, and visiting sacred sites around the world. I love visiting sacred sites, as I believe that they hold the energies of the ancients that once lived in these areas and it is an opportunity to tap into that energy and experience new levels of information. But really, all one has to do is view what is around us every day in nature and in the heavens.

Nightly, I would stare at the beautiful painting above my fireplace trusting and asking for guidance. Spirit would enter my thoughts and give me flashes on what to include in this book. I am humbled by what I have received and find it fitting that this amazing painting has become the cover of this book.

I am honored to share with you what I have learned over this time. It is my goal that the information provided within this book, will open your heart to your own truth and allow you to step out of the "box" that has been created by the world we live in, not by "Spirit".

I believe in the words of Aristotle when he wrote the opening line of *The Metaphysics*, "All men naturally desire to know". Like the great philosopher Pythagoras, I am a lover of wisdom especially since my own Greek heritage is traceable to the ancient lands where I have distant relatives living today in both Greece and Turkey.

Study to shew thyself approved unto God, a workman that needeth not to be ashamed, rightly dividing the word of truth
2Timothy 2:15

I AM a Seeker of Truth & Wisdom
Valjean Tchakirides, Ph.D.

φ α λ ι ε α ν

Placentia, CA
2010

LIST OF APPENDIXES

APPENDIX A

NICENE CREED

First Council of Nicea (325)	First Council of Constantinople (381)
We believe in one God, the Father Almighty, Maker of all things visible and invisible.	We believe in one God, the Father Almighty, Maker *of heaven and earth, and* of all things visible and invisible.
And in one Lord Jesus Christ, the Son of God, begotten of the Father [the only-begotten; that is, of the essence of the Father, God of God], Light of Light, very God of very God, begotten, not made, being of one substance with the Father;	And in one Lord Jesus Christ, the only-begotten Son of God, *begotten of the Father before all worlds (æons)*, Light of Light, very God of very God, begotten, not made, being of one substance with the Father;
By whom all things were made [both in heaven and on earth];	by whom all things were made;
Who for us men, and for our salvation, came down and was incarnate and was made man;	who for us men, and for our salvation, came down from heaven, and was incarnate *by the Holy Ghost of the Virgin Mary*, and was made man;
He suffered, and the third day he rose again, ascended into heaven;	*he was crucified for us under Pontius Pilate*, and suffered, *and was buried*, and the third day he rose again,

	according to the Scriptures, and ascended into heaven, *and sitteth on the right hand of the Father;*
From thence he shall come to judge the quick and the dead.	from thence he shall come again, *with glory,* to judge the quick and the dead;
And in the Holy Ghost.	And in the Holy Ghost, *the Lord and Giver of life, who proceedeth from the Father, who with the Father and the Son together is worshiped and glorified, who spake by the prophets.*
	In one holy catholic and apostolic Church; we acknowledge one baptism for the remission of sins; we look for the resurrection of the dead, and the life of the world to come. Amen.
[But those who say: 'There was a time when he was not;' and 'He was not before he was made;' and 'He was made out of nothing,' or 'He is of another substance' or 'essence,' or 'The Son of God is created,' or 'changeable,' or 'alterable'—they are condemned by the holy catholic and apostolic Church.]	

APPENDIX B

THE APOCRYPHA

The First Book of Esdra

The Second Book of Esdra

The Book of Tobit

The Book of Judith

The Additions to the Book of Esther

The Wisdom of Solomon

Ecclesiasticus or the Wisdom of Sirach

The Book of Baruch

The Story of Susanna

The Song of the Three Children

The Story of Bel and the Dragon

The Prayer of Manasseh

The First Book of Maccabees

The Second Book of Maccabees

APPENDIX C

72 NAMES OF GOD

8	7	6	5	4	3	2	1	
כהת	אכא	ללה	מהש	עלם	סיט	ילי	והו	1
הקם	הרי	מבה	יזל	ההע	לאו	אלד	הזי	2
ההו	מלה	ייי	נלך	פהל	לוו	כלי	לאו	3
רשר	לכב	אום	ריי	שאה	ירת	האא	נתה	4
ייז	רהע	חעם	אני	מנד	כוק	להח	יחו	5
מיה	עשל	ערי	סאל	ילה	וול	סיכ	ההה	6
פוי	מבה	נית	ננא	עמם	החש	דני	והו	7
מחי	ענו	יהה	ומב	סצר	הרח	ייל	נמם	8
מום	היי	יבמ	ראה	חבו	איע	מנק	דמב	9

EXODUS 14:19–21

YHVH
ARRANGED WITHIN THE TETRACTYS MANIFESTING THE 72 NAMES OF GOD

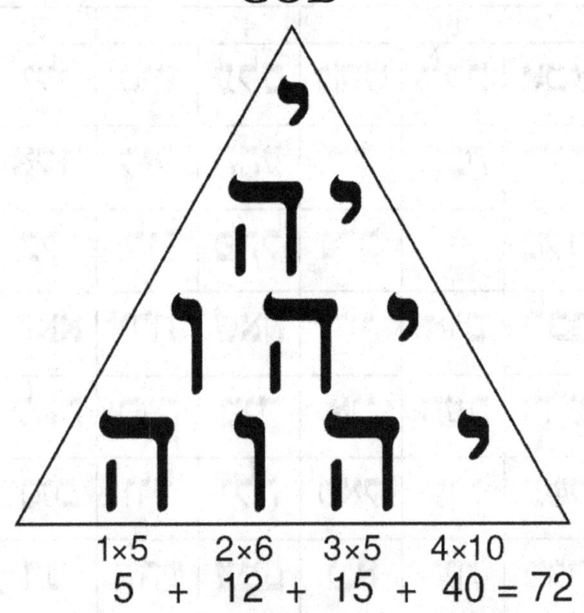

<u>READ FROM RIGHT TO LEFT:</u>

Y = 10 x 4 = 40
H = 5 x 3 = 15
V = 6 x 2 = 12
H = 5 x 1 = 5
TOTAL = 72

APPENDIX D

TABLE OF TRACTATES IN THE COPTIC GNOSTIC LIBRARY THE NAG HAMMADI LIBRARY

This is a listing of the Nag Hammadi Codices and Papyrus Berolinensis–8502. Taken from the Nag Hammadi Library Edited by James M. Robinson HarperCollins published in 1990

I, 1—The Prayer of the Apostle Paul

I, 2—The Apocryphon of James

I, 3—The Gospel of Truth

I, 4—The Treatise on the Resurrection

I, 5—The Tripartite Tractate

II, 1—The Apocryphon of John

II, 2—The Gospel of Thomas

II, 3—The Gospel of Philip

II, 4—The Hypostasis of the Archons

II, 5—On the Origin of the World

II, 6—The Exegesis on the Soul

II, 7—The Book of Thomas the Contender

III, 1—The Apocryphon of John

III, 2—The Gospel of the Egyptians

III, 3—Eugnostos the Blessed

III, 4—The Sophia of Jesus Christ

III, 5—The Dialogue of the Savior

IV, 1—The Apocryphon of John

IV, 2—The Gospel of the Egyptian

V, 1—Eugnostos the Blessed

V, 2—The Apocalypse of Paul

V, 3—The (First) Apocalypse of James

V, 4—The (Second) Apocalypse of James

V, 5—The Apocalypse of Adam

VI, 1—The Acts of Peter and the Twelve Apostles

Secrets of the Divine

VI, 2—The Thunder: Perfect Mind

VI, 3—Authoritative Teaching

VI, 4—The Concept of Our Great Power

VI, 5—Plato: Republic

VI, 6—The Discourse on the Eighth and Ninth

VI, 7—The Prayer of Thanksgiving

VI, 7a—Scribal Note

VI, 8—Aesculapius

VII, 1—The Paraphrase of Shem

VII, 2—The Second Treatise of the Great Seth

VII, 3—Apocalypse of Peter

VII, 4—The Teachings of Silvanus

VII, 5—The Three Steles of Seth

VIII, 1—Zostrianos

VIII, 2—The Letter of Peter to Philip

IX, 1—Melchizedek

The Shekhinah is Coming

IX, 2—The Thought of Norea

IX, 3—The Testimony of Truth

X—Marsanes

XI, 1—The Interpretation of Knowledge

XI, 2—A Valentinian Exposition

XI, 2a—On the Anointing

XI, 2b—On Baptism A

XI, 2c—On Baptism B

XI, 2d—On the Eucharist A

XI, 2e—On the Eucharist B

Xi, 3—Allogenes

XI, 4—Hypsiphrone

XII, 5—The Sentences of Sextus

XII, 2—The Gospel of Truth

XII, 3—Fragments

XIII, 1—Trimorphic Protennoia

Secrets of the Divine

XIII, 2—On the Origin of the World

BG, 1—The Gospel of Mary

BG, 2—The Apocryphon of John

BG, 3—The Sophia of Jesus Christ

BG, 4—The Act of Peter

APPENDIX E

THE DEAD SEA SCROLLS

The Damascus Document

Tales of the Patriarchs

Thanksgiving Psalms (The Thanksgiving Scroll)

A Commentary on Habakkuk

Charter of a Jewish Sectarian Association

Charter for Israel in the Last Days

Priestly Blessings for the Last Days

The War Scroll

The Words of Moses

The Book of secrets

Tongues of Fire

A Vision of the New Jerusalem

Festival Prayers

The Shekhinah is Coming

The Copper Scroll

Apocryphal Psalms

A Reworking of Genesis and Exodus

Ordinances

An Account of the Story of Samuel

Commentaries on Isaiah

A Commentary on Hosea

A Commentary on Nahum

Commentaries on Psalms

The Last Days: A Commentary on Selected Verses

A Collection of Messianic Proof Texts

A Commentary on Consoling Passages in Scripture

The Last Days: An Interpretation of Selected Verses

A Lament for Zion

The Ages of the World

A Sectarian History

Secrets of the Divine

Wiles of the Wicked Woman

In Praise of Wisdom

A Horoscope Written in Code

The Book of Giants

The Words of Levi

The Last Words of Naphtali

A Paraphrase of Genesis and Exodus

Israel and the Holy Land

Enoch and the Watchers

The Healing of King Nabonidus

The Vision of Daniel

A Vision of the Son of God

The Acts of a King

A Commentary on the Law of Moses

Commentaries on Genesis

Portions of Sectarian Law

The Shekhinah is Coming

Ritual Purity Laws Concerning Liquids

Rule of Initiation

The Ashes of the Red Heifer

Ritual Purity Laws Concerning Menstruation

Laws Concerning Lots

A Liturgy of Blessing and Cursing

Laws for Purification

Laws About Gleaning

The War of the Messiah

The Sage of the "Children of Dawn"

The Parable of the Bountiful Tree

The Phases of the Moon

A Divination Text (Brontologion)

Calendar of the Heavenly Signs

Synchronistic Calendars

An Annalistic Calendar

Secrets of the Divine

Priestly Service: Sabbath, Month, and Festival–Year One

Priestly Service: Sabbath, Month, and Festival–Year Four

The Sabbaths and Festivals of the Year

Priestly Service as the Seasons Change

Priestly Rotation on the Sabbath

Priestly Service on the Passover

Priestly Service on New Year's Day

A Liturgical Calendar

False Prophets in Israel

An Annotated Law of Moses

The Inheritance of the Firstborn, the Messiah of David

A Sermon on the Flood

Stories About the Tribes of Israel

A Discourse on the Exodus and Conquest

The Test of a True Prophet

The Shekhinah is Coming

A Moses Apocryphon

Psalms of Joshua

A Collection of Royal Psalms

An Apocryphon of Elijah

Prophetic Apocryphon

God the Creator

Prayers for Forgiveness

A Sectarian Manifesto

The Songs of the Sabbath Sacrifice

Prayer of Praise

A Liturgy

The Secret of the Way Things Are

A Baptismal Liturgy

A Commentary on Genesis and Exodus

A Collection of Proverbs

In Praise of God's Grace—Barki Nafshi

Secrets of the Divine

Hymns of Thanksgiving

Meditation of the Sage

In Praise of King Jonathan

Meditation on Israel's History

Lives of the Patriarchs

The Archangel Michael and King Zedekiah

Assorted Manuscripts

The Two Ways

A Record of Disciplinary Action

A Prayer for Deliverance

A Liturgy of Thanksgiving

Daily Prayers

The Words of the Heavenly Lights

The Songs of the Sage for Protection Against Evil Spirits

A Purification Ritual

The Shekhinah is Coming

Redemption and Resurrection

A Tale of Joshua

The Blessings of the Wise

The Words of the Archangel Michael

The Birth of the Chosen One

The Vision of Jacob

An Apocryphon of Judah

The Last Words of Joseph

The Last Words of Kohath

The Vision of Amram

Hur and Miriam

The Tale of Bagasraw

The Vision of the Four Trees

A Biblical Chronology

An Exorcism

An Aramaic Horoscope

Secrets of the Divine

An Aramaic Text on the Persian Period

A Priestly Vision

Thanksgivings

Apocryphal Psalms of David

An Aramaic Translation of the Book of Job

Songs to Disperse Demons

The Coming of Melchizedek

The Temple Scroll

APPENDIX F
THE HEBREW AND GREEK ALPHABETS

Hebrew Number Values

Letter	Name	Value	Letter	Name	Value
א	Aleph -	1	ל	Lamed -	30
ב	Beth -	2	מ	Mem -	40
ג	Gimel -	3	נ	Nun -	50
ד	Daleth -	4	ס	Samekh -	60
ה	Heh -	5	ע	Ayin -	70
ו	Vav -	6	פ	Peh -	80
ז	Zain -	7	צ	Tzaddi -	90
ח	Cheth -	8	ק	Qoph -	100
ט	Teth -	9	ר	Resh -	200
י	Yod -	10	ש	Shin -	300
כ	Kaph -	20	ת	Tau -	400

The Alpha-Numeric Greek Alphabet

Alpha	Beta	Gamma	Delta	Epsilon	Zeta	Eta	Theta
Α α	Β β	Γ γ	Δ δ	Ε ε	Ζ ζ	Η η	Θ θ
1	2	3	4	5	7	8	9

Iota	Kappa	Lamda	Mu	Nu	Xi	Omicron	Pi
Ι ι	Κ κ	Λ λ	Μ μ	Ν ν	Ξ ξ	Ο ο	Π π
10	20	30	40	50	60	70	80

Rho	Sigma	Tau	Upsilon	Phi	Chi	Psi	Omega
Ρ ρ	Σ σ ς	Τ τ	Υ υ	Φ φ	Χ χ	Ψ ψ	Ω ω
100	200	300	400	500	600	700	800

OBSOLETE LETTERS:

Digamma	Stigma	Koppa	Sampi
F	ϛ	ϙ	ϡ
6	6	90	900

GREEK ALPHABET SOUND EQUIVALENTS:

Greek Letter		Name	Equivalent	Sound When Spoken
Α	α	Alpha	A	al-fah
Β	β	Beta	B	bay-tah
Γ	γ	Gamma	G	gam-ah
Δ	δ	Delta	D	del-tah
Ε	ε	Epsilon	E	ep-si-lon
Ζ	ζ	Zeta	Z	zay-tah
Η	η	Eta	E	ay-tay
Θ	θ	Theta	Th	thay-tah
Ι	ι	Iota	I	eye-o-tah
Κ	κ	Kappa	K	cap-ah
Λ	λ	Lambda	L	lamb-dah
Μ	μ	Mu	M	mew
Ν	ν	Nu	N	new
Ξ	ξ	Xi	X	zzEye
Ο	ο	Omicron	O	om-ah-cron
Π	π	Pi	P	pie
Ρ	ρ	Rho	R	row
Σ	σ	Sigma	S	sig-ma
Τ	τ	Tau	T	tawh
Υ	υ	Upsilon	U	oop-si-lon
Φ	φ	Phi	Ph	figh or fie
Χ	χ	Chi	Ch	kigh
Ψ	ψ	Psi	Ps	sigh
Ω	ω	Omega	O	o-may-gah

APPENDIX G

FORMS OF THE CROSS

The ancient form of the cross was the "TAU CROSS". Its form is a horizontal bar resting on a vertical column resembling the English letter "t". This cross is often referred to as the St. Francis of Assisi cross or the St. Anthony Cross.

The second ancient form of the cross was the "ANKH CROSS". It was an Egyptian hieroglyphic character that meant "key of life" or "eternal life". It can be seen in many of the Egyptian temple and tomb drawings or on the statues of the Egyptian gods and pharaohs. They are displayed as carrying the cross by its loop or holding one in each hand as they cross their arms over their chest. It resembled the "Tau cross" surmounted by an oval shaped circle. It form is a combined cross and vesica piscis.

In Latin the cross was referred to as "CRUX ANSATA" or "cross of life"

12th Dynasty

As a symbol of life, the ankh was seen as emanating from the Sun called Aten.

From the Royal Tomb of Amarna. Familiar scene for Akhenaten and his wife Nefertiti (Cairo Museum)

The third ancient form of the cross is the "ROMAN & GREEK CROSS".

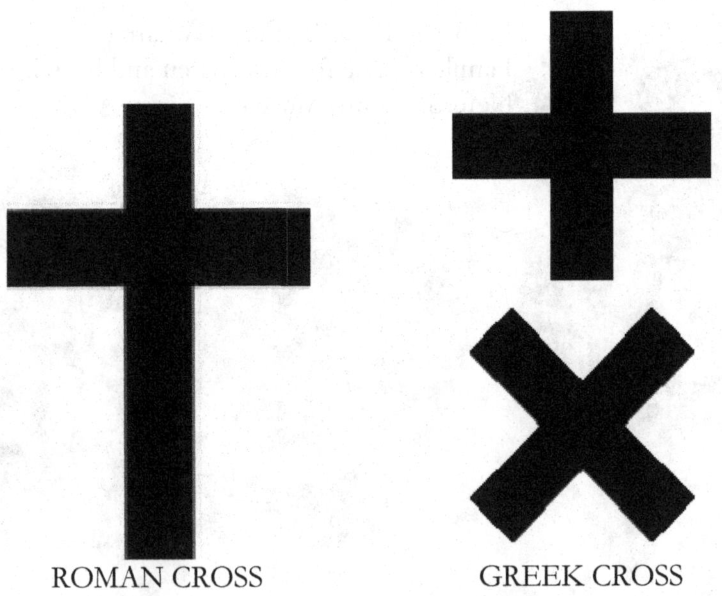

ROMAN CROSS GREEK CROSS

The Greek Cross is the symbol for many things:

- The mathematical "plus" sign for addition
- The mathematical "times" sign for multiplication
- The Roman numeral for "ten"
- The Chinese character for "ten"
- The English character for the letter "X"
- The symbol of the equinoxes and solstices
- The symbol for the elements: Water, Air, Fire, Earth
- The symbol for Earth when surrounded by a circle

From the Egyptian symbol of life, the cross became the symbol of death and crucifixion.

The cross has many variations which are shown below and taken from Wikipedia.

Cross Name	Description	Picture
Ancient Egyptian ankh	Also known as the **Egyptian Cross**, the **Key of the Nile**, the **Looped Tau Cross**, and the **Ansata Cross**. It was an Ancient Egyptian symbol of life and fertility, predating the modern cross. Sometimes given a Latin name if it appears in specifically Christian contexts, such as the ***crux ansata*** ("handled cross").	
Christian cross	Also known as the **Latin cross** or ***crux ordinaria***. It is the most common symbol of Christianity, intended to represent the death of Jesus when he was crucified on the True Cross and his resurrection in the New Testament.	

Coptic ankh

The Coptic ankh is an adaptation of the Ancient Egyptian Ankh used by early Gnostic Christians in Egypt Coptic cross.

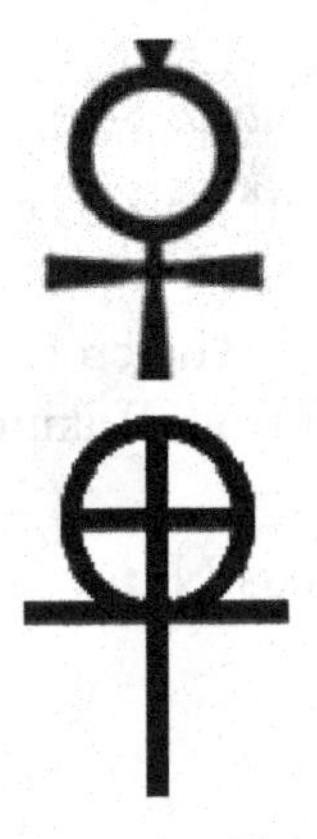

Original Coptic Cross

The original Coptic cross used by early Gnostic Christians in Egypt.

Coptic Cross

A small circle from which emanate four arms of equal length, with angled T shapes in the corners, cross-pieces outward, representing the nails used in Jesus' crucifixion. This cross receives its name from Coptic Christianity, which centered around Alexandria, Egypt.

New Coptic Cross

This new Coptic Cross is the cross currently used by the Coptic Catholic Church and the Coptic Orthodox Church of Alexandria. It evolved from the older Coptic Crosses depicted above. A gallery of Coptic Crosses can be found here.

Double Cross	Used by doctors and veterinarians as an introduction on medical prescriptions in Denmark and Norway. It is read "in nomine Dei" and followed by "rp": recipe [1]	#
Sun cross Bolgar cross	Also known as the **Bolgar cross, Sunwheel, solar cross** or **Woden's cross**. Used in Europe since the Neolithic era and by ancient and contemporary Native American culture to represent respectively Neopagan beliefs and the great Medicine Wheel of life. Was used by the Bulgarian Tzar's (emperor's)was used as symbol of the Bulgarian Orthodox Church	
High cross	Free-standing Celtic crosses commonly found in Ireland and to a lesser extent in Great Britain, very common in churches and graveyards.	

Canterbury cross	Used in the Anglican Churches. It has four arms of equal length, each widening at the outer end in a hammer shape so that their rims nearly form a circle. Each arm bears a triangular panel incised with a triquetra symbolizing the Trinity. In the center of the cross is a small square. The Anglo-Saxon original, as a brooch, dates from c. 850 A.D. and was excavated in 1867 in Canterbury, England. A stone replica can be found in Canterbury Cathedral and in many other Anglican cathedrals around the world. [1]	
Crucifix	A cross with a representation of Jesus' body hanging from it. It is primarily used in the Catholic Church, Anglican churches, and Eastern Orthodox churches, and it emphasizes Christ's sacrifice— his death by crucifixion.	

Greek cross	Used especially by Eastern Orthodoxy and Early Christianity Also known as the ***crux immissa quadrata***. Has all arms of equal length. Often the arms curve wider as they go out.	
Serbian cross (Tetragrammatic cross)	The motif of a cross between four objects is derived from Constantine's labarum and has figured on Byzantine coins, since the 6th c. Later, the 4 symbols of the cross have been interpreted as flints or firestones, but also as the initials (letters β) of the imperial motto of the Palaiologos dynasty: King of Kings, Ruling Over Kings (Greek: βασιλεύς βασιλέων, βασιλεύων βασιλευόντων - Basileus Basileōn, Basileuōn Basileuontōn). The cross has been used by Serbian states and the Serbian Orthodox Church since the Middle Ages after Dušan the Mighty was crowned Emperor (Tsar) of the Serbs and Greeks (16 April 1345). Today it is the national, religious and ethnic	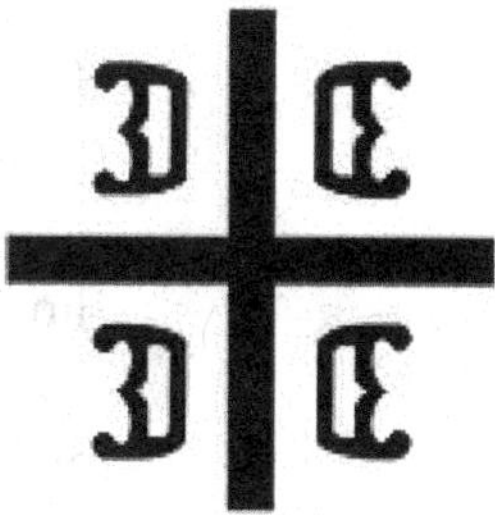

symbol of Serbs and Serbia.

Florian cross

Adopted as an emblem by the fire service, this cross is named for Saint Florian, the patron saint of Poland, Austria and firefighters. Although similar to the Maltese Cross and Cross pattée, it differs in having arms rounded outwards at the ends. Two different versions are included here; the one above is commonly found on fire service badges, patches, and emblems; the one below is typical of the St. Florian medallion or medal.

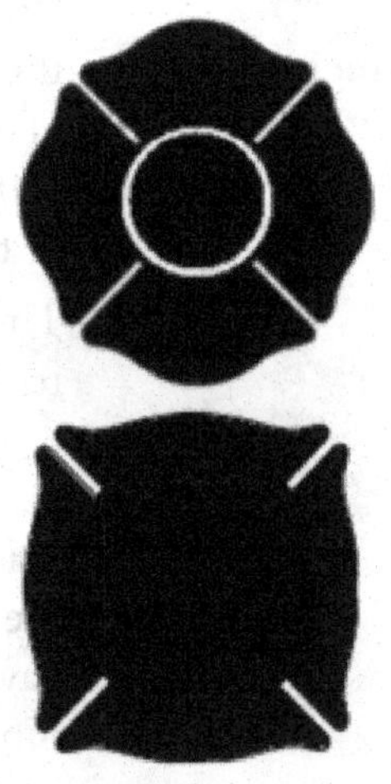

Eastern cross

Used in the Eastern Orthodox Church. The top line is said to represent the headboard, and the bottom, slanted line represents the footrest, wrenched loose by Jesus' writhing in intense agony. It is raised to the left side, because that was the side of the righteous criminal who said to Jesus: "remember me when you come into your kingdom". This symbolizes the victory

of good over evil. The letters IC XC found at the end of the main arm of most Eastern Orthodox Crosses are a Christogram, representing the name of Jesus Christ (Greek: Ιησοὺς Χριστὸς). See also the Cross of Salem

St. Brigid's Cross	This cross is found throughout Ireland. It is told that the cross was made by Brigid, daughter of a pagan king from reeds to be used as an instrument of conversion. However, Brigid's name is derived from Brigit (also spelled Brigid, Brìghde, Brìde, and Bríde), a Celtic Goddess of fire, poetry, and smith craft, and today the cross is used to protect houses from fire. This is an example of the integration of religious traditions.	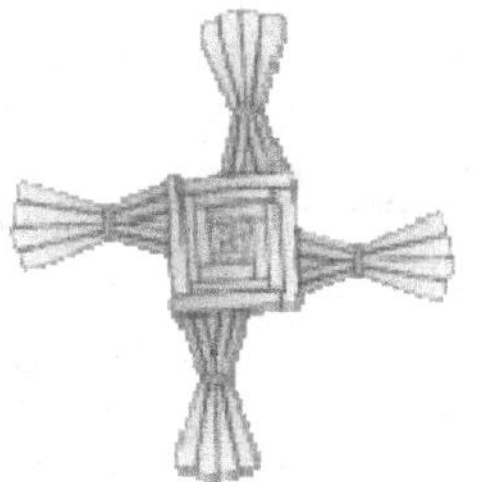
Chi-Rho	Constantine I's emblem, the Chi-Rho (from the two Greek letters that make it up) is also known as the *labarum* or Christogram. Several variants exist.	

Lorraine Cross	Used in heraldry. It is similar to a patriarchal cross, but usually has one bar near the middle and one near the top, rather than having both near the top. Is part of the heraldic arms of Lorraine in eastern France. It was originally held to be a symbol of Joan of Arc, renowned for her perseverance against foreign invaders of France.	
Marian Cross	Included on the coat of arms of Pope John Paul II, the Marian Cross is a Catholic adaptation of the traditional Latin cross to emphasize Catholic devotion to Mary.	
Nordic Cross	Used in flags descended from the Dannebrog.	

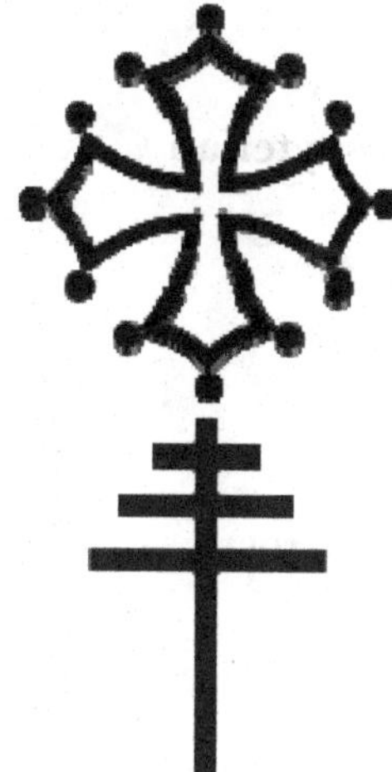

Occitan cross

Based on the counts of Toulouse's traditional coat of arms, it soon became the symbol of Occitania as a whole.

Papal Cross

The three cross-bars represent the Pope's triple role as Bishop of Rome, Patriarch of the West, and successor of St. Peter, Chief of the Apostles.

Patriarchal cross

Similar to a traditional Christian cross, but with an additional, smaller crossbar above the main one meant to represent all the Orthodox Christian Archbishops and Patriarchs. In the Eastern Orthodox Church, this cross is sometimes seen with an additional, slanted bar near the foot of the cross (see Byzantine Cross). This cross is similar to the Lorraine Cross, Caravaca Cross, and Salem Cross

Presbyterian Cross	Used by Presbyterian denominations.	
Red Cross	Used as a symbol for medical care in most of the world, the Red Crescent being used in Islamic countries and the Magen David Adom in Israel.	
Cross of Sacrifice	A Latin cross with a superimposed sword, blade down. It is a symbol used by the Commonwealth War Graves Commission at the site of many war memorials.	
Cross of Salem	Also known as a pontifical cross because it is carried before the Pope, it is similar to a patriarchal cross, but with an additional crossbar below the main crossbar, equal in length to the upper crossbar. It is also similar to the Eastern Cross.	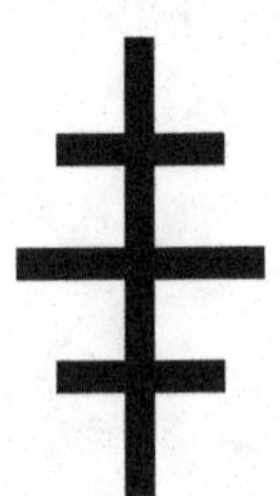

Royal Flag of Georgia	Used in Georgia as national flag, first used by Georgian King Vakhtang Gorgasali in the 5th century and later adopted by Queen Tamar of Georgia in the 13th century. The flag depicts a Jerusalem cross, adopted during the reign of George V of Georgia who drove out the Mongols from Georgia in 1334.	
St. Nune's Cross	Also known as a "Grapevine cross" and traditionally ascribed to Saint Nino, the 4th-century female baptizer of the Georgians, it is used as a symbol of the Georgian Orthodox Church.	
St. Thomas Cross	Also known as a "Mar Thoma Cross" and traditionally ascribed to Saint Thomas, the Apostle of India, it is used as a symbol of the Syro Malabar Catholic Church and venerated by all Saint Thomas Christians denominations.[2]	

Saint Andrew's Cross	Used in Scotland's national flag, the naval ensign of the Russian Navy, and the former Confederate States of America; it is also called the **Saltire**, the **Boundary Cross** (because it was used by the Romans as a barrier) and the ***crux decussata***. Saint Andrew is believed to have suffered a martyr's death on such a cross, hence its name. The cross does not have to be at this particular angle to qualify as a saltire; the symbol X can also be considered a St. Andrew's Cross.	
St George's Cross	Used in England's national flag.	
St George's Cross (in Scandinavia)	The definition of a St George's cross is, in Scandinavia, extended to also include a centered cross, normally red but not necessarily, with triangular arms that do not fill the square. The example beside is the cross of the Swedish	

	Order of Freemasons.	
Saint Peter's Cross/Inverted Cross	An upside-down Latin cross, based on a tradition that holds that Saint Peter was martyred by being crucified upside-down. Today it is often associated with anti-Christian or Satanic groups.	
Tau Cross	Also known as **Saint Anthony's Cross**, the **Egyptian Cross** and the ***crux commissa***. It is shaped like the letter T. Francis of Assisi used it as his signature.	
Thieves' Cross	Also known as the **Furka Cross**. The fork, shaped like the letter Y. [2]	
Mariner's Cross	The **Mariner's Cross** is a stylized cross in the shape of an anchor. The Mariner's Cross is also referred to as *St. Cement's Cross* in reference to the way he was martyred.	

Order of Christ Cross	Cross originally used by the Portuguese Order of Christ. Since then it has become a symbol of Portugal, used on the sails of the carracks during the Discoveries Era, and currently by the Madeira Autonomous Region of Portugal and the Portuguese Air Force.	
Hands of God	The Hands of God (Slavic: ręce boga) is a pre-Christian symbol in central Europe.	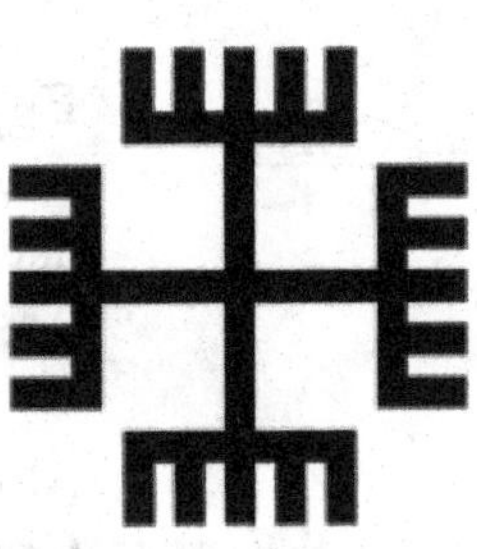
Extreme-right variant of the Celtic Cross	Some white nationalist and neo-fascist groups adopted this variation of the Celtic cross, made up of simple lines, without any of the ornamental complexity of traditional Celtic crosses. It is thought that this basic variation's minor resemblance to the swastika [citation needed] is the reason it has become popular in such circles. This variation was also used by the Zodiac killer	

at the scenes of his crimes.

Swastika

The **swastika** is an equilateral cross with its arms bent at right angles, in either right-facing (卐) form or its mirrored left-facing (卍) form. Archaeological evidence of swastika-shaped ornaments dates from the Neolithic period. It occurs mainly in the modern day culture of India, sometimes as a geometrical motif and sometimes as a religious symbol. It remains widely used in Eastern religions / Dharmic religion such as Hinduism, Buddhism and Jainism. Though once commonly used all over much of the world without stigma, because of its iconic usage in Nazi Germany the symbol has become stigmatized in the Western world.

Chakana

The **Chakana** or **Tawa Chakana** (or Inca Cross) symbolizes for Inca mythology what is known in other mythologies as the World Tree, Tree of Life and so on. The stepped cross is made up of an equal-armed cross indicating the cardinal points of the compass and a superimposed square. The square represents the other two levels of existence. The three levels of existence are *Hana Pacha* (the upper world inhabited by the superior gods), *Kay Pacha*, (the world of our everyday existence) and *Ucu* or *Urin Pacha* (the underworld inhabited by spirits of the dead, the ancestors, their overlords and various deities having close contact to the Earth plane). The hole through the centre of the cross is the Axis by means of which the shaman transits the cosmic vault to the other levels. It also represents Cuzco, the center of the Incan empire.

Skull and crossbones	Not a cross as such, but a saltire made of bones, with an overlaid skull. While traditionally associated with pirates, it was actually relatively rarely used by them, each ship having its own design, often involving an hourglass.	

APPENDIX H
PERIODIC TABLE OF ELEMENTS

PERIODIC TABLE OF THE ELEMENTS

Key: 1 — ATOMIC NUMBER; H — SYMBOL; 1.008 — ATOMIC WEIGHT

1	2	3	4	5	6	7	8	9	10	11	12	13	14	15	16	17	18
1 H 1.01																	2 He 4.00
3 Li 6.94	4 Be 9.01											5 B 10.81	6 C 12.01	7 N 14.01	8 O 16.00	9 F 19.00	10 Ne 20.18
11 Na 22.99	12 Mg 24.31											13 Al 26.98	14 Si 28.09	15 P 30.97	16 S 32.07	17 Cl 35.45	18 Ar 39.95
19 K 39.10	20 Ca 40.08	21 Sc 44.96	22 Ti 47.88	23 V 50.94	24 Cr 52.00	25 Mn 54.94	26 Fe 55.85	27 Co 58.93	28 Ni 58.69	29 Cu 63.55	30 Zn 65.39	31 Ga 69.72	32 Ge 72.61	33 As 74.92	34 Se 78.96	35 Br 79.90	36 Kr 83.80
37 Rb 85.47	38 Sr 87.62	39 Y 88.91	40 Zr 91.22	41 Nb 92.91	42 Mo 95.94	43 Tc 97.91	44 Ru 101.07	45 Rh 102.91	46 Pd 106.42	47 Ag 107.87	48 Cd 112.41	49 In 114.82	50 Sn 118.71	51 Sb 121.75	52 Te 127.60	53 I 126.90	54 Xe 131.29
55 Cs 132.91	56 Ba 137.32	57 La* 138.91	72 Hf 178.49	73 Ta 180.95	74 W 183.85	75 Re 186.21	76 Os 190.20	77 Ir 192.22	78 Pt 195.08	79 Au 196.97	80 Hg 200.59	81 Tl 204.38	82 Pb 207.20	83 Bi 208.98	84 Po 208.98	85 At 209.99	86 Rn 222.02
87 Fr 223.02	88 Ra 226.03	89 Ac‡ 227.03	104 Rf 261	105 Db 262	106 Sg 263	107 Bh 262	108 Hs 265	109 Mt 266	110 Ds 281	111 Dec.1994 272	112 Dec.1996 277	113 Uut 284	114 Dec.1999 289	115 Uup 288	116 Not Discovered 289	117 Not Discovered	118 Not Discovered 293
58 Ce 140.12	59 Pr 140.91	60 Nd 144.24	61 Pm 144.91	62 Sm 150.36	63 Eu 151.97	64 Gd 157.25	65 Tb 158.93	66 Dy 162.50	67 Ho 164.93	68 Er 167.26	69 Tm 168.93	70 Yb 173.04	71 Lu 174.97				
90 Th 232.04	91 Pa 231.04	92 U 238.05	93 Np 237.05	94 Pu 244.06	95 Am 243.06	96 Cm 247.07	97 Bk 247.07	98 Cf 251	99 Es 252.08	100 Fm 257.10	101 Md 258.10	102 No 259.10	103 Lr 260.11				

THE ELEMENTS
SONG BY: TOM LEHRER
1959

In 1959, Tom Lehrer, a musical humorist put the then known 102 chemical elements to the tune of the *Major General's Song* from *The Pirates of Penzance* by Gilbert and Sullivan.

Lehrer ordered the elements in the lyrics to fit the meter of the song. Lehrer was a Harvard math instructor so the last lines of the lyrics are done with a Boston accent to emphasize the Harvard connection. The complete lyrics and chords are:

There's antimony, arsenic, aluminum, selenium
And hydrogen and oxygen and nitrogen and rhenium
And nickel, neodymium, neptunium, germanium
And iron, americium, ruthenium, uranium
Europium, zirconium, lutetium, vanadium
And lanthanum and osmium and astatine and radium
And gold and protactinium and indium and gallium
And iodine and thorium and thulium and thallium

D—A7—D—A—E7—A—A7—Dm—C7—F—A7—Dm—Bb7—A7

There's yttrium, ytterbium, actinium, rubidium
And boron, gadolinium, niobium, iridium
And strontium and silicon and silver and samarium
And bismuth, bromine, lithium, beryllium, and barium

D—A7—D—A7—D—A7—D—G—D—A7—D

There's holmium and helium and hafnium and erbium
And phosphorus and francium and fluorine and terbium
And manganese and mercury, molybdenum, magnesium
Dysprosium and scandium and cerium and cesium
And lead, praseodymium, and platinum, plutonium
Palladium, promethium, potassium, polonium
And tantalum, technetium, titanium, tellurium
And cadmium and calcium and chromium and curium

There's sulfur, californium, and fermium, berkelium
And also mendelevium, einsteinium, nobelium
And argon, krypton, neon, radon, xenon, zinc, and rhodium
And chlorine, carbon, cobalt, copper, tungsten, tin, and sodium

These are the only ones of which the news has come to Ha'vard and there may be many others, but they haven't been discavard

D—A7—D—G—D—A7—D

There are many web sites where you can actually listen to the song as it is being sung.

APPENDIX I
THE BOAZ & JACHIN PILLARS

Artist Depiction of Solomon's Temple

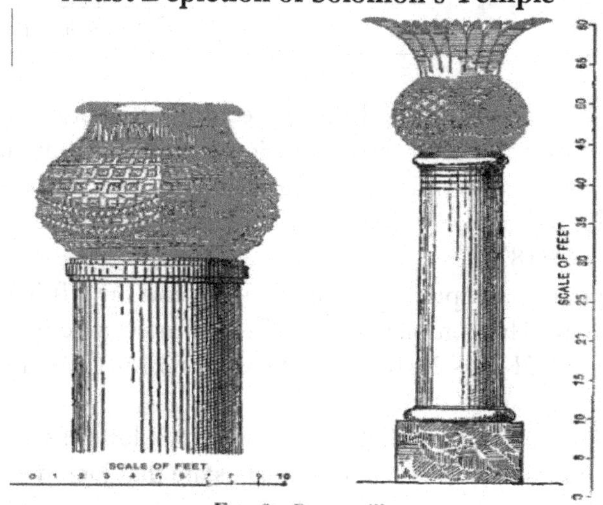

FIG. 5—Brazen pillars.

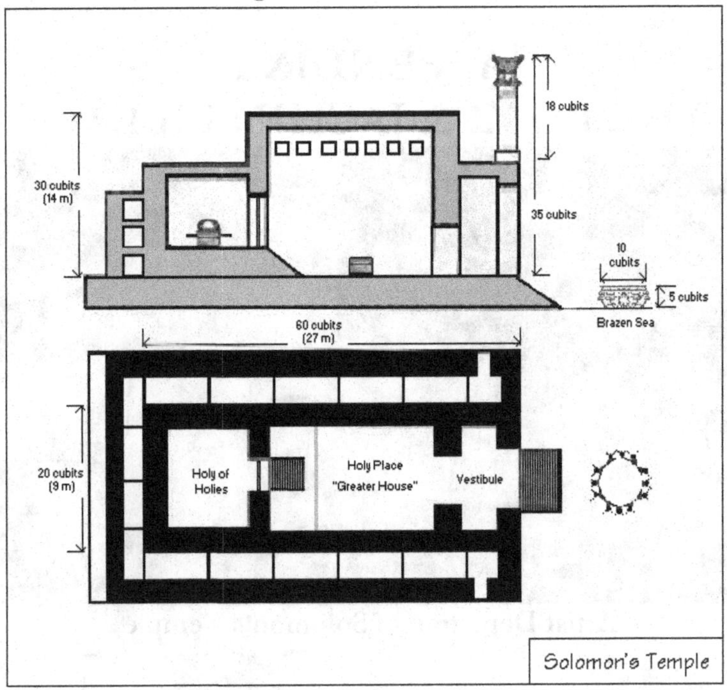

Solomon's Temple

The Temple faced due East to greet the rising Sun where the two copper pillars stood on the porch. Some Bible versions state that the columns were brass or bronze instead of copper. One of the Dead Sea Scrolls known as Brontologion makes reference to "the secret of the pillars" (4Q318:59).

The right hand pillar was called Jachin and the left hand pillar was called Boaz. The complete detail of the pillars can be found in 1Kings 7:15–22, 2Kings 25:16–17, 2Chronicles 3:15–17, and Jeremiah 52:17.

Jachin was the first High Priest of King Solomon's Temple also known as the First Temple. Some scholars state that Jachin means "he shall establish" and others define Jachin as meaning "one only" or "Unity". As the High Priest, his duty was to establish righteousness.

Boaz, who came from Bethlehem, was the husband of Ruth whose son was Obed, the father of Jesse. Jesse was the father of King David. Boaz' character was one of love and knowing how to treat others. Some scholars state that Boaz means "in it is strength".

Simply, the pillars represented the exact teachings of Jesus who said "Love the One God and Love thy neighbor".

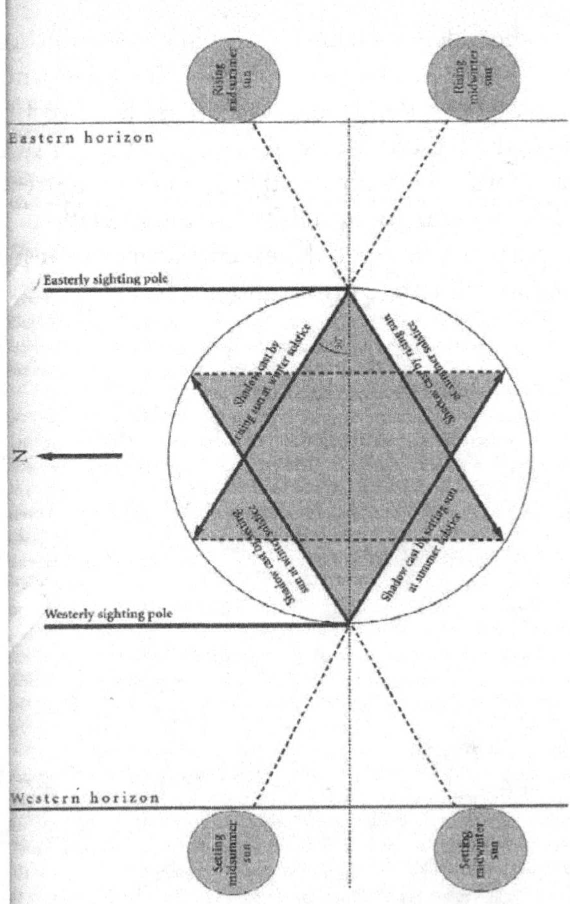

Figure 1 How the symbol of the Seal of Solomon, or Star of David, derives from the solstice sunrises and sunsets at the latitude of Jerusalem

Drawing from *Solomon's Power Brokers* (Christopher Knight 2007, 15)

APPENDIX J
THE DENDERA ZODIAC
TEMPLE OF HATHOR

the Ancient Egyptians named the Constellation 'Virgo' after the AE Holy Mary the 'Virgin'

http://www.mazzaroth.com/ChapterOne/TranslateDenderah.htm

APPENDIX K

TABLE OF ANCIENT COPTIC NAMES BY ULUGH BEG

Latin Names	Coptic Names	Explanations	Hebrew Roots	
VIRGO	Aspolia, Statio Amoris	Aspolia, ears of corn, the seed		Gen 41:5
LIBRA	Lambadia, Statio propitiationis	Lam, Arab. gracious	Mhl	
		Badia, branch	db	Eze 17:6
SCORPIO	Isias, Statio Isidis	Isias, salvation		Psa 35:3
SAGITTARIUS	Pi Maere, Statio Amenitatis	Amenity, graciousness, beauty of the appearing or coming forth	hrm	Gen 24:16
CAPRICORNUS	Hupenius, Brachium sacrificii	Hupe, place or chamber	Px	Psa 19:5
		Nius, of Him	wn	Zech

		having salvation		9:9
AQUARIUS	Hupei Tirion	Hupei, place or chamber		
		Tirion, of Him coming down as rain	hry	Hosea 6:3
PISCES	Pi-cot Orion, Piscis Hori	Cot, fish, the congregation, or company of	twyx	Psa 104:25; 68:30
		Orion, Him who cometh (Arab. form, or formative of the noun), wayfaring men	xr	Jer 9:2
		Hori, of Horus, Him who cometh, as above.		
ARIES	Tametouris Ammon, Regnum Ammonis	Reign, dominion, government	hrm	Isa 9:6,7 EV
		Ammon, established	Nm	Isa 7:9 Jer 42:5
TAURUS	Isis or Apis, Horias, Statio	Isis, who saves or		Zech 9:9

	Hori	delivers		
		Apis, the head. Apes, Egyptian; as Aleph, Heb.; captain, chief	Pl	Jer 13:21
		Horias, who cometh, traveler,	xr	2 Sam 12:4
		Horias, to save	y	
GEMINI	Clusus, Claustrum Hori	The place of Him who cometh, wayfaring man	xr	Isa 33:8
CANCER	Klaria, Statio Typhonis	Klaria, cattle-folds	hlk	Psa 50:9
		Statio Typhonis, who smites, is smitten	Ppx	Nahum 2:7
LEO	Pi Mentekeon, Cubitus Nili	Mentekeon, the pouring out	Ktn	Exo 9:33

VIRGO

Decans. Names	Egyptian	Noetic		Used in

now in use, and Hieroglyphic Names	Hieroglyphic Names and Figures*	Roots traced by the Hebrew		the Hebrew Bible
COMA, the desired	Figured as the infant held by a woman seated beneath			
SHES-NU	Shes-nu: Shes, son or offspring (B); Nu, desired, Heb.	Offspring	h	Exo 12:5
		Desired	hw	Isa 26:9
CENTAURUS, the appointed offering himself as a sacrifice	A human figure with the tail, "this cometh," and with the head of a calf or lamb of sacrifice.			
KNEMU	Knemu: Mu, to die. (B)	Mnk, appointed, established	Nk	1 Kings 7:21
	The appointed dieth, is bruised	To die	twm	Gen 2:17
BOOTES, who cometh	A human figure, as coming, holding the ploughshare, to break or bruise the enemy.	Ploughshare	t	Joel 3:10
SMAT	Smat, who rules, subdues. (B.)	M#, makes		
	Comes, ht)	Ordain, place	M	Exo 13:16

		Comes	ht	Deut 33:2

LIBRA

Decans .Names now in use, and Hieroglyphic Names	Egyptian Hieroglyphic Names and Figures*	Noetic Roots traced by the Hebrew		Used in the Hebrew Bible
THE SOUTHERN CROSS SERA	The figure of a lion, hyr), who cometh to tear, to gain the victory. His tongue is out of his mouth, as in thirst.* A female figure offers a cup. He holds the usual hieroglyphic for running waters.	Who comes	b	
		To draw water, to drink, Arab. sense	b	Gen 24:11
	Sera, victory. (B)	Who rules, Heb.	r	
		Sets free	hr	Job 37:3
THE VICTIM, held by the Centaur SURA	The emblem called Harpocrates, a child or youth with the finger on the lip.	Lip, hp	h	Song 4:3, &c.
		Break or bruise	Pw	Job 9:17
	Sura, a sheep or lamb. (B.)	Lamb	h#	Gen 3:15
THE CROWN	The enthroned figure	Who	r)	

API-AATL	above	cometh		
	Api-aatl: Api, head or chief (B); Aatl, noble (B), strong, Heb.	The Ruler	Nd Nt	Gen 42:30 Num 24:21

SCORPIO

Decans .Names now in use, and Hieroglyphic Names	Egyptian Hieroglyphic Names and Figures*	Noetic Roots traced by the Hebrew		Used in the Hebrew Bible
THE SERPENT, enemy of Him who cometh, held by Ophiuchus KHU-OR-BAKH	Figured as the serpent under the foot of the throne figure.			
	Khu, ruled (B.); Or, enemy; Bakh, bows down, ruled. (B.)	Enemy	r	Psa 139:20
		Caused to . fail	qb	Jer 19:7
OPHIUCHUS, the serpent conqueror API-BAU	A throne human figure with the hawk's head, as enemy of the serpent.		hp	
	Api-bau, the chief or head who cometh. (B.)	Api, head, face	wb	Psa 96:13
		Bau, who cometh		

HERCULES, who bruiseth the head, and is bruised in the heel	He who bruises a human figure with the club, as Hercules.			
BAU	Bau, who cometh. (B.)	Who cometh	wb	

SAGITTARIUS

Decans. Names now in use, and Hieroglyphic Names	Egyptian Hieroglyphic Names and Figures*	Noetic Roots traced by the Hebrew		Used in the Hebrew Bible
LYRA, or the harp, held by the eagle, the triumph	Figured as a hawk or eagle, the enemy of the serpent in triumph.			Job 20:16
FENT-KAR	Fent-kar, the serpent, worm (B.), ruled.	Fent, worm or serpent, viper	h(p)	Isa 30:6, 59:5
ARA, the altar of the sacrifice BAU	A throne human figure holding the flail, the implement of bruising. In the modern sphere this decan is very obscure. There seems here to have been a victim in the Persian sphere. To the throne figure the	Bau, he cometh	b	Isa 63:1

	Egyptian name seems to refer.			
	Bau, He cometh, as in Scorpio			
DRACO, the serpent enemy HER-FENT	The serpent, or dragon, under the forefoot of Sagittarius.			
	Her-fent, the serpent, or the serpent accursed.	Her, cursed	r	Gen 3:14
		Fent, as above.		

CAPRICORNUS

Decans. Names now in use, and Hieroglyphic Names	Egyptian Hieroglyphic Names and Figures*	Noetic Roots traced by the Hebrew		Used in the Hebrew Bible
THE ARROW, of slaying FENT-KAR	A tailed figure with the hawk's head, standing over the junction of the head of the kid with the body of the fish.	Fent, serpent; suphon, Arab.	zpyp	Gen 49:17
	Fent-kar, serpent			
	Kar, enemy. Heb. enemy.	Kar, enemy	r	Psa 139:20
AQUILA, the	A bird, goose of the			

falling eagle	Nile, apparently.			
SU-AT	Su-at, He cometh Su, He (B); At, cometh, Heb.	Cometh	ht	Job 3:25
DELPHINUS, the dolphin	A fish			
KHAU	Khau, multitude, fish; goat? (B.), or hoped for, Heb.	Khau, longed for	hwq	Job 7:2

AQUARIUS

Decans. Names now in use, and Hieroglyphic Names	Egyptian Hieroglyphic Names and Figures*	Noetic Roots traced by the Hebrew		Used in the Hebrew Bible
THE SOUTHERN FISH AAR	The figure seems to include both the fish and the stream of water on it. Aar, a stream.	Iar, a stream	ry	Gen 41:1
PEGASUS, the winged horse	The ascending node, of which the headless horse is an emblem.**	sws, a horse	sws	Job 39:18
CYCNUS, the swan	The swan			
TES-ARK	Tes-ark, this from afar, Kr), Heb.	Tes, this (B), afar	Kr	Gen 6:15

PISCES

Decans. Names now in use, and Hieroglyphic Names	Egyptian Hieroglyphic Names and Figures*	Noetic Roots traced by the Hebrew		Used in the Hebrew Bible
THE BAND U-OR	A tailed human figure walking			
	U-or* (B.), who cometh, r), Heb.	To flow forth	r	
		Flood	rw	Amos 8:8
CEPHEUS, the crowned king, the branch PE-KU-HOR	The wolf lying on the fore-leg of a beast	Wolf, b)z, who cometh; foreleg, rz, also the seed	rz	Gen 3:15
	Pe-ku-hor, this (B.), to rule (B.), cometh (B. and Heb.)			
ANDROMEDA, the Church set free	A female figure, either that in the circle holding a victim, or that holding the band of Pisces, under which are the characters, S-r, as of Sirra, one name of Andromeda, which therefore seems most likely.	Lady or Princess	hr	Gen 17:15
SET	Set, set up	Appointed	tw	Job 14:13
	Sutn being "a king"	Set up as		

	(B.), this may be "queen," as the spouse of Perseus the deliverer	king		

ARIES

Decans. Names now in use, and Hieroglyphic Names	Egyptian Hieroglyphic Names and Figures*	Noetic Roots traced by the Hebrew		Used in the Hebrew Bible
CASSIOPEIA, the throne woman SET	Set, set up.	Set, set up, appointed	t	Gen 4:25
	A female figure, under which are the hieroglyphic signs denoting a female, an oval or egg, hcyb, and a half-circle or hill, lt, for Beth, *a daughter.* According to Albumazer this decan was anciently called "the daughter of splendor."			
CETUS, the sea-monster or serpent-enemy.	Knem, subdued	Triumph	hg	Exo 15:1,21 &c.
	Kanu-nu, victory. (B.)	Established	Nwk	Gen

				41:32
KNEM	Here figured as a monstrous head, trodden under foot by the swine, the natural enemy of the serpent, united to which is the wolf,^ whose name b)z signifies *He cometh*. The hawk, also a natural enemy of the serpent, crowned with the mortar, the emblem of *bruising*, is over this figure. It corresponds to the head of Medusa, carried by Perseus.	Swine	ryzx	Lev 11:7
		Who turns		Eze 1:9,12,17
		Mortar, to bruise	tk	Prov 27:22
		Medusa, trodden on	wd	Job 39:15
PERSEUS, He who breaks or bruises KAR KNEM	Kar Knem			1 Sam 28:16
	Kar, who fights. (B.)	Who fights	r	Psa 139:20
	The figure of a man with the tail of a quadruped appended as to a girdle, signifying *This cometh*, by the word *tail*, bnz, *this cometh*, or shall be sent forth.	Who destroys, subdues, Arabic		Dan 4:16
		this	hz	Gen 5:9
		Cometh	)wb	Gen 2:22
	He has a royal diadem or fillet round his head.	Or is sent forth	bn	

TAURUS

Decans. Names now in use, and Hieroglyphic Names	Egyptian Hieroglyphic Names and Figures*	Noetic Roots traced by the Hebrew		Used in the Hebrew Bible
ORION HA-GA-T	Ha-ga-t, who triumphs	Ha, the chief. (B) g, ga, triumphs	)g	Exo 15:1,21
	In the lower circle are hieroglyphic characters that read Oar, Orion having been anciently spelt Oarion.			
	T is the article affix, the or this. (Bunsen)			
ERIDANUS, the river. PEH-TA-T	Peh-ta-t, mouth of the river, originating from the urn of Aquarius, figured by water in Pisces.	Mouth, hp; river, y) (t); water, Aa. (B)	Mym	Gen 8:9
AURIGA, the shepherd TUM	Tum, scepter, power. (B)	Subdued, put to silence, tame. (Heb)	hmd	Psa 94:17
	Who subdues, tames. He carries the head of an animal (Ba, He cometh) on a cross or			

	scepter.			
	The cross was said to be emblematic of life, divine life, among the Egyptians, whose belief in the immortality of the soul is well known.			

GEMINI

Decans. Names now in use, and Hieroglyphic Names	Egyptian Hieroglyphic Names and Figures*	Noetic Roots traced by the Hebrew		Used in the Hebrew Bible
LEPUS, (Arnebeth, the enemy of Him that cometh)	The enemy of Him who cometh, trodden under foot, here figured as the hoopoe, an unclean bird, standing over the serpent under the foot of Orion.			
BASHTI-BEKI	Bashti-beki, confounded, failing. (B)	Bashti, confounded	b	Job 6:20
		Beki, failing	qb	Isa 19:3
SIRIUS, the prince	The prince, figured by the hawk,* enemy of the serpent, the Egyptian substitute for the eagle	Swiftly coming down	Cn	Lev 11:16
APES		Victory or a vulture. (B)	rn	Deut 32:11

	Nesir; called in the Greek sphere the first or great dog, but anciently the wolf, whose name b)z, *this cometh*, denoted the coming to reign. On his head is the pestle and mortar, denoting who shall bruise the head of the enemy.	Eagle, coming down,		
	Apes, the head. (B)	Apes, the face or head, commanding	hp	Gen 45:21 Exo 17:1 Eccle 8:2
PROCYON, the deliverer from evil SEBAK	The lesser dog or wolf, representing the first coming to redeem, by a human figure with the hawk's head, and the appendage of the tail			
	Sebak, conquering, victorious. (B.)	Shebah, making captive, Heb.	hb	Exo 22:10

CANCER

Decans. Names now in use, and Hieroglyphic Names	**Egyptian Hieroglyphic Names and Figures**	**Noetic Roots traced by the Hebrew**		**Used in the Hebrew Bible**
URSA MINOR API-FENT	The chacal, or wolf, standing on the ploughshare, which comes, tearing or bruising the ground.	Ploughshare	t	Isa 2:4
		Coming	t	Deut 33:2
	Api, head; Fent, of the serpent. (B)	Head, hp; Fent, serpent, adder	h(p)	Job 20:16
		Siphon, Arab.		
URSA MAJOR FENT-HAR	A female swine, enemy of the serpent, holding a ploughshare, implement of bruising, emblem of coming.	Swine	ryzx	Lev 11:7
		Who turns		Eze 1:9
	Fent-har, enemy of the serpent	Enemy, Chaldeans	r	Psa 139:20
	Har, who terrifies. (B.)			Dan 4:16
	Kark, to smite, with a scimitar, to strike. (B)	Enraged against	rrx	Gen 18:30

	This figure holding a ploughshare will account for that title having been given to Ursa Major.	Ploughshare		
		Coming	ht)	Job 3:25
		Bruising, crushing	rh	Job 1:14
ARGO, or Canopus, the possession of Him who cometh	A beeve with the crux ansata, cross with handle, or emblem of life, round its throat.	Ba, who cometh	b	
		Rejoicing	y	Job 3:22
SHES-EN-FENT	Shes-en-fent, rejoicing over the serpent. (B, worm)	Fent, serpent, adder	h(p)	Job 20:16

LEO

Decans. Names now in use, and Hieroglyphic Names	Egyptian Hieroglyphic Names and Figures*	Noetic Roots traced by the Hebrew		Used in the Hebrew Bible
HYDRA	The serpent under the lion's foot. The name is not given in Mr. Birch's list; but hieroglyphics that read Knem (He who triumphs, who conquers, or is conquered) are underneath these	Knem, from Khan, whence King and Khan, established, fixed.	Nwk	Psa 93:2

	figures.			
CRATER	A plumed female figure, holding a vase or cup in each hand, while responding to the constellation Crater, may be a memorial that at the arrangement of the emblems, the invention of astronomy, the summer solstice was there, and consequently the pouring forth of the inundation of the Nile.	There are characters below, which may be "sent forth," as water from the vase. Her seat is figured as the thighs of a beast.	hry	Exo 15:4
CRATER		Thigh	Kry	Psa 45:3
CRATER		To send forth	hry	Hosea 6:3
CORVUS HER-NA	The bird perched on the serpent at the heel of the lion.			
CORVUS HER-NA	Her-na, great enemy. (B)	Her, as in Cancer	r	
CORVUS HER-NA	Her-na, great enemy. (B)	Na, fail, break, enemy failing	n	Num 32:7

(Taken from *Mazzaroth* by Frances Rolleston)

APPENDIX L

BOOK OF JOB
CONSTELLATION & STAR REFERENCES

Job 9:9——Which maketh Arcturus, Orion, and Pleiades, and the chambers of the south.

Job 26:13——By his spirit he hath garnished the heavens; his had hath formed the Crooked serpent.

Job 38:4——Where wast thou when I laid the foundations of the Earth?

Job 38:5——Who hath laid the measures thereof? Or who hath stretched the line upon it?

Job 38:7——When the morning stars sang together and all the sons of God shouted for joy.

Job 38:31——Canst thou bind the sweet influences of Pleiades, or loose the bands of Orion?

Job 38:32——Canst thou bring forth Mazzaroth in his season? Or canst thou guide Arcturus with his sons?

Job 38:33——Knowest thou the ordinances of Heaven?

The Shekhinah is Coming

Job 39:2——Canst thou number the months that they fulfill? Or knowest thou the time when they bring forth?

Job 41:1——Canst thou draw out leviathan with a hook?

APPENDIX M

THE BRIGHTEST STARS

NK	STAR	CONSTELLATION	LOCATION	MAGNITUD
	The Sun			**-26.74**
	Sirius	Canis Major	Dog's Mouth	-1.46
	Canopus	Argo—now Carina	Oar in Keel	-0.72
	Arcturus	Boots	Left Knee	-0.04
	Toliman	Centaurus	Left Front Hoof	-0.01
	Vega	Lyra	Top of Harp	0.03
	Rigel	Orion	Left Knee	0.12
	Procyon	Canis Minor	Dog's Throat	0.34
	Betelgeuse	Orion	Right Shoulder	0.42
	Archenar	Eridanus	Mouth of Fish	0.46
	Hadar, Agena	Centaurus	Right Foreleg	0.60

11	Capella	Auriga	Body of Goat	0.71
12	Altair	Aquila	Eagle's Breast	0.77
13	Aldebaran	Taurus	Bull's Eye	0.85

APPENDIX N

THE SEVEN WONDERS OF THE ANCIENT WORLD

According to Manly P. Hall, the Seven Wonders of the World were "monuments erected to perpetuate the arcana of the Mysteries. They were symbolic structures, placed in peculiar spots, and the real purpose of their erection can be sensed only by the initiated" (Hall 1928, 188).

Great Pyramid of Giza

Hanging Gardens of Babylon

Statue of Zeus at Olympia

Temple of Artemis at Ephesus

Mausoleum of Maussollos at Halicarnassus

Colossus of Rhodes

Lighthouse of Alexandria

APPENDIX O

THE TWELVE LABORS OF HERCULES

(Δωδεκαθλος, dodekathlos)

Hercules was considered the greatest of the Greek heroes and his feats were recorded in a poem by Peisander from Rhodes around 648–645 BC. The poem has since been lost with only a few lines preserved by others. However, the labors were carved in stone in Olympia at the Temple of Zeus around 470–456 BC.

Hercules was the son of Zeus and a mortal woman. Zeus' wife, Hera was jealous of Zeus' transgression and made Hercules lose his mind. In his stupor, Hercules killed his own wife and children.

Hercules was very sadden and sought the advice of Apollo's oracle at Delphi. As punishment and repentance, Hercules was required to serve Eurystheus, King of Mycenae for twelve years. Originally, there were only 10 tasks for Hercules to complete, but two were added as he had been helped by others, especially Hermes and Athena. In the end, Hercules was granted immortality.

Apollodorus of Athens (ca. 180–120 BC) is cited for the traditional order of the twelve labors:

1. Slay the Nemean Lion (offspring of Typhon & Echidna)
2. Slay the 9-headed Hydra of Lerna (offspring of Typhon & Echidna)
3. Capture the animal known as the Golden Hind of Artemis
4. Capture the Erymanthean Boar

5. Clean King Augeas stables in a single day
6. Slay the Symphalian Birds
7. Capture the Cretan Bull
8. Steal the Mares of Diomedes/Thrace (4 man-eating horses)
9. Obtain the magical Girdle of Hippolyta, the Amazon Queen
10. Obtain the Cattle of the Monster Geryon, the grandson of Medusa
11. Steal the Golden Apples from the Garden of the Hesperides
12. Capture and bring back Cerberus who guards the gates of Hades

There is some documentation that the twelve labors of Hercules represented the Sun's progress through the twelve signs of the zodiac. That discussion is beyond the scope of this writing, but might be important for some to follow-up with on their own. Could this be a comparison to Jesus and his journey?

APPENDIX P

SONG:
"WHEN YOU WISH UPON A STAR"

When you wish upon a star
Makes no difference who you are
Anything your heart desires
Will come to you

If your heart is in your dream
No request is too extreme
When you wish upon a star
As dreamers do

Fate is kind
She brings to those who love
The sweet fulfillment of
Their secret longing

Like a bolt out of the blue
Fate steps in and sees you through
When you wish upon a star
Your dreams come true

Written by: Leigh Harline and Ned Washington
1940 Disney film: *Pinocchio*

Secrets of the Divine

BIBLIOGRAPHY

Amen, Daniel. *Change Your Brain Change Your Life*. New York, NY: Three Rivers Press, 1998.

Andrews, Ted. *Sacred Sounds: Transformation through Music & Word.* St. Paul, MN: Llewellyn Publications, 2001.

Babbitt, Edwin. *The Principles of Light and Color as Revealed by the Material and Spiritual Universe.* New York, NY: Babbitt & Co, 1878.

Bauval, Robert and Adrian Gilbert. *The Orion Mystery.* New York, NY: Crown Trade Paperbacks, 1994.

Beckman, Petr. *A History of Pi.* New York, NY: The Golem Press, 1971.

Booth, Mark. *The Secret History of the World.* Woodstock, NY: The Overlook Press, 2008.

Braden, Gregg. *Awakening to Zero Point: The Collective Initiation.* Bellevue, WA: Radio Bookstore Press, 1993.

———.*Fractal Time.* Carlsbad, CA: Hay House, Inc, 2009.

Breese-Whiting, Kathryn. *The Miracle of the Phoenix.* Phoenix, NY: The Phoenix Press, 1995.

The Shekhinah is Coming

Budge, E. A. Wallis. *The Book of the Dead.* Mineola, NY: Dover Publications, Inc, 1967.

Bullinger, E. W. *Number in Scripture: Its Supernatural Design and Spiritual Significance.* Grand Rapids, MI: Kregel Publications, 1967.

———.*The Witness of the Stars.* Grand Rapids, MI: Kregel Publications, 1967.

Burnham, Robert, Alan Dyer, Robert A. Garfinkle, Martin George, Jeff Kanipe, David H. Levy. *A Guide to Backyard Astronomy: Your Guide to Starhopping and Exploring the Universe.* San Francisco, CA: Fog City Press, 1997.

Campbell, Joseph. *The Hero with a Thousand Faces.* Novato, CA: New World Library, 1949.

———.*The Inner Reaches of Outer Space.* Novato, CA: New World Library, 1986.

Campbell, Joseph and Bill D. Moyers. *The Power of Myth.* New York, NY: Doubleday, 1988.

Case, Paul F. *The True and Invisible Rosicrucian Order.* York Beach, MA: Samuel Weiser, Inc, 1981.

Charles, R.H. *The Book of Enoch the Prophet.* York Beach, MA: Samuel Weiser, Inc, 2003.

Childress, David Hatcher. *Technology of the Gods: The Incredible Sciences of the Ancients.* Kempton, IL: Adventures Unlimited Press, 2000.

Clow, Barbara Hand and Christopher Cudahy Clow. *Catastrophobia: The Truth behind Earth Changes in the Coming Age of Light.* Rochester, VT: Bear & Company, 2001.

Columbia Encyclopedia: Sixth Edition. New York, NY: Columbia University Press, 2000.

Cotterell, Arthur. *The Encyclopedia of Mythology: Classical, Celtic, Norse.* London, England: Anness Publishing Limited, 1996.

———.*The Ultimate Encyclopedia of Mythology.* London, England: Anness Publishing Limited, 1999.

D'Aoust, Maja and Adam Parfrey. *The Secret Source.* Los Angeles, CA: Process Media, 2007.

David, Earl Avraham. *Code of the Heart.* Matawan, NJ: Mazal & Bracha Inc, 2003.

Davis, Kenneth. *Don't Know Much About Mythology.* New York, NY: HarperCollins Publishers, 2005.

Devlin, Keith. *Mathematics: The Science of Patterns.* New York, NY: Scientific American Library, 1994.

Dispenza, Joe. *Evolve Your Brain.* Deerfield Beach, FL: Health Communications, Inc, 2007.

Emerald Tablets of Thoth the Atlantean, The. Translated by Doreal, Brotherhood of the White Temple. Castle Rock, CO: Light Technology Publishing, 1939.

The Shekhinah is Coming

Emerson, Ralph Waldo. *The Conduct of Life, Nature & Other Essays.* Whitefish, MT: Kessinger Publishing, 2007.

Fideler, David R. *Jesus Christ, Sun of God: Ancient Cosmology and Early Christian Symbolism.* Wheaton, IL: Quest Books, 1993.

Fontana, David. *The Secret Language of Symbols: A Visual Key to Symbols and Their Meanings.* San Francisco: Chronicle Books, 1994.

Forinash, Kyle. *Galileo's Mathematical Language of Nature, 2000.*

Friedlander, Gerald. *Hellenism and Christianity.* London, England: P. Vallentine & Sons, 1912.

Galilei, Galileo. *The Assayer (Il Saggiatore).* Rome, 1623.

Gillings, Richard J. *Mathematics in the Time of the Pharaohs.* Boston, MA: MIT Press, 1972.

Godwin, David. *Godwin's Cabalistic Encyclopedia: A Complete Guide to Cabalistic Magic.* St. Paul, MN: Llewellyn Publications, 2003.

Goldman, Jonathan. *The 7 Secrets of Sound Healing.* Carlsbad, CA: Hay House, Inc, 2008.

Goodspeed, Edgar J. *The Apocrypha.* Chicago, IL: University of Chicago Press, 1938.

Gospel of Thomas: The Hidden Sayings of Jesus. Translated by Marvin Meyer. San Francisco, CA: Harper San Francisco, 1992.

Guant, Bonnie. *Beginnings: The Sacred Design.* Kempton, IL: Adventures Unlimited Press, 1995.

———.*Jesus Christ: The Number of His Name.* Kempton, IL: Adventures Unlimited Press, 1998.

———.*The Coming of Jesus.* Kempton, IL: Adventures Unlimited Press, 1999.

———.*The Bible's Awesome Number Code.* Kempton, IL: Adventures Unlimited Press, 2000.

———.*Genesis One.* Kempton, IL: Adventures Unlimited Press, 2003.

Haanel, Charles F. *The Master Key System.* New York, NY: Atria Books, 2008.

Hall, Manley P. *The Secret Teachings of All Ages.* Los Angeles, CA: Philosophical Research Society, 1928.

Halpern, Steven and Louis M. Savary. *Sound Health: The Music and Sound that Makes Us Whole.* New York, NY: HarperCollins Publishers, 1985.

Hamilton, Edith. *Mythology.* Boston, MA: Little, Brown and Company, 1942.

Hancock, Graham and Robert Bauval. *The Message of the Sphinx.* New York, NY: Three Rivers Press, 1996.

Hancock, Graham. *Finger Prints of the Gods.* New York, NY: Three Rivers Press, 1995.

Hartmann, Franz. *The Doctrines of Jacob Boehme.* New York, NY: McCoy Publishing Co, 1919.

Heath, Richard. *Sacred Number and the Origins of Civilization: The Unfolding of History through the Mystery of Number.* Rochester, VT: Inner Traditions, 2007.

Hislop, Alexander. *The Two Babylons.* Brooklyn, NY: A & B Distributors, 1999.

Hoffman, Edward. *The Hebrew Alphabet: A Mystical Journey.* San Francisco, CA: Chronicle Books, 1998.

Holy Bible: King James Version. Translated. New York, NY: Thomas Nelson Publishers, 1976.

Hone, William. *The Lost Books of the Bible.* New York, NY: Bell Publishing Company, 1820.

Hulse, David Allen. *The Western Mysteries (Key of It All).* St. Paul, MN: Llewellyn Publications, 2000.

Hunt, Valerie. *Infinite Mind.* Malibu, CA: Malibu Publishing Co, 1989.

Hurtak, J. J. *An Introduction to the Keys of Enoch.* Los Gatos, CA: The Academy for Future Science, 1975.

Huxley, Aldous. *Proper Studies.* London, England: Chatto & Windus, 1929.

Kaplan, Aryeh. *The Bahir.* York Beach, MA: Samuel Weiser, Inc, 1979.

———.*Sefer Yetzirah: The Book of Creation.* Boston, MA: Weiser Books, 1997.

Knight, Christopher and Alan Butler. *Solomon's Power Brokers: The Secrets of Freemasonry, the Church and the Illuminati.* London, England: Watkins Publishing, 2007.

Knight, Christopher and Robert Lomas. *The Hiram Key: Pharaohs, Freemasonry, and the Discovery of the Secret Scrolls of Jesus.* London, England: Century Books, Random House, 1996.

———.*Uriel's Machine: Uncovering the Secrets of Stonehenge, Noah's Flood and the Dawn of Civilization.* Gloucester, MA: Fair Winds Press, 2001.

Koran, The. Translated by J. M. Rodwell. Mineola, NY: Dover Publications, Inc., 2005.

Kush, Indus Khamit. *Enoch the Ethiopian: The Lost Prophet of the Bible: Greater Than Abraham, Holier Than Moses.* Brooklyn, NY: A&B Publishers Group, 2000.

Laurence, Richard. *The Book of Enoch the Prophet.* Kempton, IL: Adventures Unlimited Press, 1883.

Lawlor, Robert. *Sacred Geometry (Illustrated Library of Sacred Imagination).* New York, NY: Thames and Hudson Ltd, 1982.

Lea, Thomas Simcox and Frederick Bligh Bond. *Gematria: A Preliminary Investigation of the Cabala.* Thame, England: Essex House, 2005.

Levy, David. *A Guide to Skywatching.* San Francisco, CA: Fog City Press, 1994.

Lewis, James R. *Astrology Encyclopedia.* Canton, MI: Visible Ink Press, 1994.

Littleton, C. Scott. *Mythology.* London, England: Duncan Baird Publishers, 2002.

Lundy, Miranda. *Sacred Geometry.* Wales, England: Wooden Books Ltd, 1998.

Martin, Richard P. *Bullfinch's Mythology: The Age of the Fable, The Age of Chivalry, Legends of the Classics.* New York, NY: HarperCollins Publishers, 1991.

Mathers, Samuel L. MacGregor. *The Book of the Sacred Magic of Abramelin the Mage.* Mineola, NY: Dover Publications, Inc, 1975.

Matt, Daniel Chanan. *Zohar: The Book of Enlightenment.* Mahwah, NJ: Paulist Press, 1983.

McDowell, A. G. *Village Life in Ancient Egypt.* Oxford, NY: Oxford University Press, 1999.

Mercatante, Anthony S. *The Facts on File Encyclopedia of World Mythology and Legend–Volume I & II.* New York, NY: Facts on File, Inc, 2004.

Metaphysics–Aristotle. Translated by W. D. Ross. London, England: Penguin Books, 1998.

Michell, John. *The Temple at Jerusalem: A Revelation.* London, England: Gothic Image Publications, 2000.

———.*The Dimensions of Paradise: The Proportions and Symbolic Numbers of Ancient Cosmology.* Kempton, IL: Adventures Unlimited Press, 2001.

Miller, Harnish and Paul Broadhurst. *The Sun and the Serpent.* Launceston, Cornwall: Pendragon Press, 1989.

Moore, Patrick. *Philip's Atlas of the Universe.* London, England: Octopus Publishing Group Ltd, 2000.

Morison, Ian and Margaret Penston. *Pocket Guide to Stars & Planets.* London, England: New Holland Publishers, 2005.

Nozedar, Adele. *The Element Encyclopedia of Secret Signs and Symbols.* London, England: HarperElement, 2008.

O'Connell, Mark and Raje Airey. *The Complete Encyclopedia of Signs & Symbols: Identification and Analysis of the Visual Vocabulary That Formulates Our Thoughts and Dictates Our Reactions to the World Around Us.* London, England: Hermes House, 2008.

Pawson, Marke. *Gematria: The Numbers of Infinity*. Sutton Mallet, England: Green Magic, 2004.

Pearson, Carol S. *Awakening The Heroes Within: Twelve Archetypes to Help Us Find Ourselves and Transform Our World.* New York, NY: HarperCollins Publishers, 1991.

Pennick, Nigel. *Sacred Geometry: Symbolism and Purpose in Religious Structures.* United Kingdom: Capall Bann Publishing, 1994.

Plato: Republic. Translated by Desmond Lee. New York: Penguin Books, Ltd, 1987.

Plato: Timaeus and Critias. Translated by Desmond Lee. New York: Penguin Books, Ltd, 1977.

Plato: The Laws. Translated by Trevor J. Saunders. New York: Penguin Books, Ltd, 1970.

Regardie, Israel. *A Garden Of Pomegranates: Skrying on the Tree of Life.* St. Paul, MN: Llewellyn Publications, 1932.

———.*The Tree of Life: An Illustrated Study in Magic.* St. Paul, MN: Llewellyn Publications, 1932.

Rey, H.A. *The Stars: A New Way to See Them.* Boston, MA: Houghton Mifflin Company, 1952.

Robins, Gay and Charles Shute, C. *The Rhind Mathematical Papyrus: An Ancient Egyptian Text.* New York, NY: Dover, 1990.

Savedow, Steve. *Sepher Rezial Hemelach: The Book of the Angel Rezial.* York Beach, MA: Samuel Weiser, Inc, 2000.

Seiss, Joseph A. *Gospel in the Stars or Primeval Astronomy.* Whitefish, MT: Kessinger Publishing, 1910.

Shesso, Renna. *Math for Mystics: From the Fibonacci Sequence to Luna's Labyrinth to the Golden Section and Other Secrets of Sacred Geometry.* San Francisco, CA: Red Wheel/Weiser, LLC, 2007.

Silver, Steve, Joseph Peterson, and Mark Wysocki. *The Alchemy Secret Code.* Pomona, NY: Trafford Publishing, 2008.

Strudwick, Nigel. *Hieroglyph Detective: How to Decode the Sacred Language of the Ancient Egyptians.* London, England: Duncan Baird Publishers Ltd, 2010.

Toomer, G. J. and Owen Gingerich. *Ptolemy's Almagest.* Princeton, NJ: Princeton University Press, 1998.

Turnbull, Grace H. *The Essence of Plotinus: Extracts from the Six Enneads and Porphyry's Life of Plotinus.* Eugene, OR: Wipf & Stock Publishers, 1934.

Unknown. *Urania's Mirror.* New York, NY: Barnes & Noble Books, 1832.

Upanishads. Translated by Juan Mascaro. New York, NY: Penguin Books, Ltd, 1965.

Washburn, Del. *Theomatics II.* Lanham, MA: Scarborough House, 1994.

Weber, John. *An Illustrated Guide to the Lost Symbol.* New York, NY: Pocket Books, 2009.

Weigel, James. *Mythology.* New York, NY: Wiley Publishing, Inc, 1973.

Wilhelm, Richard. *The I Ching or Book of Changes.* Translated by Cary F. Baynes. London, England: Arkana, 1950.

Wilkinson, Philip. *Myth & Legends: An Illustrated Guide to Their Origins and Meanings.* New York, NY: DK Publishing, 2009.

Zolar. *Zolar's Encyclopedia of Ancient and Forbidden Knowledge.* New York, NY: Arco Publishing, Inc, 1970.